AF594398

FACES OF ANCIENT EGYPT

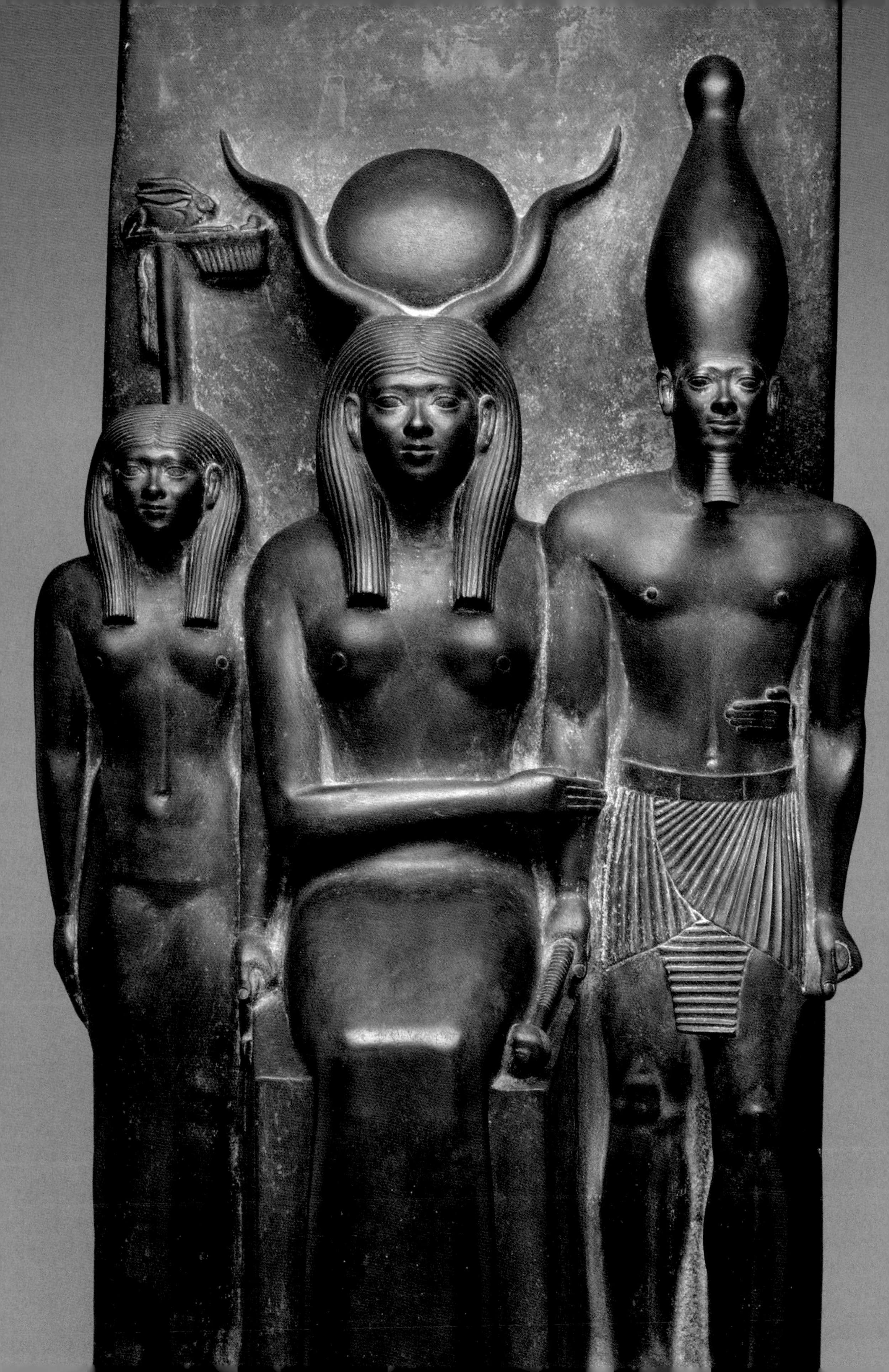

FACES *of* ANCIENT EGYPT

PORTRAITS FROM THE MUSEUM OF FINE ARTS, BOSTON

Lawrence M. Berman

MFA PUBLICATIONS
Museum of Fine Arts, Boston

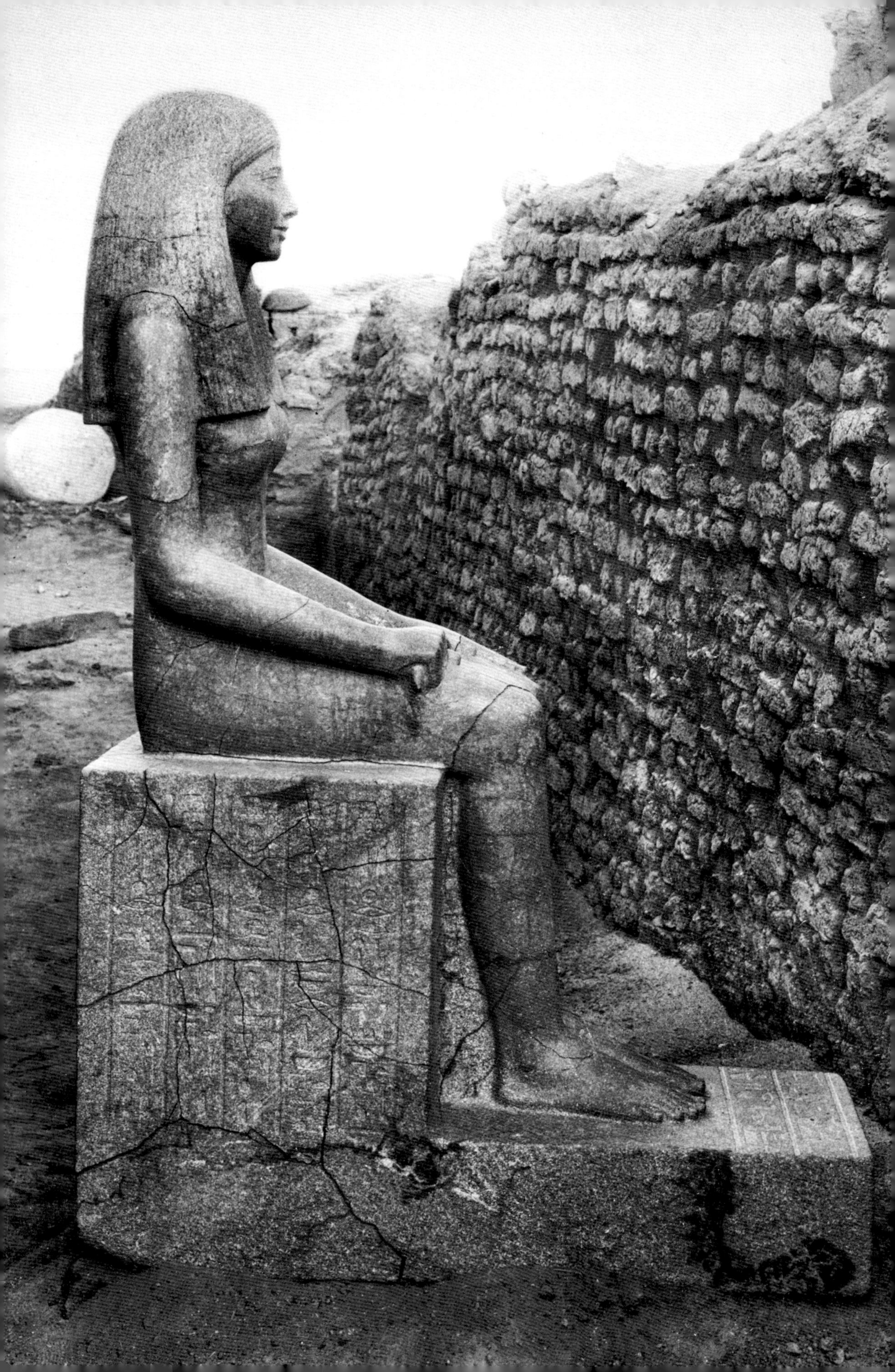

CONTENTS

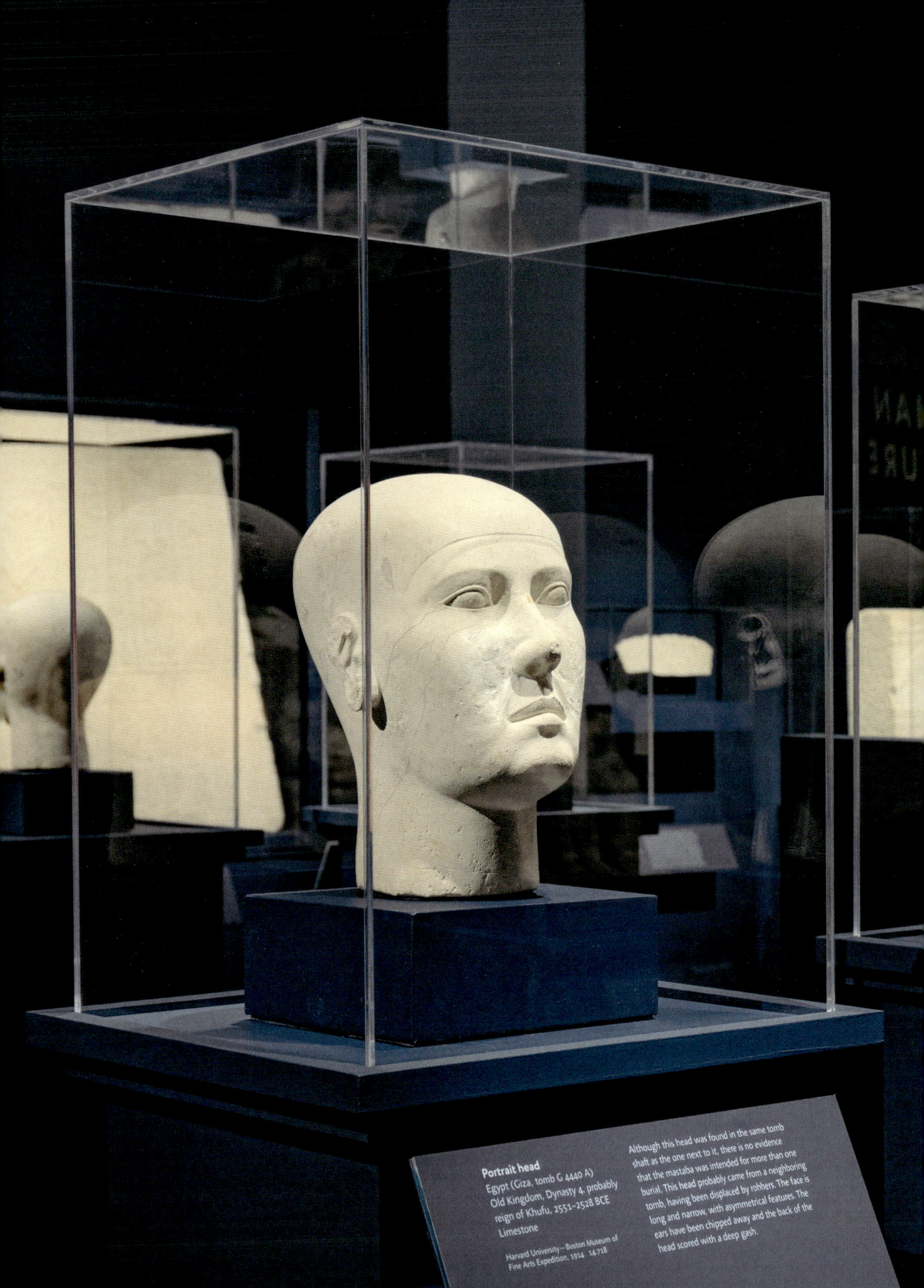
Portrait head
Egypt (Giza, tomb G 4440 A)
Old Kingdom, Dynasty 4, probably
reign of Khufu, 2551–2528 BCE
Limestone
Harvard University—Boston Museum of
Fine Arts Expedition, 1914 14.718
Although this head was found in the same tomb
shaft as the one next to it, there is no evidence
that the mastaba was intended for more than one
burial. This head probably came from a neighboring
tomb, having been displaced by robbers. The face is
long and narrow, with asymmetrical features. The
ears have been chipped away and the back of the
head scored with a deep gash.

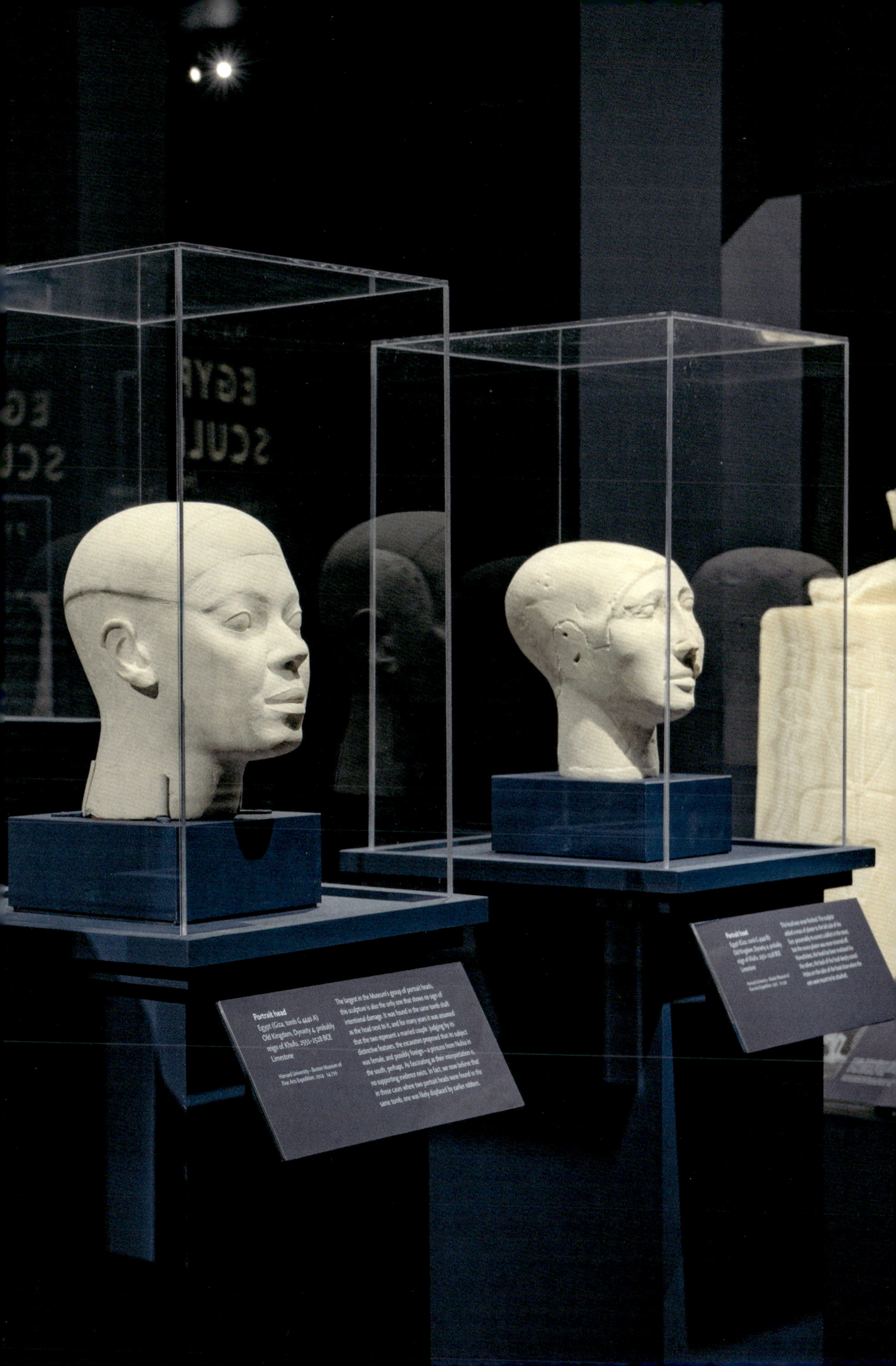
Portrait head
Egypt (Giza, tomb G 4440 A)
Old Kingdom, Dynasty 4, probably
reign of Khufu, 2551–2528 BCE
Limestone

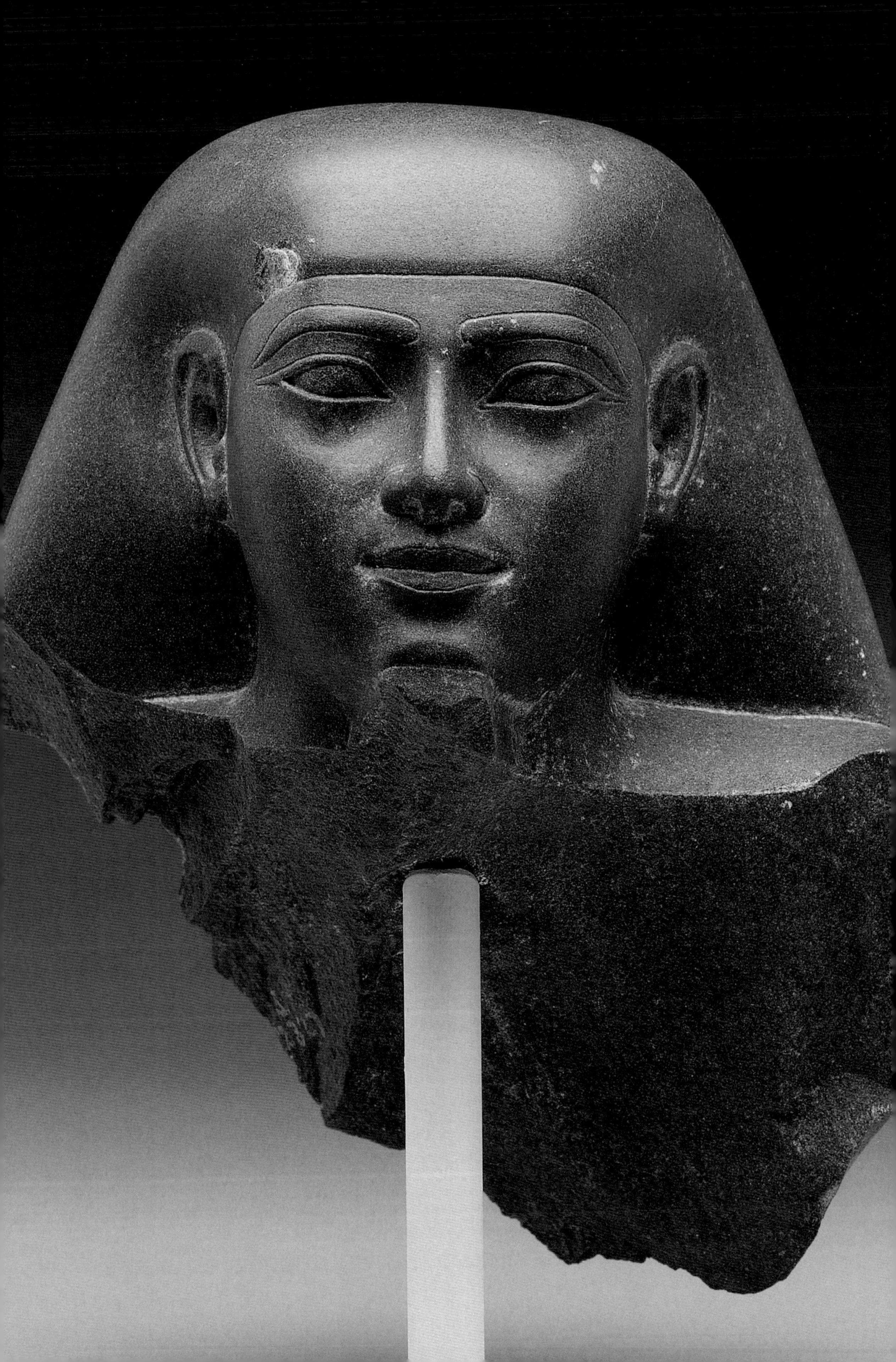

FACES OF ANCIENT EGYPT

PREFACE

In most cases a catalogue or companion book comes before the exhibition. In this case it is the reverse: the galleries came first. In February 2021 the Museum of Fine Arts, Boston, opened two new galleries of Egyptian art. The larger one, "Masterpieces of Egyptian Sculpture from the Pyramid Age," focuses on the works of art for which the MFA's Egyptian collection is best known: the statuary from the pyramid complex of King Menkaura at Giza and the adjacent cemeteries of the Fourth, Fifth, and Sixth dynasties. The smaller gallery, "Faces of Ancient Egypt," explores the theme of portraiture in Egyptian art with ten portraits from the Middle Kingdom, New Kingdom, and Late periods chosen to complement the Old Kingdom masterpieces in the larger gallery.

For the purposes of this book, the existence of portraiture in ancient Egypt is taken for granted. The definition of portraiture is a broad one that encompasses both those works of art—and every portrait is a work of art—that rely primarily on physical resemblance, and those where personal identity is conveyed through coded facial features (as when a private individual is shown with the ruler's features), pose, dress, or hairstyle. To say a work of art is not a "true" portrait "in our sense" implies that portraiture is a property of Western art to the exclusion of all other artistic traditions, that only Western artists can do portraits, and that only Westerners understand them.

Although the approach of this book is intended to be thematic and not chronological, certain themes are most prevalent at certain periods. Others develop over time, so thematic and chronological narratives may coincide and overlap. Thus, we start with the Fourth Dynasty, not only the earliest period covered here but also the one that saw the creation of the first portraits with individualized features. And we conclude with a realist masterpiece from twenty-two hundred years later.

A close-knit team worked together seamlessly to meet the challenge of re-presenting the finest Egyptian art of the Old Kingdom outside of Cairo to our visitors. The exhibition designers Chelsea Garunay and Nick Pioggia came up with a striking architectural design that pulls the works together and also enables the visitor to engage with each individual sculpture on its own aesthetic merits. Adam Tessier helped formulate the conceptual framework, and along with Catherine Johnson-Roehr edited the labels and text panels.

Installing these important and demanding sculptures in the time of Covid presented a challenge, to say the least, and I am grateful to conservators Mei-An Tsu and LeeAnn Gordon, collection engineers Dante Vallance and Neal Johnson, and our dedicated crew of utility workers, carpenters, painters, and electricians.

In MFA Publications, I am most of all grateful to Jennifer Snodgrass. It was she who came up with the idea of this book as a companion to the new galleries and encouraged me to write it. Thanks are due also to Hope Stockton and Diana Sibbald. Debra LaKind supported the book's publication, and Tom Eykemans of Lucia | Marquand contributed the elegant design.

The staff of the William Morris Hunt Library facilitated my work in every way and gave me a quiet and congenial environment to write during the pandemic. I am most grateful to Hee Jung Lee and her staff, particularly Paul McAlpine, Jordan Barnes, and Marie Oedel. I will always have fond memories of my regular Wednesdays at Horticultural Hall.

My fellow curator in the Department of Ancient Egyptian, Nubian, and Near Eastern Art, Denise Doxey, bore with patience and grace my numerous interruptions and was always ready to discuss and evaluate new ideas. She also kindly filled in for me when I was busy with the book. My friend and colleague Danny Cashman took time from his studies to read the bulk of the manuscript in its first draft. His spot-on comments and astute observations were both helpful and encouraging.

In the end, however, this is a very personal book, born of many years working with these wonderful objects and reflecting on portraiture in ancient Egypt, and the opinions expressed are my own.

Lawrence M. Berman
Norma Jean Calderwood Senior Curator of
Ancient Egyptian, Nubian, and Near Eastern Art

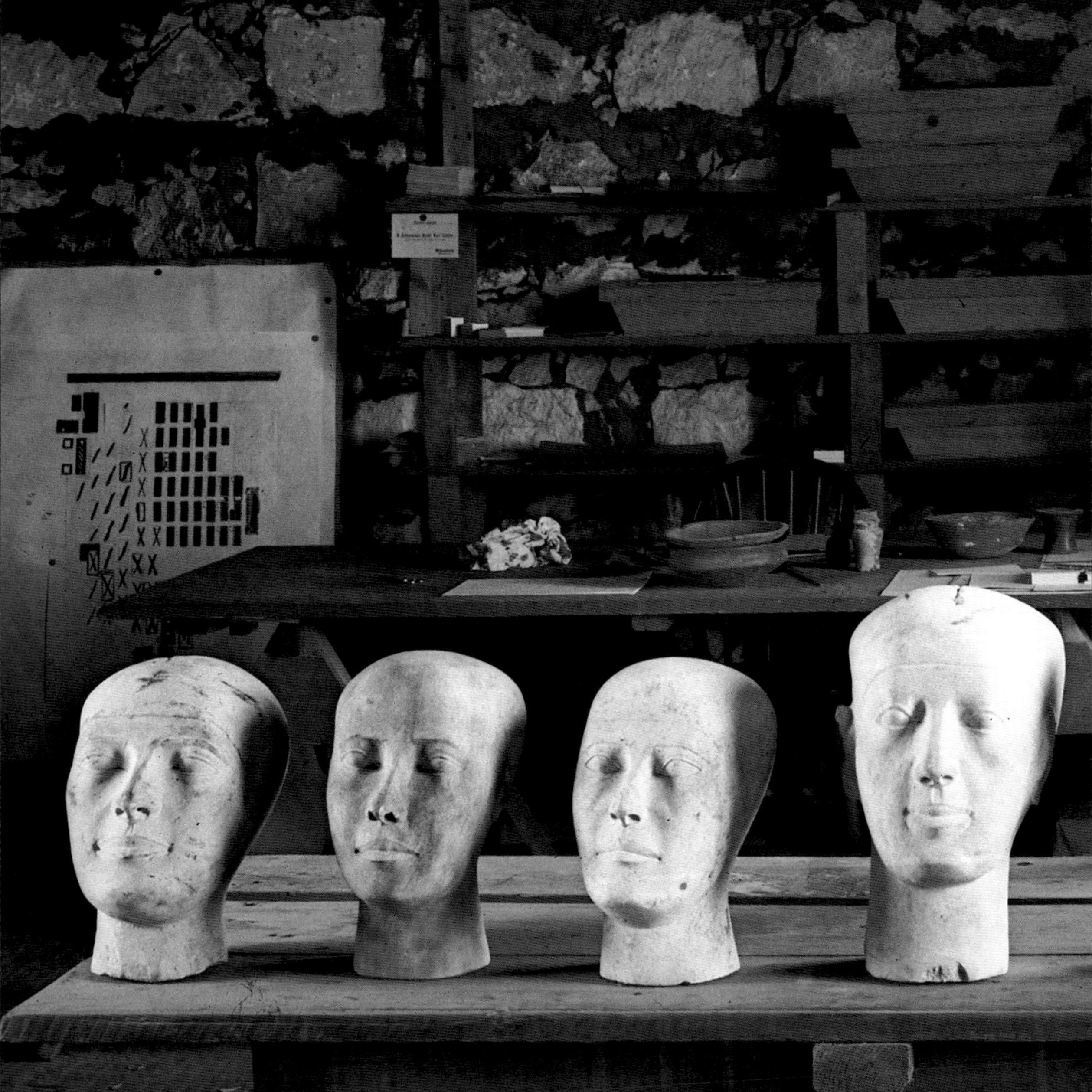

DÉCEMBRE
17
MERCREDI

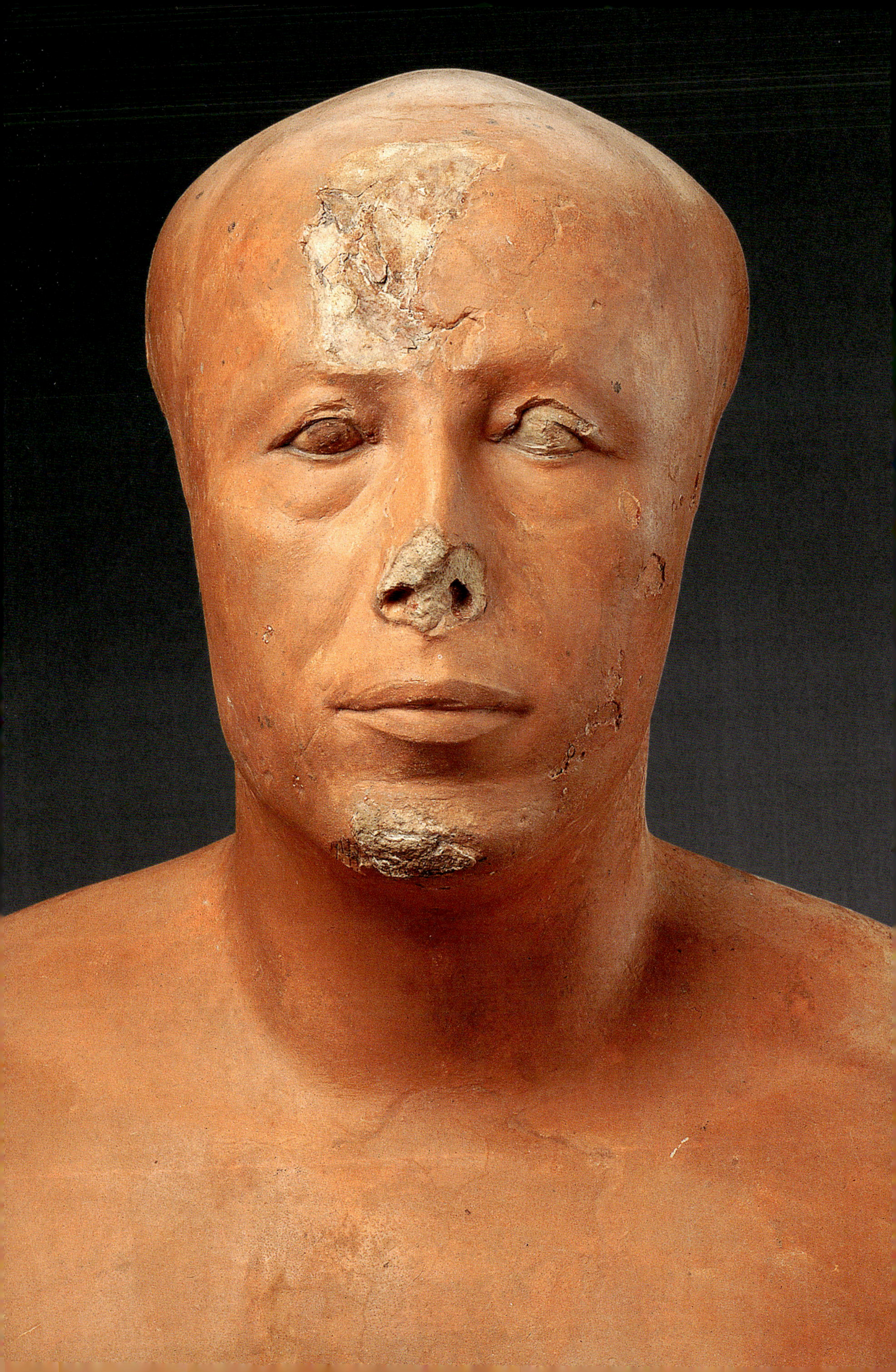

ONE

The Case of Ankhhaf

On February 8, 1925, the Harvard University–Boston Museum of Fine Arts Expedition made one of its greatest discoveries:

> *This morning at 7:30 was made the very important find of a fine limestone portrait bust of Ankhhaf which had fallen from its pedestal at the north of room I in the Exterior Chapel of G 7510. This is an almost perfect piece and displays the most amazing technique and beauty of form. It is life-size and painted the usual red, the bones of shoulder and back and skull are shown with admirable skill and restraint, and the expression is very lifelike. It was found lying on its back on the floor.*[1]

At that time, the Harvard-Boston expedition was excavating the cemetery east of the Great Pyramid of Khufu at Giza. The tomb of Ankhhaf, known as G 7510, was the largest construction in that area, which was reserved for the most important members of the royal family. Shaped like an enormous stone bench with sloping sides, 100 meters (328 feet) long by 51.8 meters (170 feet) at the base, the tomb had a brick offering chapel built against its eastern side. Egyptian tombs of this type are known as *mastabas*, after the Arabic word for bench. The owner of this mastaba, Ankhhaf, was the most powerful man in Egypt after the king—a royal prince, the half-brother of Khufu, vizier (prime minister), and overseer of all royal construction works. Obviously, the most important building project of the reign of Khufu was the king's pyramid complex, and Ankhhaf was very much in charge. Documents on papyrus dated to the last year of Khufu's reign, around 2528 BCE, record the shipment of

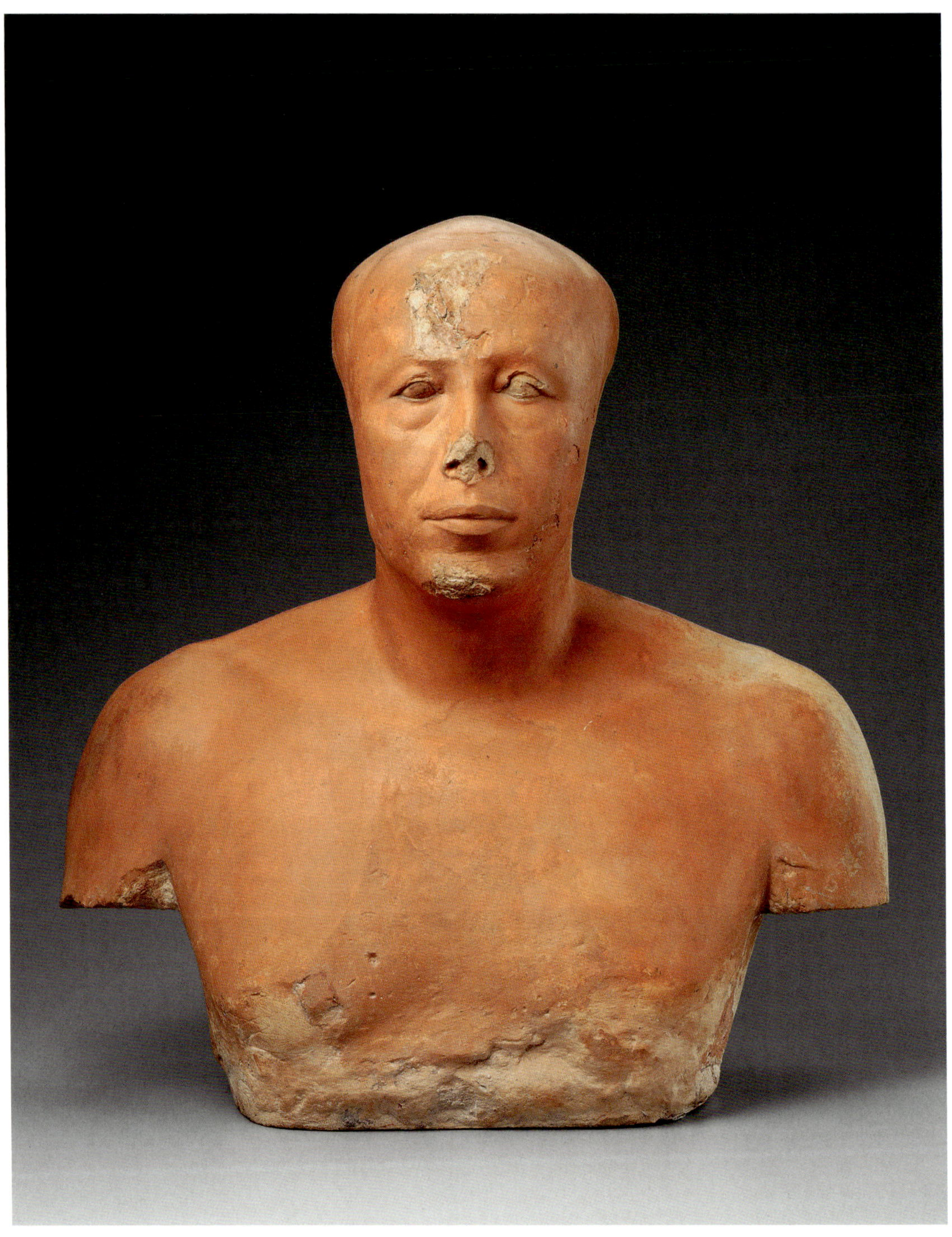

1 Bust of Ankhhaf, 2520–2494 BCE. Painted limestone, h. 50.5 cm (19⁷⁄₈ in.)

fine limestone from the Tura quarry to the pyramid construction site across the Nile at Giza.[2] Ankhhaf is named in these papyri as overseer of "the harbor of Khufu," where the massive, fine white limestone blocks for the pyramid casing were delivered and offloaded. They supplied the finishing touch to one of the greatest and most durable monuments of all time.

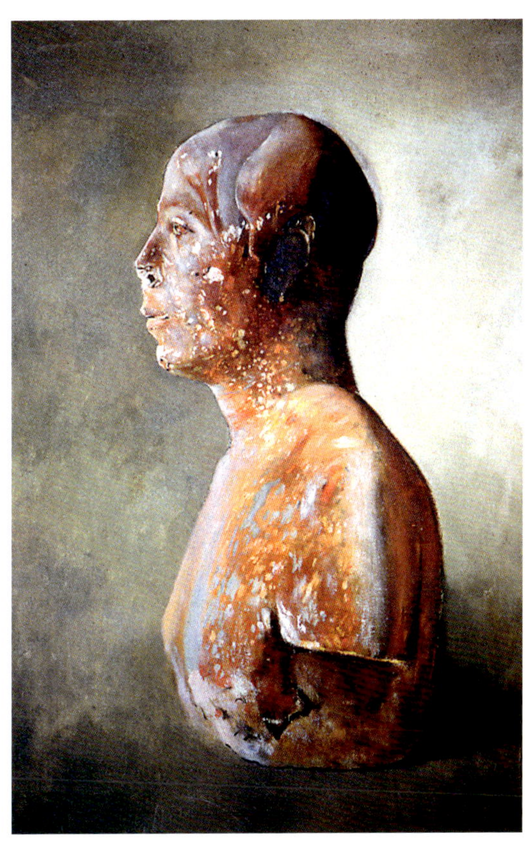

2 Joseph Lindon Smith, *Bust of Prince Ankhhaf, Profile View*, 1925. Oil on canvas, 86 × 54.5 cm (33⅞ × 21½ in.)

His ears are missing, his nose is damaged, and he has a big gash on his forehead. It hardly matters. Ankhhaf's painted bust is the most convincing example of realistic portraiture to have survived from ancient Egypt and was clearly done by a master sculptor (fig. 1). The subject's body is cut off flat below the chest, his arms at armpit level. He looks straight ahead, turning neither to the left nor to the right. He's not particularly young, well-built, or handsome. The great man wears no fancy clothes, no ornaments, and no insignia of rank.

The subtlety and naturalness of the modeling was helped by coating the fine white limestone with a coat of plaster, which gives the surface an extra degree of plasticity, as observed in the pouches beneath the eyes, the folds of flesh alongside the nose, and the muscles around the mouth. The skin appears almost soft, as though it would yield to the touch. The underlying bone structure is apparent in the salient cheekbones, strong chin, and firm jaw. The eyes are small and close-set. The tip of the nose has broken off; the missing ears were made separately and attached to the head. In contrast to the extraordinary sensitivity of the carving, Ankhhaf's skin was painted a uniform brick red, the conventional skin color for men; women's skin was mustard yellow.

Egyptian sculpture was almost always painted, even—though more selectively—works made of colored stones with beautiful surfaces.[3] The paint was applied flat, without shading or gradations of tone. To the Egyptians, this was more realistic. Although to us it appears jarring, we have to accept that for the Egyptians there would have been no disconnect between the naturalness of the carving and the flatness of the painting. Whoever painted Ankhhaf's bust, however, was overzealous. Although his hairline clearly shows typical male-pattern baldness, his entire head has been slathered with red paint, whereas normally the hair would have been painted black.[4] Ankhhaf's upper body is powerful though not muscular:

the collarbones protrude, and the chest muscles sag. The back is as naturalistic as the front. The shoulder blades are rounded and natural, the spine indented. He has the presence of a living human being.

On March 28, 1925, the painter Joseph Lindon Smith arrived at Harvard Camp, the expedition's headquarters behind the Great Pyramid, and promptly got to work on two oil paintings of the bust.[5] Smith excelled at reproducing the time-ravaged surfaces of ancient sculptures. George Andrew Reisner, director of the expedition and curator of Egyptian art at the MFA, much appreciated the value of Smith's reproductions of ancient monuments at a time when color photography was not readily available, and had begun collecting them for the Museum in 1911 (fig. 2).[6] Reisner arranged for Smith to spend part of his time at Giza to document the excavations.[7] Smith's paintings of Ankhhaf give the most accurate record of its appearance at the time it was discovered, particularly since the paint is largely restored.[8] Visitors came to Harvard Camp especially to admire it. The Egyptologist Georg Steindorff of Leipzig University, echoing Smith's own appraisal of the sculpture, compared it to "the splendid Florentine portrait busts of the Medicis."[9]

Indeed, nothing like the bust of Ankhhaf had been seen in Egyptian art before, and with its truncated arms and torso it does bear a certain formal resemblance to Italian Renaissance busts and their ancient Roman forebears. The Egyptians hardly ever made busts or heads as such. Ankhhaf and the so-called reserve heads, complete in themselves, are the exceptions. The closest thing to this portrait is not a freestanding statue but a relief bust carved in a niche below the false door in the tomb of Idu, from the reign of Pepy I (2289–2255 BCE), some 275 years later than Ankhhaf, showing the deceased with arms outstretched to receive offerings (fig. 3).[10] The bust of Ankhhaf may originally have had a separately made base with outstretched arms just like Idu's—though no trace of any such base was found in the tomb of Ankhhaf.[11]

Ankhhaf is Egyptian art at its most approachable. But the ancient Egyptians did not make statues just to admire them as works of art. Statues were places where the living spirits of the departed could reside. The ritual of "opening of the mouth," which involved a priest using a set of special implements (a fishtail knife, a set of dummy vessels), brought the statue to life, enabling it to receive offerings in tomb or temple (fig. 4). The same ritual was performed on statues of deities and on wrapped mummies. For a statue to serve this purpose, it did not have to be a realistic portrait; an inscription identifying the subject by name would do. However, the religious function of statuary did not preclude portraiture. The Egyptians were perfectly capable of making individualized portraits, and in some periods a likeness was considered desirable, even essential. The Fourth Dynasty (2575–2465 BCE), during which Ankhhaf lived, was such a time. As William Stevenson Smith, who wrote the first comprehensive

3 False door of Idu, with engaged bust of Idu in lower section, from Giza tomb G 7102

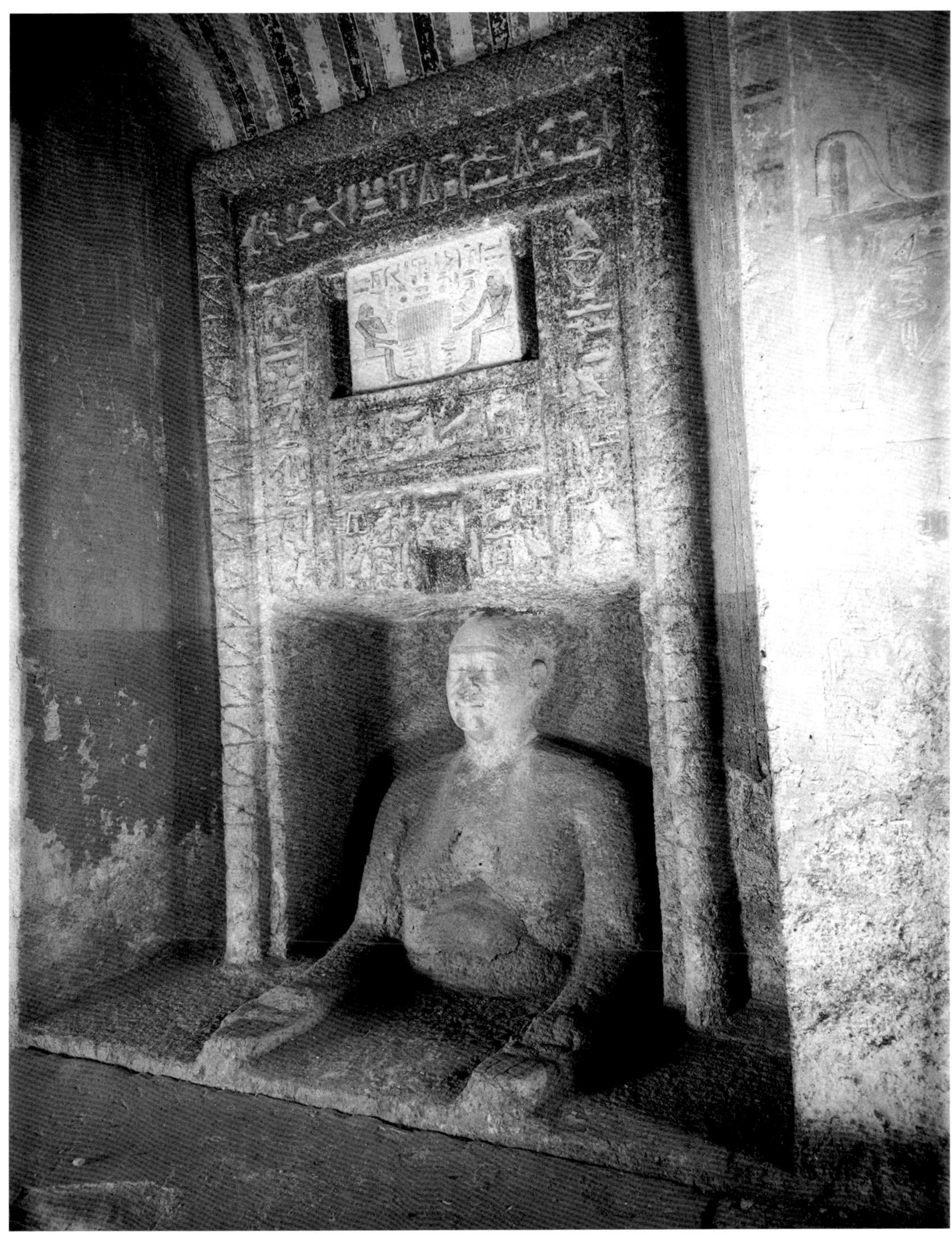

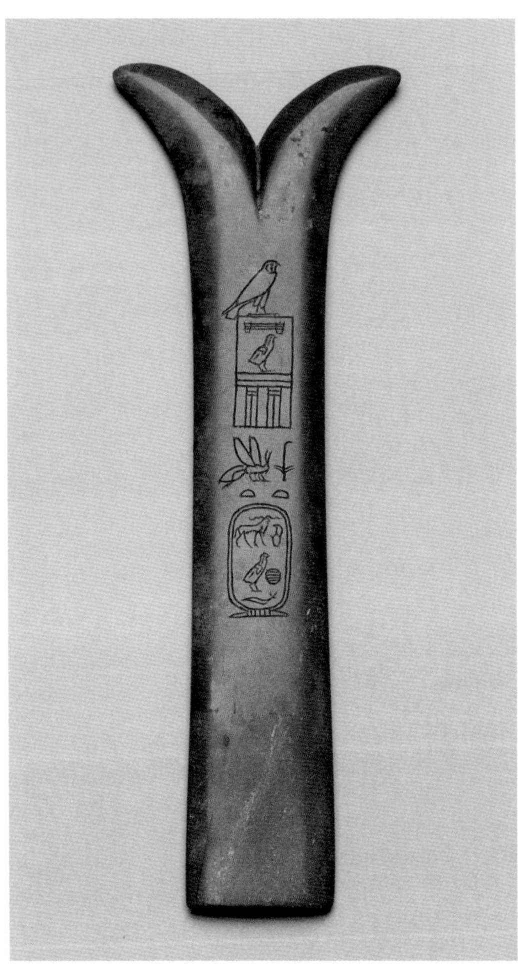

4 Fishtail knife inscribed for Khufu, 2551–2528 BCE. Flint, 18.3 × 2.8 cm (7½ × 1⅛ in.). This fishtail knife found in Menkaura's valley temple would have been the very one used in the "opening of the mouth" ritual for the king's statues. By Menkaura's time, it was already an heirloom, at least fifty years old.

survey of Old Kingdom sculpture based on the finds from Giza, observes, "I can find no evidence that would make one think that the owner would not prefer to have the statue look like him, that is, within the boundaries of what he expected a statue to look like, to begin with, and providing he had obtained the services of a sculptor who was capable of achieving this."[12] Only a very restricted group of people—basically the king and his officials—had statues made, and these were individual portraits by the finest artists available.

The mastaba of Ankhhaf had an interior chapel built into the stone core on its eastern side, and an exterior mudbrick chapel added in front of the interior chapel. The eastern side faced the Nile Valley, the land of the living, from which visitors would come with prayers and offerings to the cemetery. The bust was found lying on the ground in a rear room of the exterior mudbrick chapel.[13] Judging from its position, and as shown in the photographs taken at the time, the bust would have sat on a plastered mudbrick platform—the "pedestal" mentioned in the diary—right opposite the door. You walked in, and there it was, big as life, looking right at you.

Found under the bust were ninety-four tiny model vessels and offerings of bread and cake made of plaster (fig. 5). The models may have been placed on a low extension of the platform to the right. The conical loaves of bread (imitating real bread baked in molds) look like wizards' hats. The close juxtaposition of the bust and the models makes explicit the role of the statue in the offering cult of the deceased. Even though the deceased has been reborn as an *akh*, or effective spirit, he still needs food and drink; the model offerings and vessels were there to provide continuous service in the afterlife.

The bust of Ankhhaf was assigned to the Harvard-Boston expedition on April 8, 1927, a signal gesture of appreciation on the part of the Egyptian government.[14] Reisner considered it one of the three pieces on which the future fame of the MFA's Egyptian collection would be based, the other two being the pair statue of Menkaura and queen (see fig. 12) and the beautifully painted outer coffin of Governor Djehutynakht from Deir el-Bersha.[15] In 1942, shortly after the United States entered World War II,

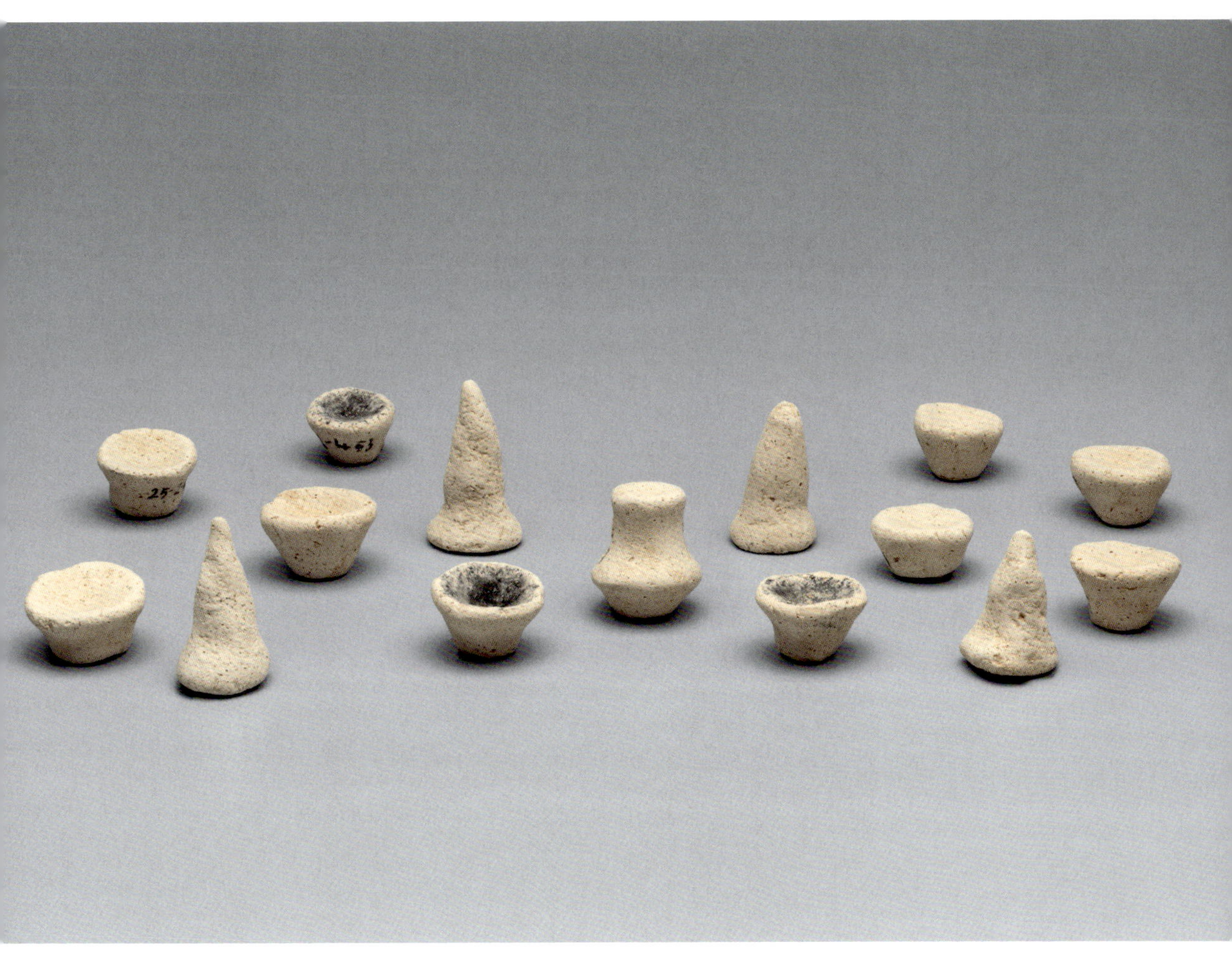

5 Model vessels and offerings found under the bust of Ankhhaf, 2520–2494 BCE. Plaster, largest object h. 4.1 cm (1⅝ in.)

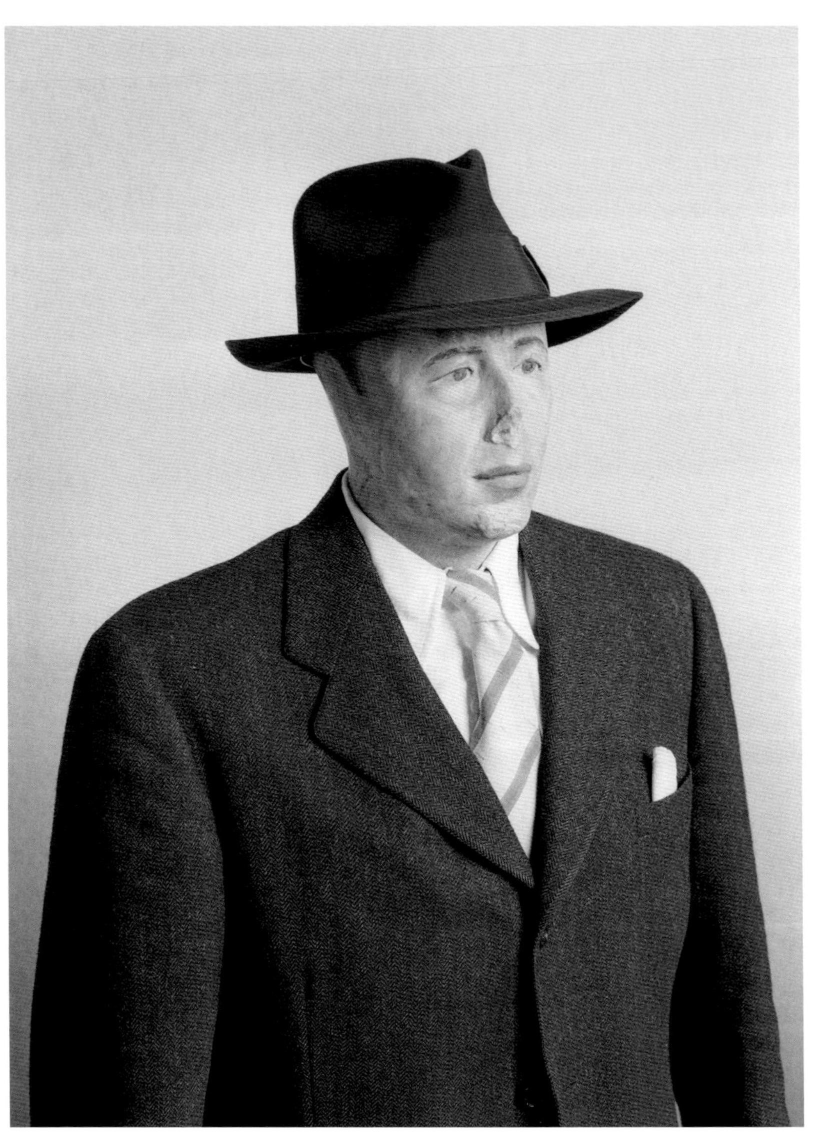

6 Cast of bust of Ankhhaf in modern clothing, about 1943

the Trustees of the Museum decided to remove certain key works of art, including the pair statue of Menkaura and queen and the bust of Ankhhaf, from the galleries and send them into the countryside as a safety precaution against possible damage from enemy bombardment. To maintain appearances, painted plaster casts prepared by MFA conservators were substituted for the originals in the galleries. The director of the Museum at the time, George Edgell, remarked: "These were colored so skillfully that in some cases only an expert could distinguish the reproduction from the original unless he rapped it with his knuckles to test the sound."[16] Dows Dunham, the Curator of Egyptian Art, took advantage of this occasion to perform an experiment. He took a defective duplicate cast of Ankhhaf, repainted it, and dressed it in his own hat, coat, shirt, and tie (fig. 6).[17] Thus disguised, the forty-five-hundred-year-old Egyptian prince looked like a man you might meet on the street—if you could overlook the missing ears and broken nose (the fedora covered up damage to the forehead).

Why was it necessary to prove this at all? When the first realistic portraits from the Pyramid Age came to light in the 1850s and 1860s, connoisseurs were astonished.[18] Portraiture was supposed to have been invented by the Greeks, and here were realistic portraits with individual features, created hundreds or even thousands of years before the first Greek portrait sculptures.[19] This rocked the establishment: Egyptian art was not supposed to look like this. Indeed, most of it doesn't; as Dunham explains, "It is the misfortune of most people today that their impression of Egyptian art is based in no small degree on objects which, whatever their archaeological and historic importance, are distinctly mediocre as works of art, and they are disappointed with their stiffness and lack of vitality."[20]

The portraits presented in this book span some twenty-five hundred years, from the Pyramid Age to the first century BCE. Not all of them are realistic, but not one is mediocre. Verisimilitude is only one aspect of portraiture, Egyptian or otherwise, and not necessarily the most important one. Many of these works express their subject's identity in ways beyond physical likeness. Different approaches to portraiture arose in response to developments in politics and religion and changing ideas of the self over time. Whereas in Western art individual portraiture comes at the end of a long development—from the simple to the complex, from the general to the specific—in Egyptian art it comes at the beginning, with the bust of Ankhhaf in the Fourth Dynasty, at the height of the Pyramid Age.

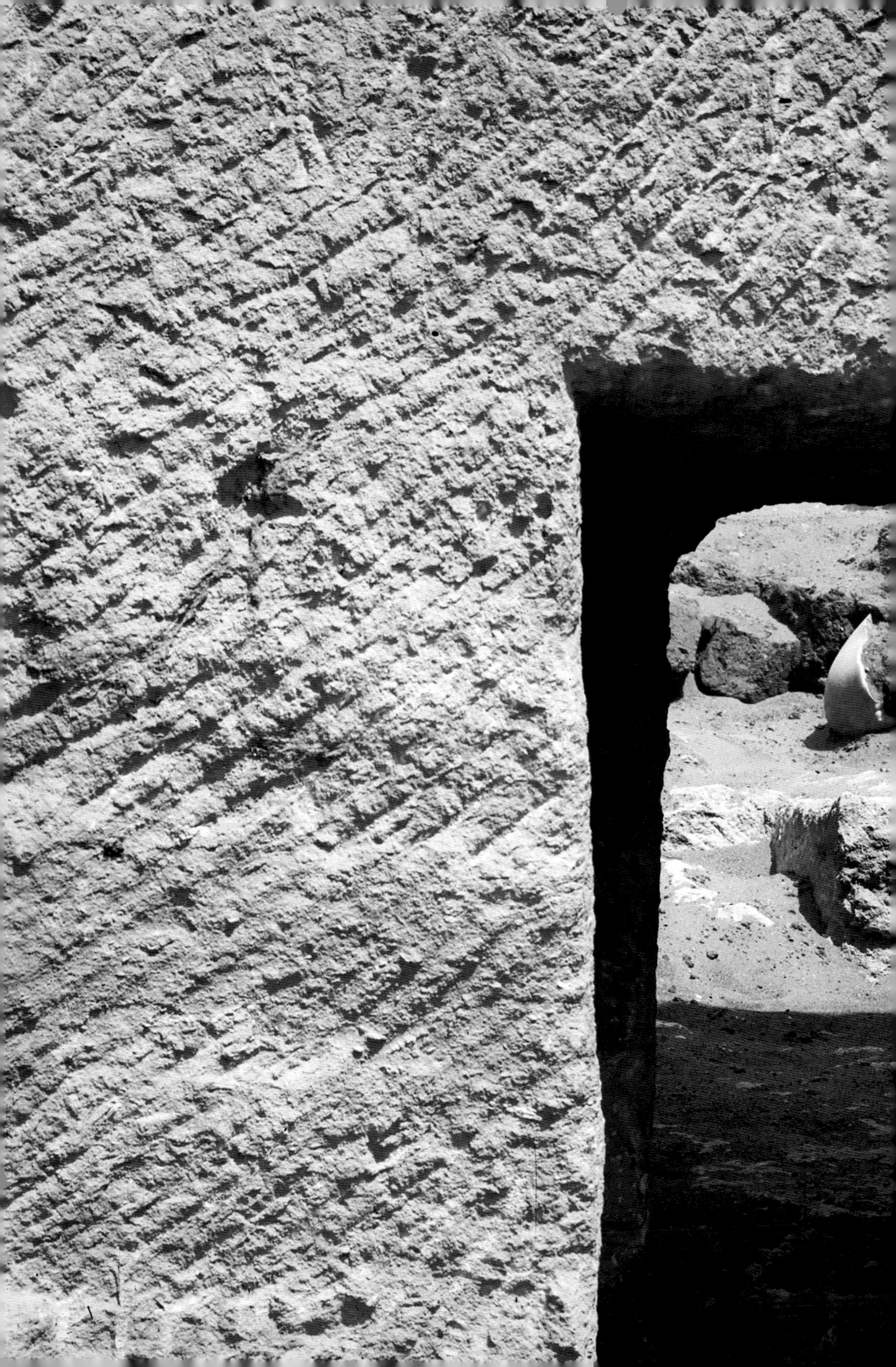

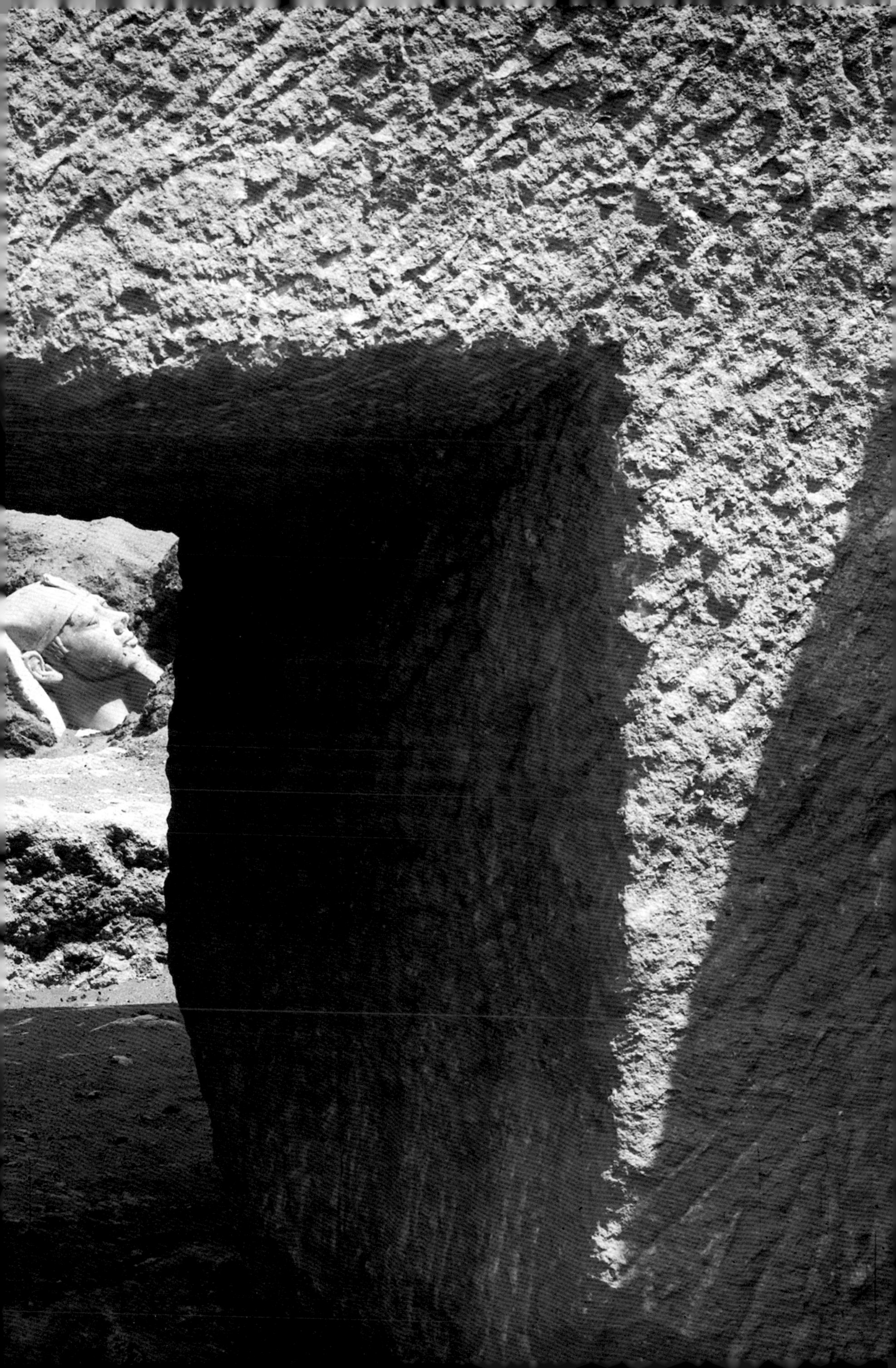

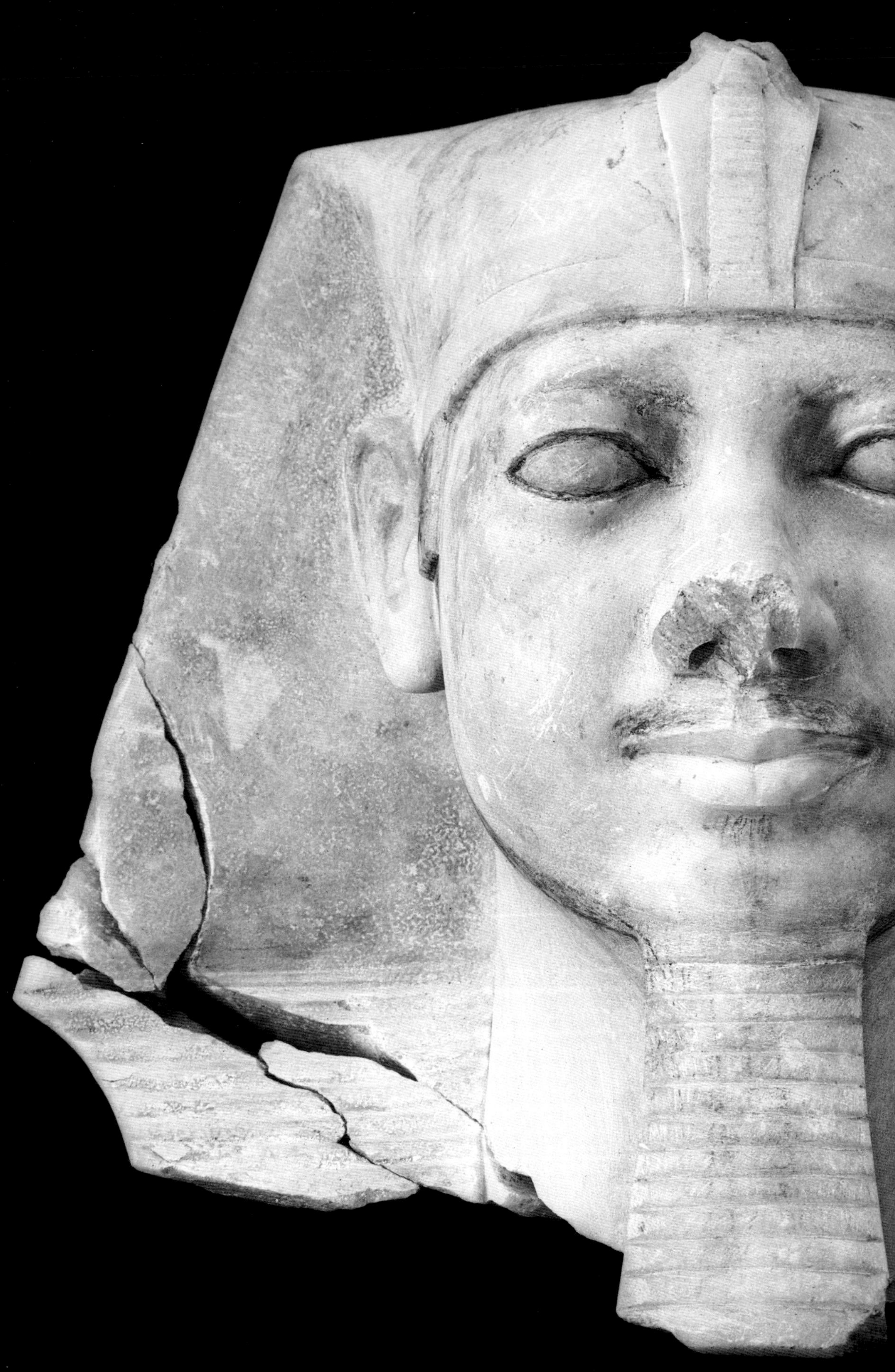

TWO

INDIVIDUALITY

For all the grandeur of their tombs, we know very little about the lives of the great pyramid builders. It is an irony of history that the only completely preserved image of Khufu (Cheops in Greek), who built the largest of all pyramids, is a tiny seated statuette in ivory, just three inches tall.[1] The face of Khafra (Chephren), who built the Second Pyramid at Giza, is known around the world as that of the Great Sphinx, and appears on a few well-preserved statues from his pyramid temple, notably the famous seated statue of the king with a falcon behind his head.[2] But it is Menkaura (Mycerinus), who built the smallest of the three pyramids, who is represented by the largest number of statues. This is entirely due to the work of the Harvard-Boston expedition at the Third Pyramid in 1906–9, which more than doubled the number of Fourth Dynasty royal statues known at the time, from thirteen to thirty.[3]

Nearly eight feet tall and weighing approximately five thousand pounds, the colossal seated statue of Menkaura is one of the largest sculptures from the Pyramid Age (fig. 7). Made of travertine (or Egyptian alabaster), the statue was found in pieces scattered about the king's pyramid temple. One large fragment with the knees, hands, and legs was found in January 1907 in a long corridor providing access to the storerooms in the northern part of the temple. Already the beauty and fine workmanship of the statue was apparent, particularly the perfect modeling of the knees. Not until April were the head, left shoulder, and upper part of the torso located outside the building, having been unceremoniously dragged out of a storeroom through a drain hole (fig. 8).[4] The head lay just a few inches below the surface, according to Reisner, "near the path formerly used by travelers visiting the pyramid [where it] might have been discovered any

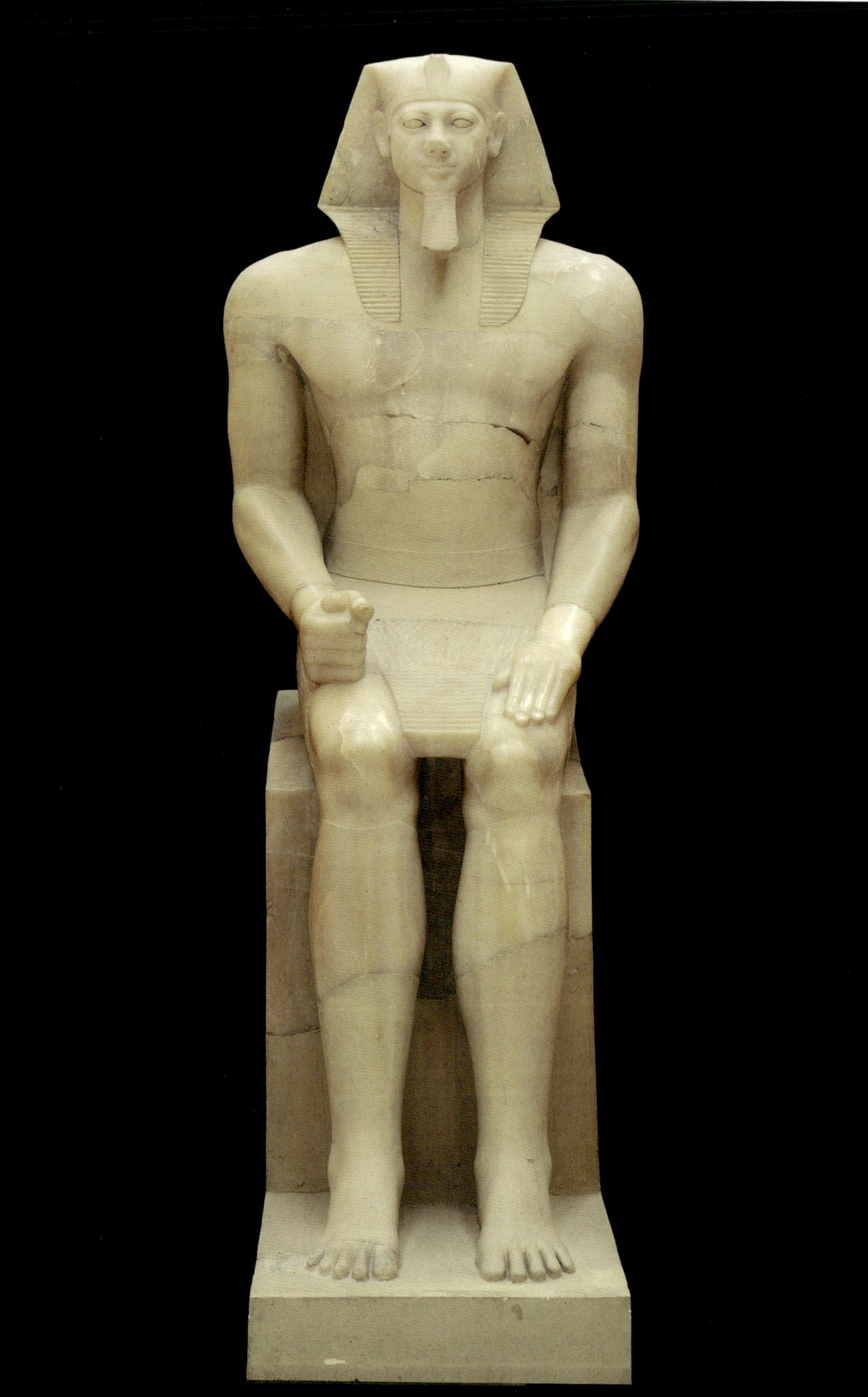

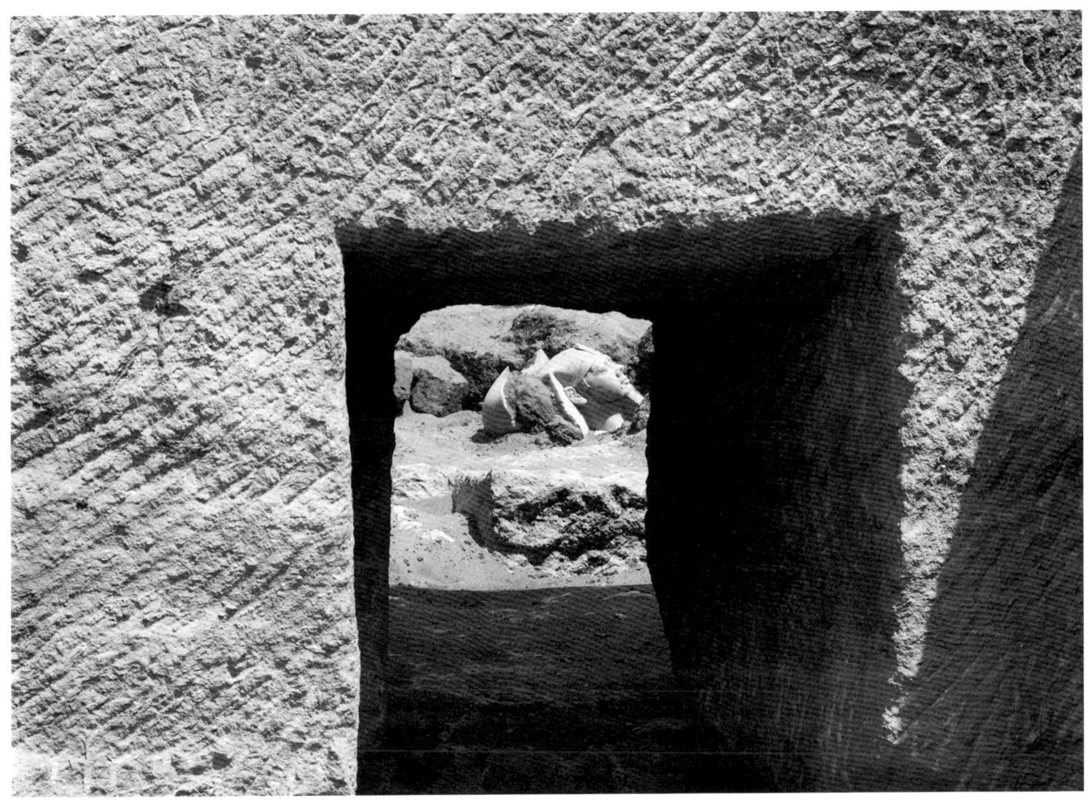

7 Colossal statue of Menkaura, 2490–2472 BCE. Travertine (Egyptian alabaster), 243.8 × 115.6 × 83.8 cm (96 × 45½ × 33 in.)

8 Head of Menkaura seen through a drain hole, 1907

time in the last thousand years by some stroller casually prodding the sand with stick or parasol."[5]

The expedition waited two years in the hope of finding additional fragments of the statue before shipping the pieces to Boston. A 1907 photograph, with Reisner's five-year-old daughter Mary included for scale, clearly shows which parts were missing or not yet identified (fig. 9). After arriving at the MFA, the statue was reconstructed based on a study of complete examples in Boston and Cairo.[6] Although the reconstruction cannot claim absolute accuracy, it gives a very good idea of how the statue would have originally appeared.

Except for the tip of the nose, the head is intact, and it is a marvel. Menkaura has a full mouth with drooping lower lip, a round nose, and bulging eyes. His face is youthful, almost chubby. The modeling is of the utmost delicacy. Photographs from the time of discovery show that he had black eyeliner, a moustache, and sideburns. Black chinstraps hold in place the narrow false beard (fig. 10). Yet even this much color was abhorrent to those who did not appreciate the use of pigment on ancient sculptures; the 1911 handbook of the Museum observes, "Fortunately the traces of the black beard and hair are all that remain of the coloring."[7]

9 Fragments of statue of Menkaura, with Mary Reisner, 1907

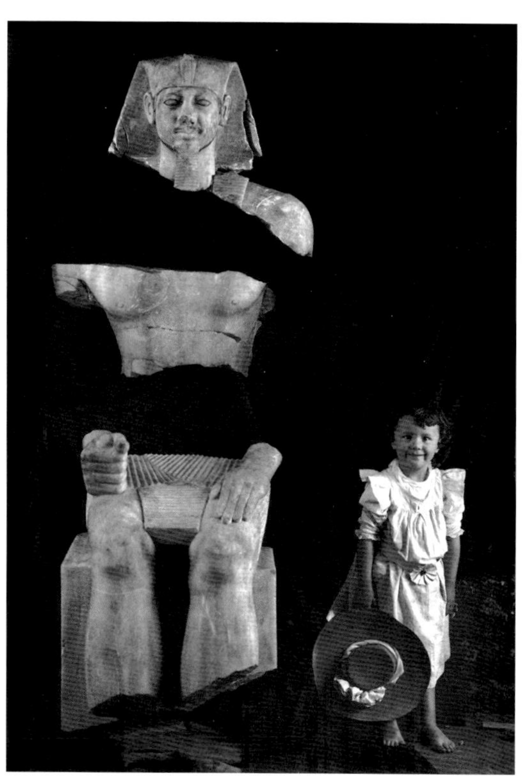

The false beard, *nemes*-headcloth with lappets, rearing cobra, and pleated kilt with tab in front are royal attributes. They tell us we are looking at a king. The folded linen cloth in the king's right hand was a status item shared by kings and commoners.[8] The base was inscribed, and part of Menkaura's name remains beside his right foot. But even without the inscription there would be no doubt which king we are looking at, for his facial features are unmistakable. The king's shoulders are immense. He is barechested and muscular, with huge pectorals and a physique that would not be out of place on a modern body builder. It is an image of might and power. Modern viewers have commented on the small size of the head in relation to the body.[9] Some see it as a miscalculation on the part of the artist, but for others, it contributes to the overall effect.[10]

Yet very few people would have seen this imposing image once it was finished. The statue was probably intended to sit in the back of the long, narrow offering hall of the temple.[11] From this lordly position, the divine ruler would have looked down the axis of the temple

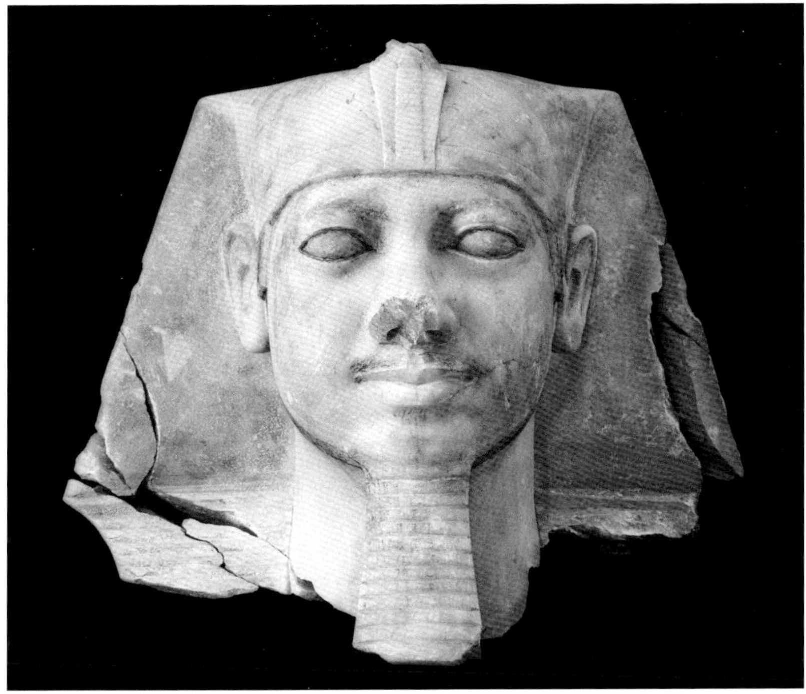

10 Head of Menkaura shortly after discovery, showing traces of original paint, 1907

complex straight through the causeway to the valley, to greet the rising sun as it appeared on the eastern horizon. But the great statue was never installed in the offering hall. Menkaura died before he could complete his pyramid complex. His temples, conceived to be erected entirely in stone, were finished in mudbrick by his successor, Shepseskaf. Services for the king's spirit continued to be performed there for three hundred years after his death, although in greatly reduced circumstances. At some point, the mudbrick temple was badly damaged by a flash flood, after which it was rebuilt, probably in the reign of Pepy II (2246–2152 BCE). Meanwhile, settlers had moved in, crowding the courtyard with their huts, storage bins, and silos, and turning the temple into a small town. Services for the king's spirit continued, though now confined to the sanctuary and offering hall.

Much later, beginning in the seventh century BCE, the site of Giza experienced a revival, as the Egyptians drew new inspiration from their ancient past. Menkaura once again became a focus of attention. His pyramid was restored, and his mummy provided with a new wooden coffin.[12] In 1837, the first person to enter the pyramid in modern times, the Englishman Howard Vyse, found the king's hard stone sarcophagus lying open and empty, the burial having been plundered long before. Vyse extracted the sarcophagus and put it on a ship bound for England. The

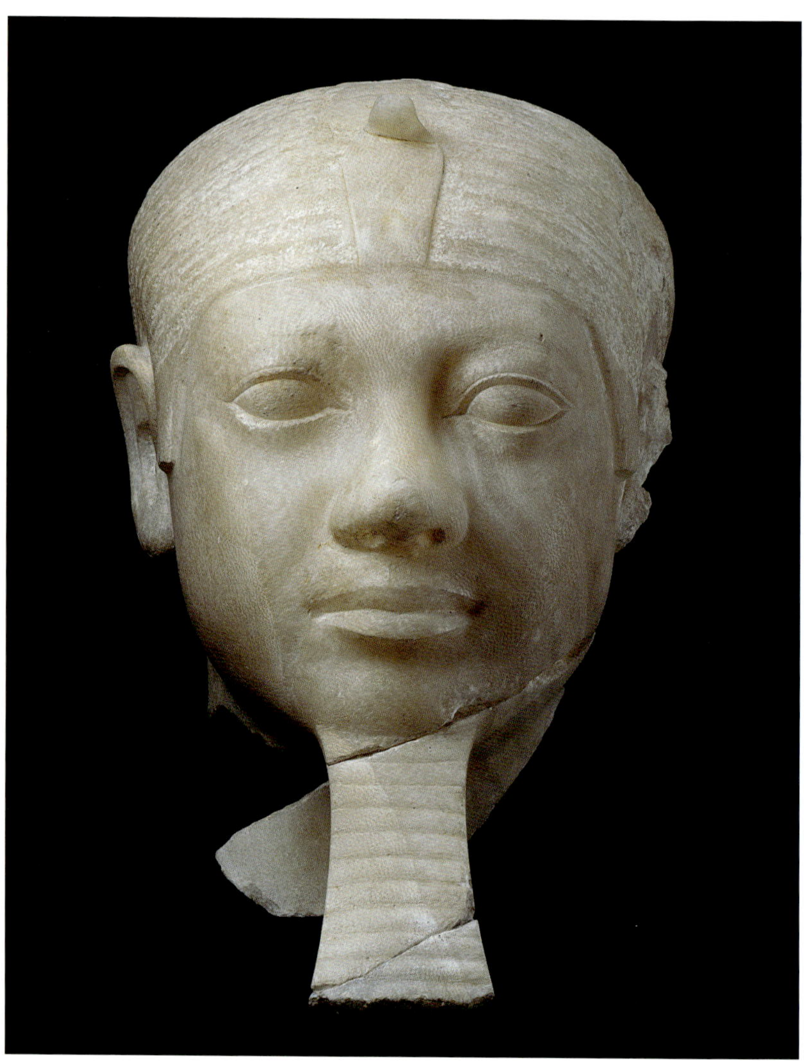

11 Head of Menkaura, 2490–2472 BCE. Travertine (Egyptian alabaster), 29.2 × 19.6 × 21.9 cm (11½ × 7¾ × 8⅝ in.)

ship sank off the coast of Spain, and Menkaura's sarcophagus still lies at the bottom of the Mediterranean, all attempts to retrieve it having so far failed.

Menkaura's facial features are consistent on all his statuary. They appear in even more youthful form on another royal head in Egyptian alabaster, where the nose is well preserved, and in the graywacke triad of Menkaura, the goddess Hathor, and the Hare nome (fig. 11; see fig. 26). The face of the king in the pair statue of Menkaura and queen, also in graywacke, is leaner and bonier, with more pronounced cheekbones (fig. 12). These portraits would appear to be the work of different sculptors.[13]

12 Pair statue of Menkaura and queen, 2490–2472 BCE. Graywacke, 142.2 × 57.1 × 55.2 cm (56 × 22½ × 21¾ in.)

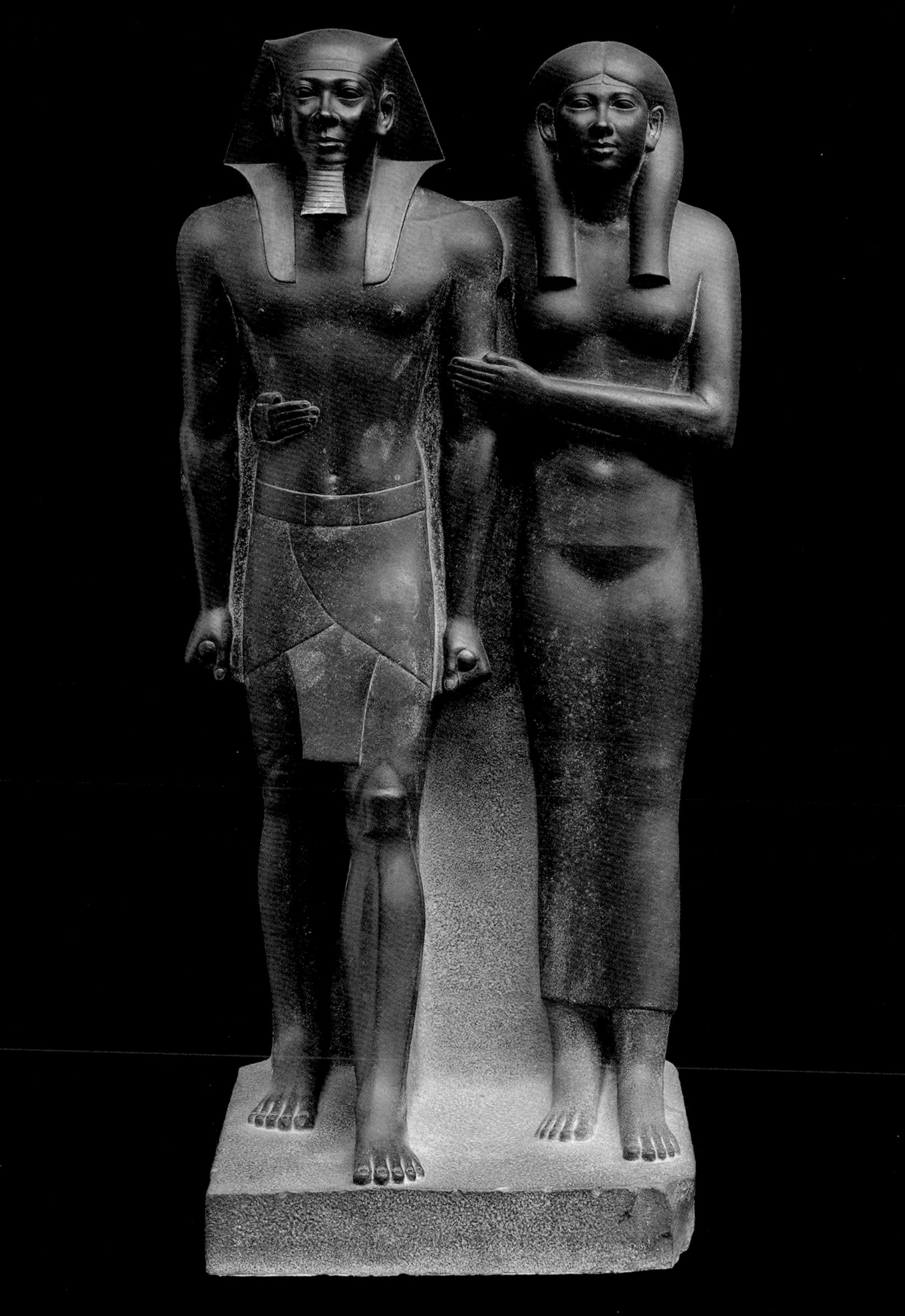

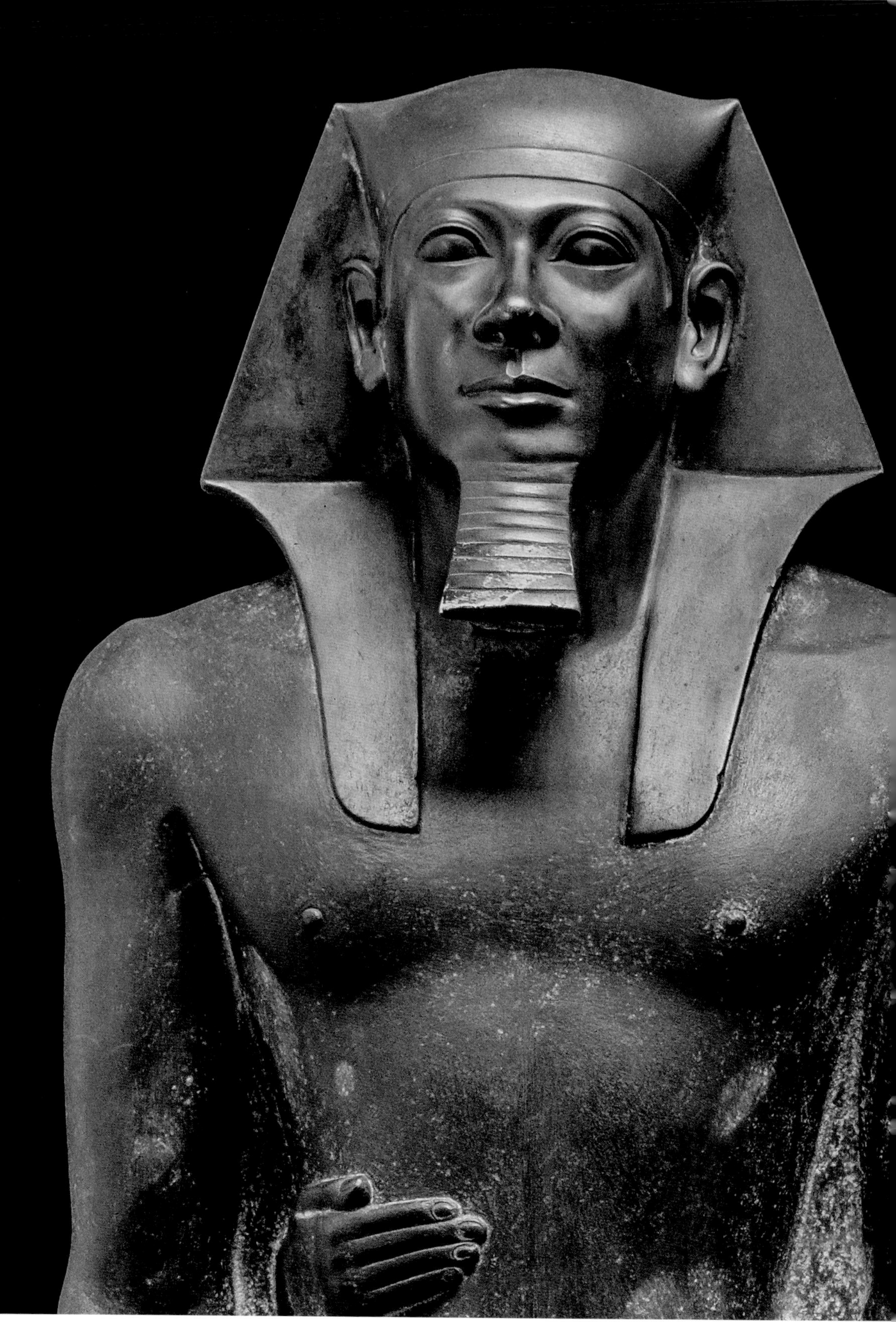

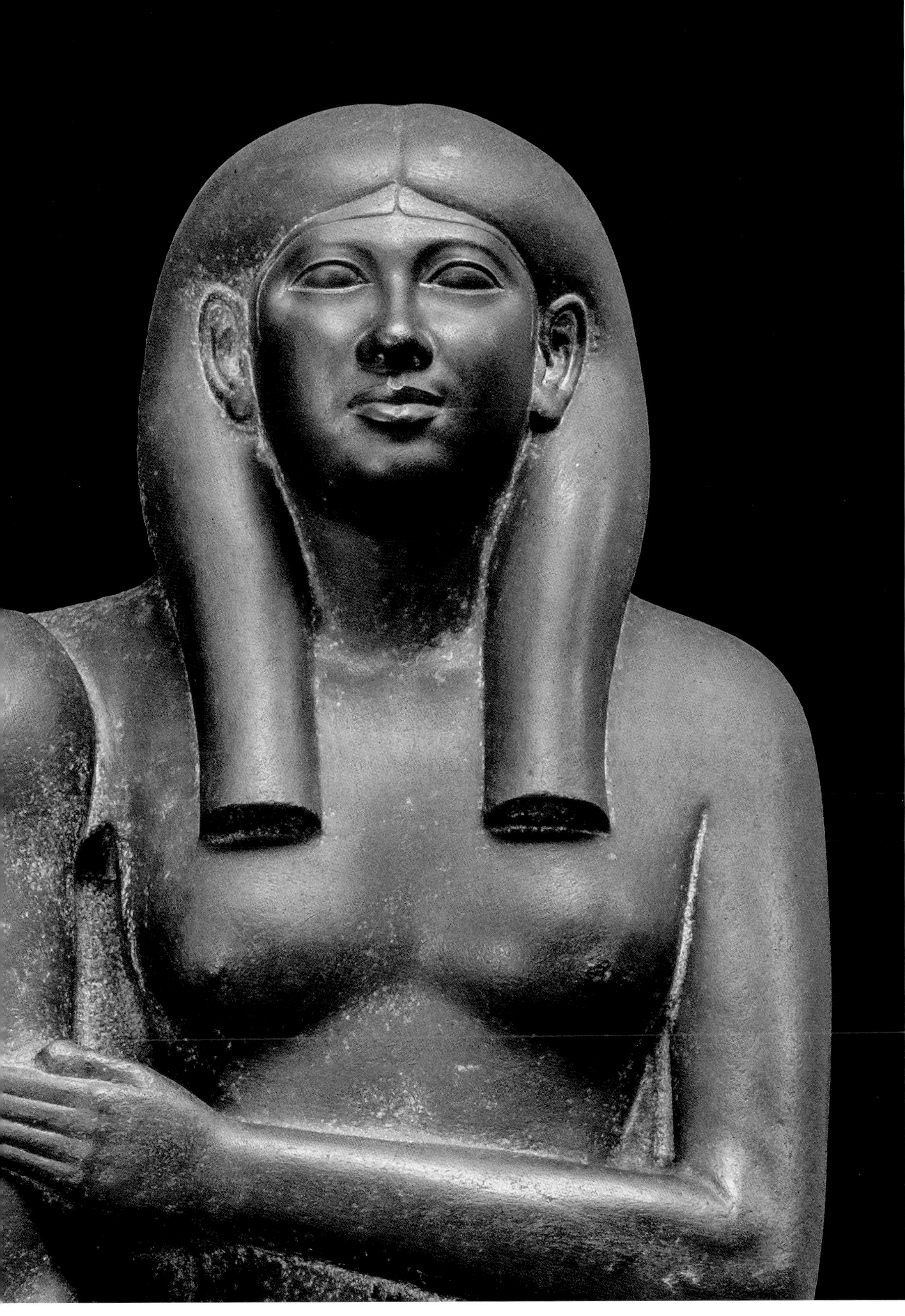

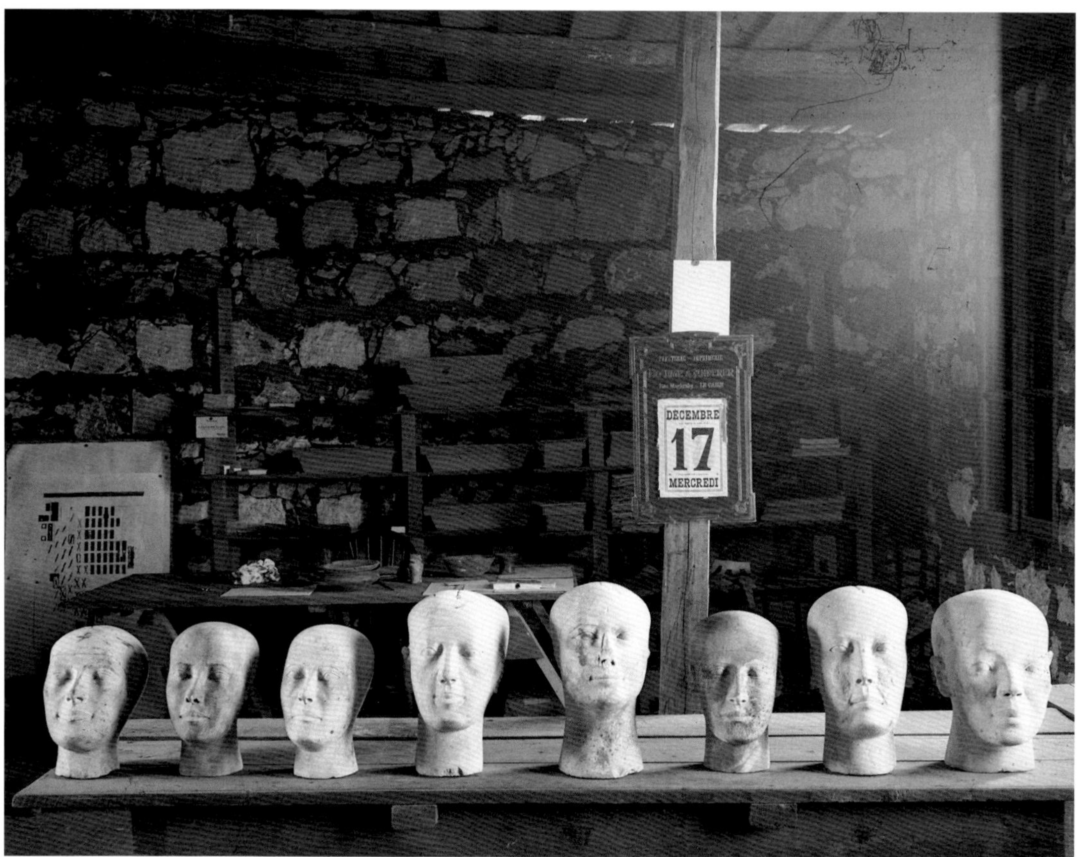

13 Portrait heads lined up in Harvard Camp workroom, December 17, 1913

Unfortunately, we will probably never know the names of these great artists, whose work had such a profound influence on Egyptian sculpture.

The pair statue and the triad also include three female portraits: a queen and two goddesses. The queen's face resembles the king's, except that her cheeks are fuller and her mouth smaller. Her face in turn provided the model for Hathor and the nome goddess. The king was considered the image of god on earth, and deities regularly appear in Egyptian art with the features of the reigning monarch.

These sculptures are Menkaura's legacy. We know next to nothing about him as a person. Menkaura was the grandson of Khufu, who built the First Pyramid, and the son of Khafra, who built the Second Pyramid. His mother's identity is not certain.[14] Three small subsidiary pyramids south of the king's pyramid contained the burials of Menkaura's principal queens, but we do not know their names. Another queen, Khamerernebty II, was buried in a rock-cut tomb behind Khafra's valley temple. She bore Menkaura a son, Khuenra.[15] Khuenra never became king, however; the next king after Menkaura was Shepseskaf. Even the length of Menkaura's reign is uncertain. It may have been as short as six years or as long as twenty-eight, so scanty and uncertain are the written sources. The chronology used by the MFA allots Menkaura eighteen years of rule (2490–2472 BCE).[16]

Ironically, the small size of Menkaura's pyramid compared to his father's and grandfather's was to the benefit of Menkaura's posthumous reputation. Whereas Khufu and Khafra went down in history as tyrants, forcing their subjects to perform hard labor to build their gargantuan funerary monuments, Menkaura was remembered as a benevolent ruler. "Of all kings who ruled in Egypt," wrote the mid-fifth-century BCE Greek historian Herodotus, "he had the greatest reputation for justice . . . and for this the Egyptians gave him higher praise than any other monarch."[17]

The nonroyal tombs at Giza were built in clusters, laid out in organized rows like housing developments for the living spirits of the dead.[18] The cemetery to the east of the Great Pyramid (where Ankhhaf was buried) was reserved for close relatives of the king, while the larger cemetery to the west of the Great Pyramid was reserved for high officials and more distant royal relations. Khufu set out to regulate the design and layout of the tombs, as well as the funerary equipment they included. The earliest mastabas had only a rectangular slab stele carved in low relief, showing the deceased seated at an offering table. It was enclosed by a mudbrick chapel on the east face of the superstructure, and a portrait head was deposited in the burial chamber below ground.

These heads are among the most remarkable portraits from ancient Egypt (fig. 13). The Egyptians hardly ever made standalone busts or heads, and these life-size heads, cut off flat at the base of the neck so that they can stand upright, are a brief phenomenon in the history of Egyptian art

14 Mummy from Giza tomb 2220B

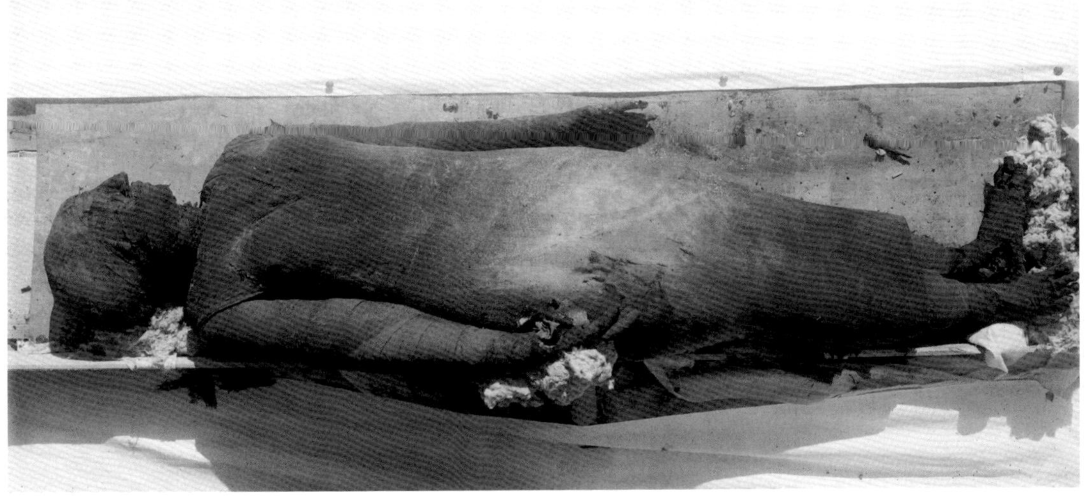

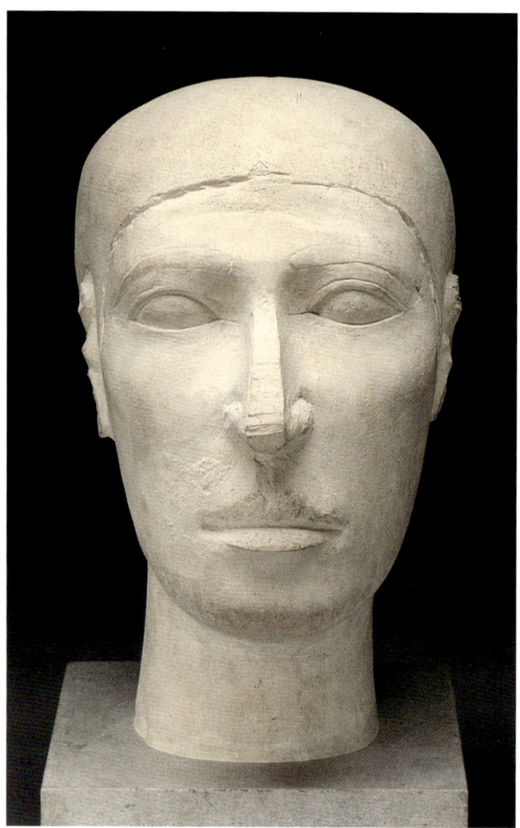

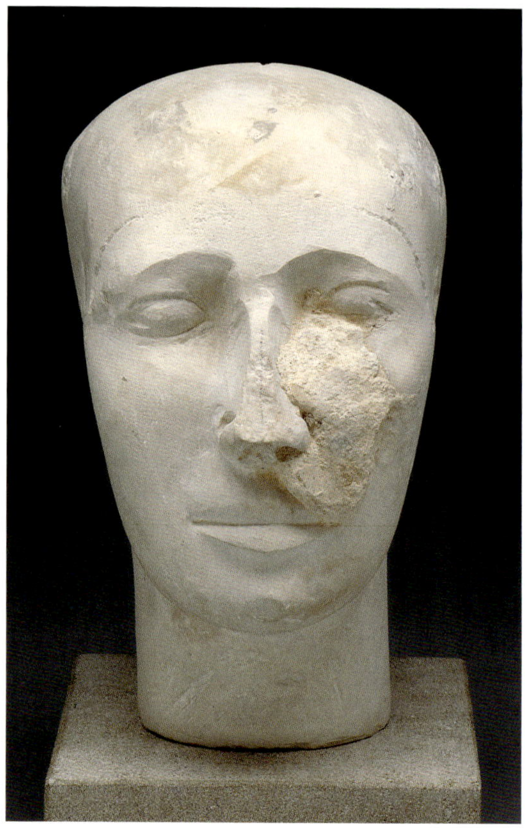

15 Portrait head of Nofer, 2551–2528 BCE. Limestone, h. 27.1 cm (10⁵⁄₈ in.)

16 Portrait head, 2551–2528 BCE. Limestone, h. 27.4 cm (10³⁄₄ in.)

and funerary practices. Of about thirty heads that have been found, most come from tombs in the western cemetery at Giza that date from the earliest construction phases in the reign of Khufu.[19] They are often called "reserve heads," after a theory introduced by German scholars in the early twentieth century that they were made to be replacements for the actual head of the deceased in case the mummy was damaged or destroyed.[20] As their purpose is still not clearly understood, however, a better and more neutral term is "portrait heads"—for whatever else they are, they are portraits. No two look like; they are distinct individuals. These people lived side-by-side and were buried in the same place. They all knew one another. These people saw the Great Pyramid being built and the transformation of the Giza plateau into a vast city of the dead, a regal court in stone with the pharaoh at its apex.

Because all but one of the tombs in which portrait heads were found had been ransacked by robbers, none were in their original position. Most of the heads were located amid the debris at the bottom of the burial shaft or in the burial chamber itself, and it seems likely that they had originally been placed in the burial chamber. Egyptian tomb sculptures were usually placed in the chapel (like Ankhhaf's) or in a sealed statue chamber, or *serdab* (after the Arabic word for cellar), hidden behind the chapel in the superstructure. Visitors made offerings to the statues in the chapel, while the mummy of the deceased rested in the burial chamber below. The placement of the portrait heads in the burial chamber suggests they had a special function in connection with the mummy.

Mummification in the Old Kingdom was essentially sculpting a body out of linen (fig. 14).[21] The limbs and torso were padded out with rolls of fabric and modeled to give the body a lifelike appearance, and facial

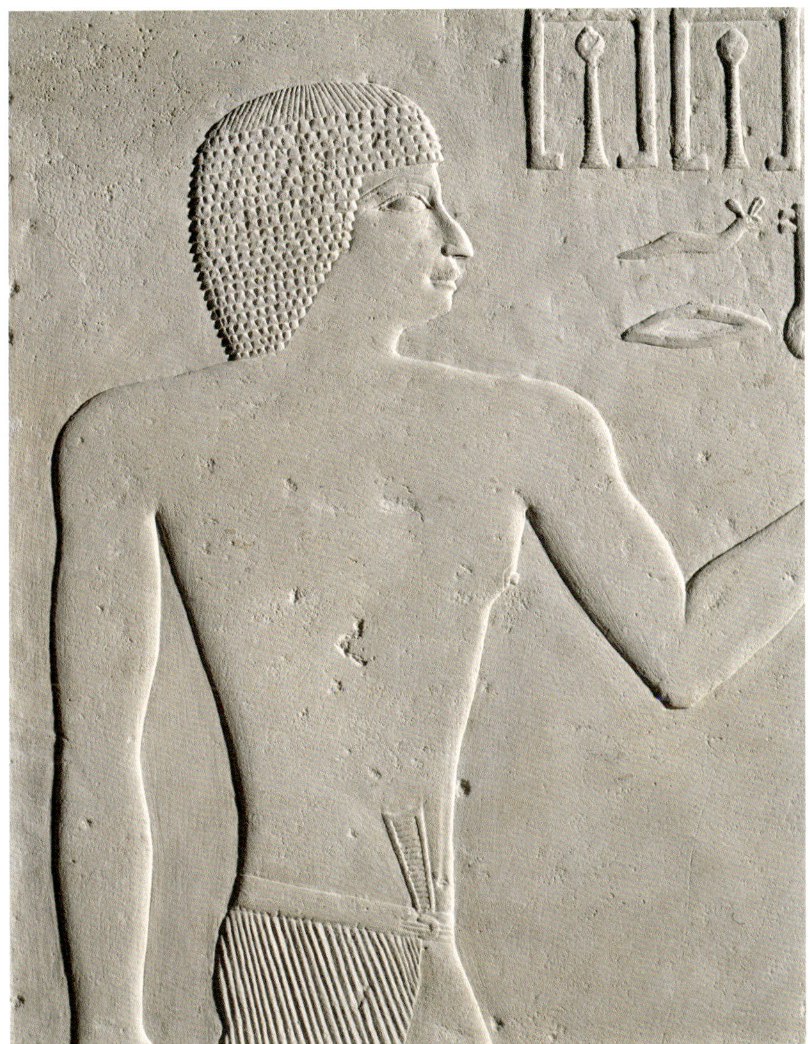

17 Relief of Nofer, 2551–2494 BCE (detail). Limestone, 95 × 109.5 cm (37 3/8 × 43 1/8 in.)

features were added in paint on the linen. The result was to turn the mummy into a statue, an everlasting simulacrum of the departed. Mummies and statues had a lot in common, and the same ritual of "opening of the mouth" was performed for both. Although the limestone portrait heads of course contain no human remains, it can be tempting to see them as related to the plaster face masks and body coverings molded directly over the outer linen wrappings of mummies in the Fifth and Sixth dynasties, which in turn have been regarded as the precursors of the cartonnage mummy masks and anthropoid cases of the Middle Kingdom, around 2140 BCE, four hundred years later.[22]

Many of the portrait heads show signs of what looks like intentional damage, inflicted after they were finished but before the tomb was sealed. Most often, the ears have been chopped off and the back of the skull has been scored with a deep gash—presumably as part of some ritual, although no satisfactory explanation has been put forward to account for it. One of the earliest of these heads to be discovered, and the first to enter the collection of the Museum back in 1906, is the head of Nofer, a treasury official. The portrait was vaunted at the time as "probably the most important piece of Egyptian sculpture in America."[23] And no doubt it was, at that time.

This is a distinct and not overly flattering portrait of a specific individual, one who could not be mistaken for anyone else (fig. 15). Nofer has a long face with high cheekbones, a short forehead, and a strong chin, but unquestionably the most striking aspect of his physiognomy is his large nose. The nose was apparently never finished: the bridge has been flattened and its straight edges have not been smoothed out. In addition, the sculptor has adjusted the length of the right sideburn but has not covered up his initial attempt. Another feature of this head, found on others as well, is that the hairline is indicated on the front and sides but not in back. This puzzling combination of finished and unfinished, polished and unpolished is typical of these portraits. One of the heads has a huge lump of plaster on the left side of the face, presumably to correct a defect in the stone, which was never trimmed off (fig. 16). Others are quite perfect, without even any ritual mutilation. Unlike other Egyptian statues, the portrait heads were never painted—another anomaly.[24]

A relief from Nofer's tomb chapel offers an opportunity to compare portraits of the same individual in the round and in relief. A block from the right jamb of the doorway portrays Nofer with the same distinctive, sharply aquiline nose as the portrait head (fig. 17). Other reliefs from the chapel, however, even the one from the opposite jamb, exhibit this feature to a lesser degree or not at all.[25]

The case of Hemiunu provides another opportunity to compare individualized portraits of the same person in two and three dimensions.[26] One of the most important figures in Khufu's court, Hemiunu probably

18 Relief of Hemiunu, 2551–2528 BCE (detail). Limestone, 12.1 × 39.5 cm (4¾ × 15½ in.)

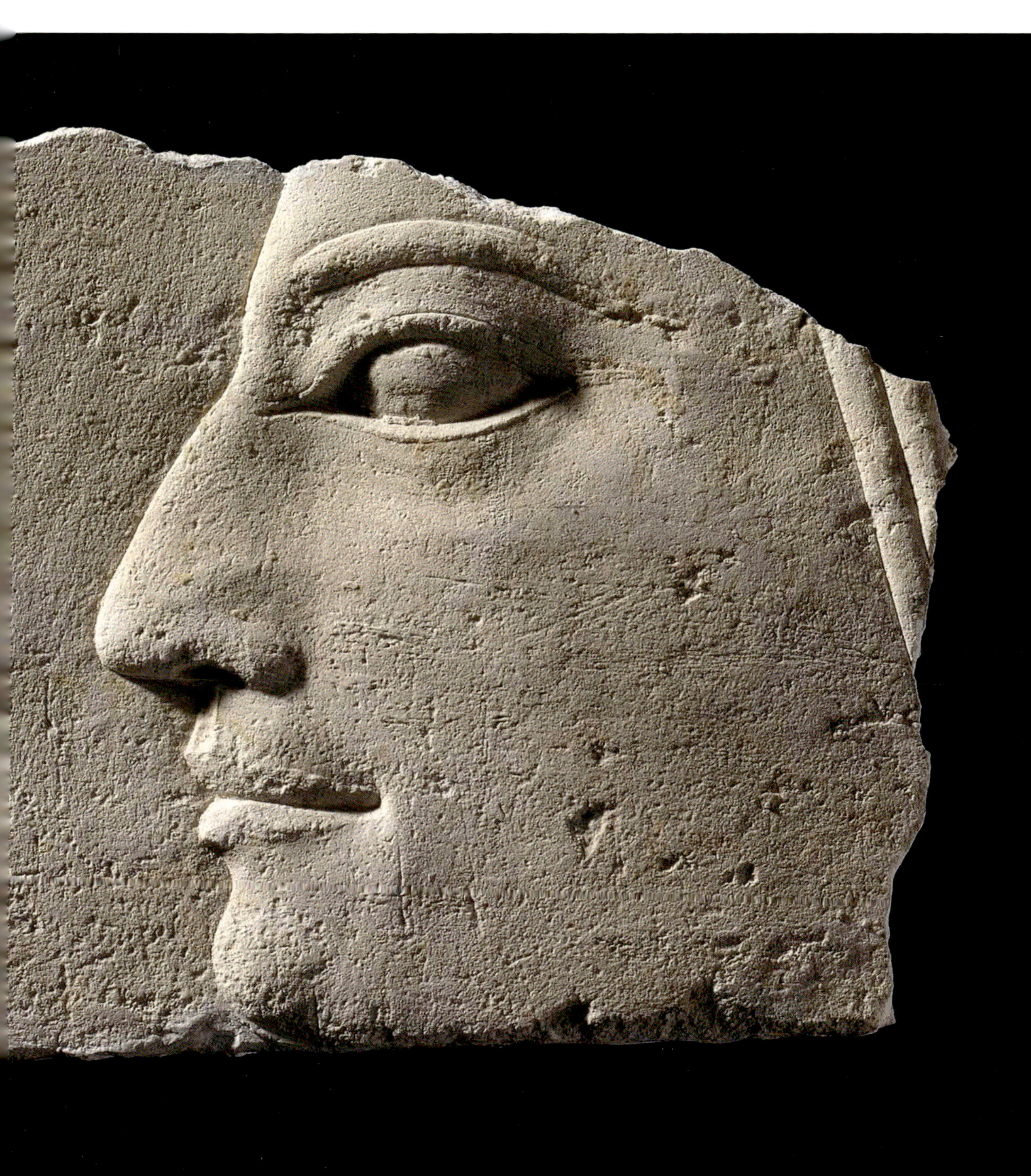

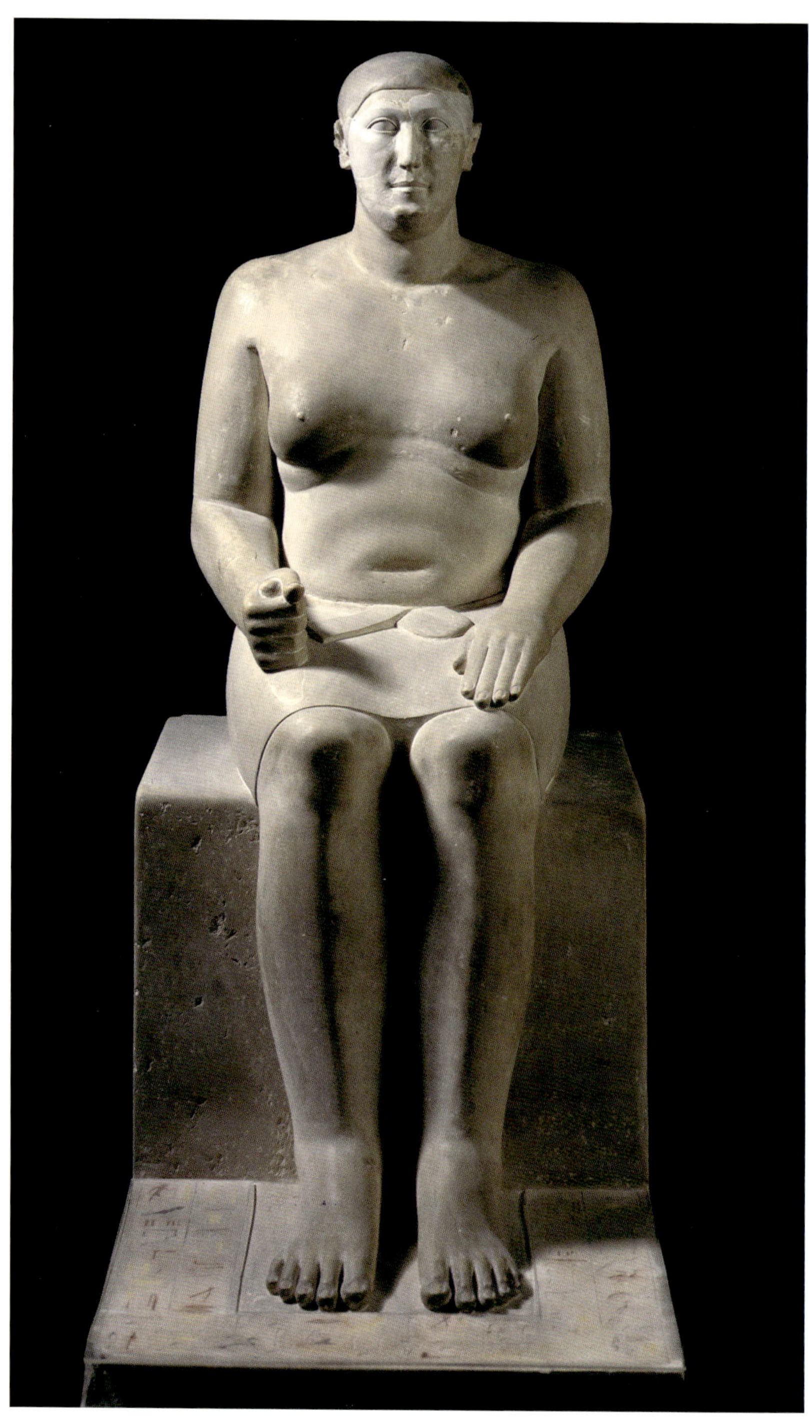

19 Seated statue of Hemiunu, 2551–2528 BCE. Limestone, h. 155.5 cm (61¼ in.)

preceded Ankhhaf as vizier and overseer of all royal construction works. He would have begun the work on the Great Pyramid, which Ankhhaf saw to completion. As befits his status, Hemiunu had the largest mastaba in the cemetery west of the Great Pyramid. Only fragments remain of the superlative low relief carving that decorated the walls of his tomb chapel. On one of them, Hemiunu's relief portrait features a prominent nose, a subtly modeled pocket under the eye, and full, undulating outlines of the lip and chin (fig. 18).

The same facial features occur on his life-size portrait statue, excavated by the Germans and now in Hildesheim.[27] It is the body of this statue that rivets attention, however: Hemiunu appears as a man of immense girth, fat and flabby, with pendulous breasts, heavy limbs, and thick ankles (fig. 19). Men of wealth and station were often portrayed in this manner, and the same man might appear in one scene as youthful and fit and in another as old and fat, representing two different stages in life or two different ideas of success. For instance, Prince Kawab, the eldest son of Khufu, appears as a portly old gentleman in a scene in the tomb of his daughter, Queen Meresankh.[28] Yet many a successful official would have looked like this, and there is no disputing the anatomical accuracy of Hemiunu's abundant folds of flesh. The statue was originally painted, like Ankhhaf, and the eyes were inlaid with rock crystal, so the effect would have been extraordinarily vivid. Unlike the bust of Ankhhaf, however, the statue of Hemiunu was not set up in the chapel where visitors could see it, but in the serdab, where it communicated with the outside through a hole in the wall at eye level, the so-called serdab-slit.[29] Tomb robbers managed to squeeze through the hole to pry out the valuable eye inlays, smashing the face to bits in the process. The restoration of the eyes is conjectural, but the form of the nose is confirmed by the relief portrait.

There can be no greater contrast than that between the heroic physique of Menkaura and the corpulent figure of Hemiunu. Not until a brief episode in the fourteenth-century BCE reign of Akhenaten would a king's body be shown in such an apparently unflattering manner, in public for all to see.

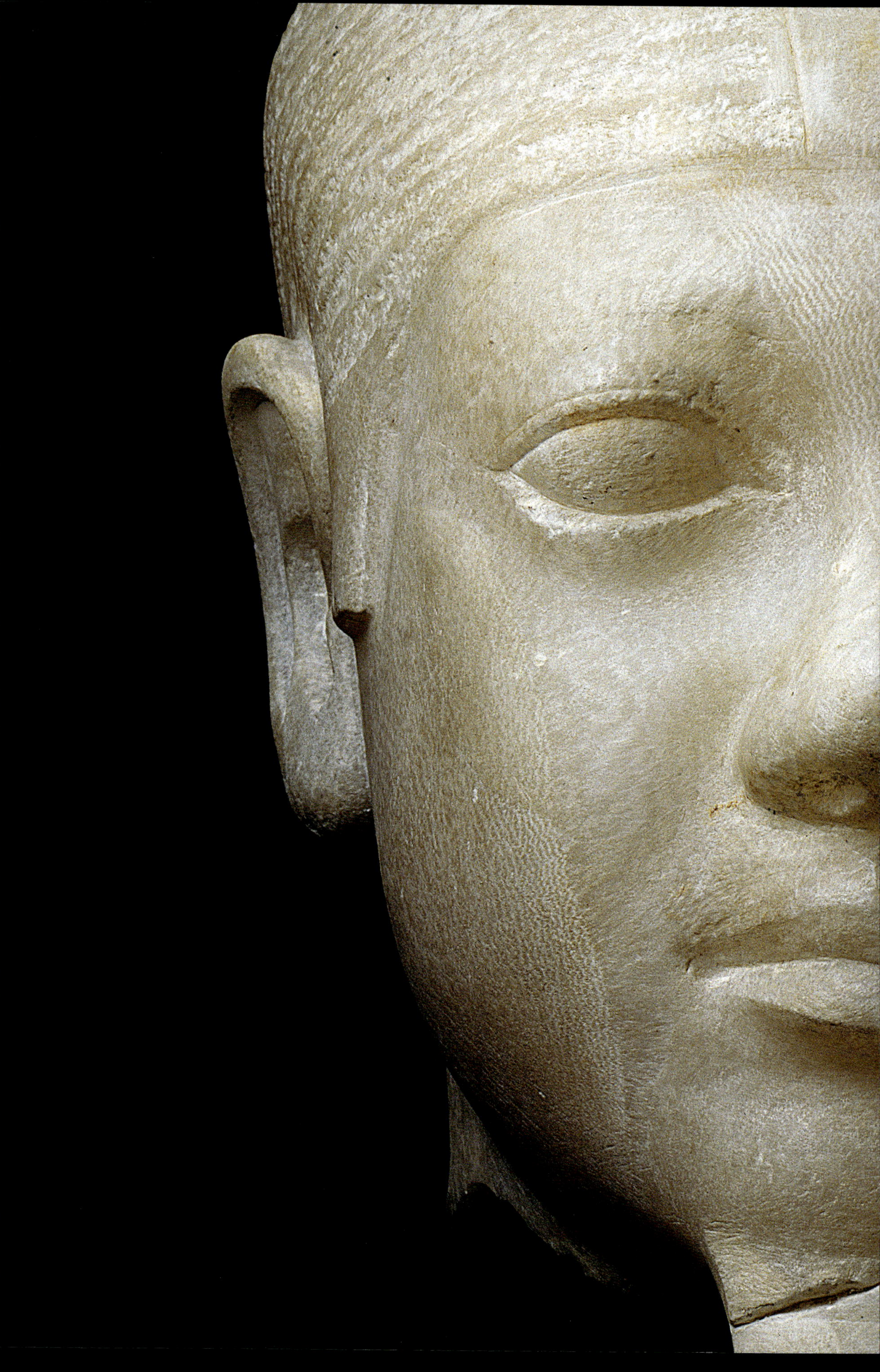

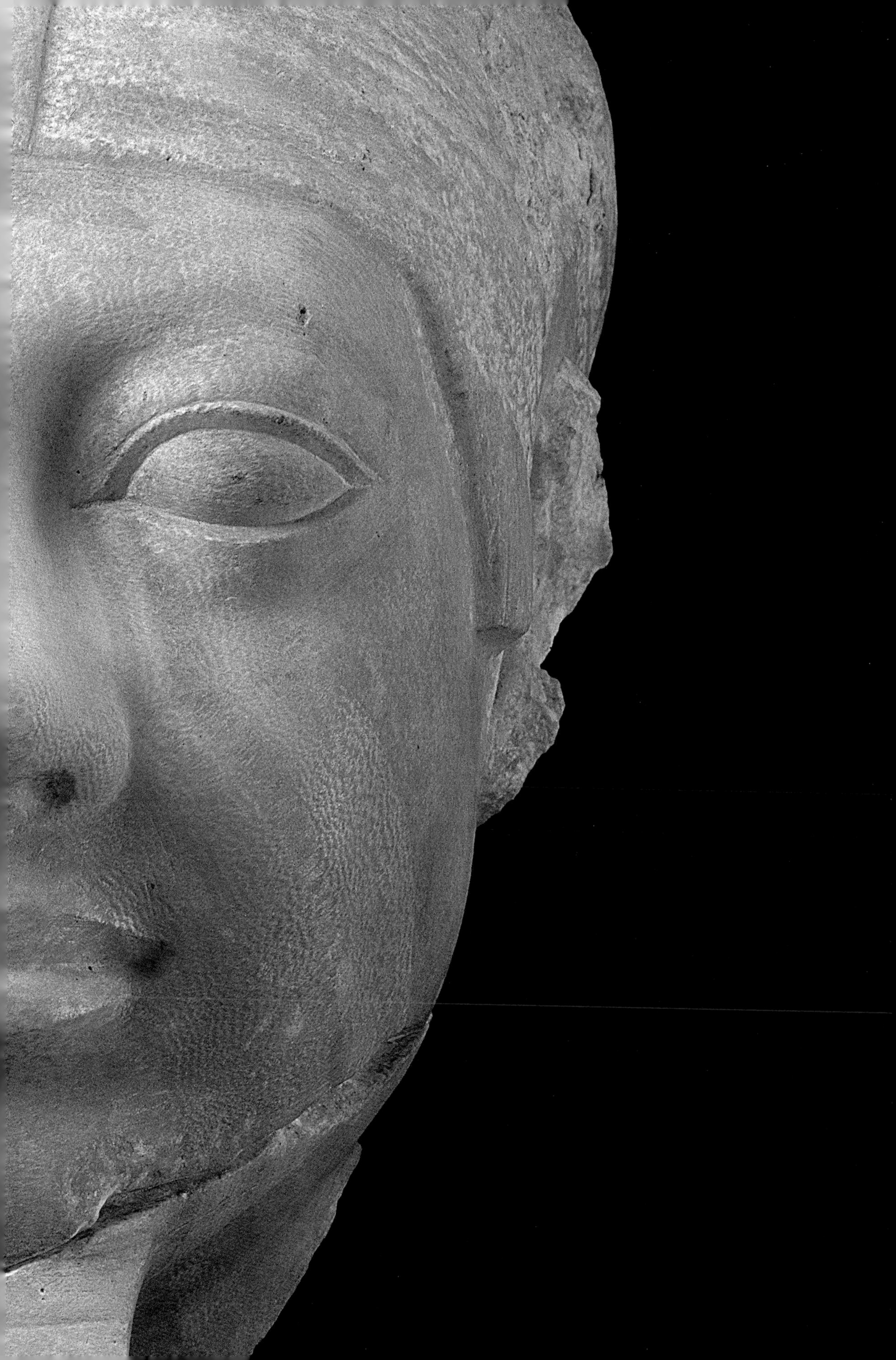

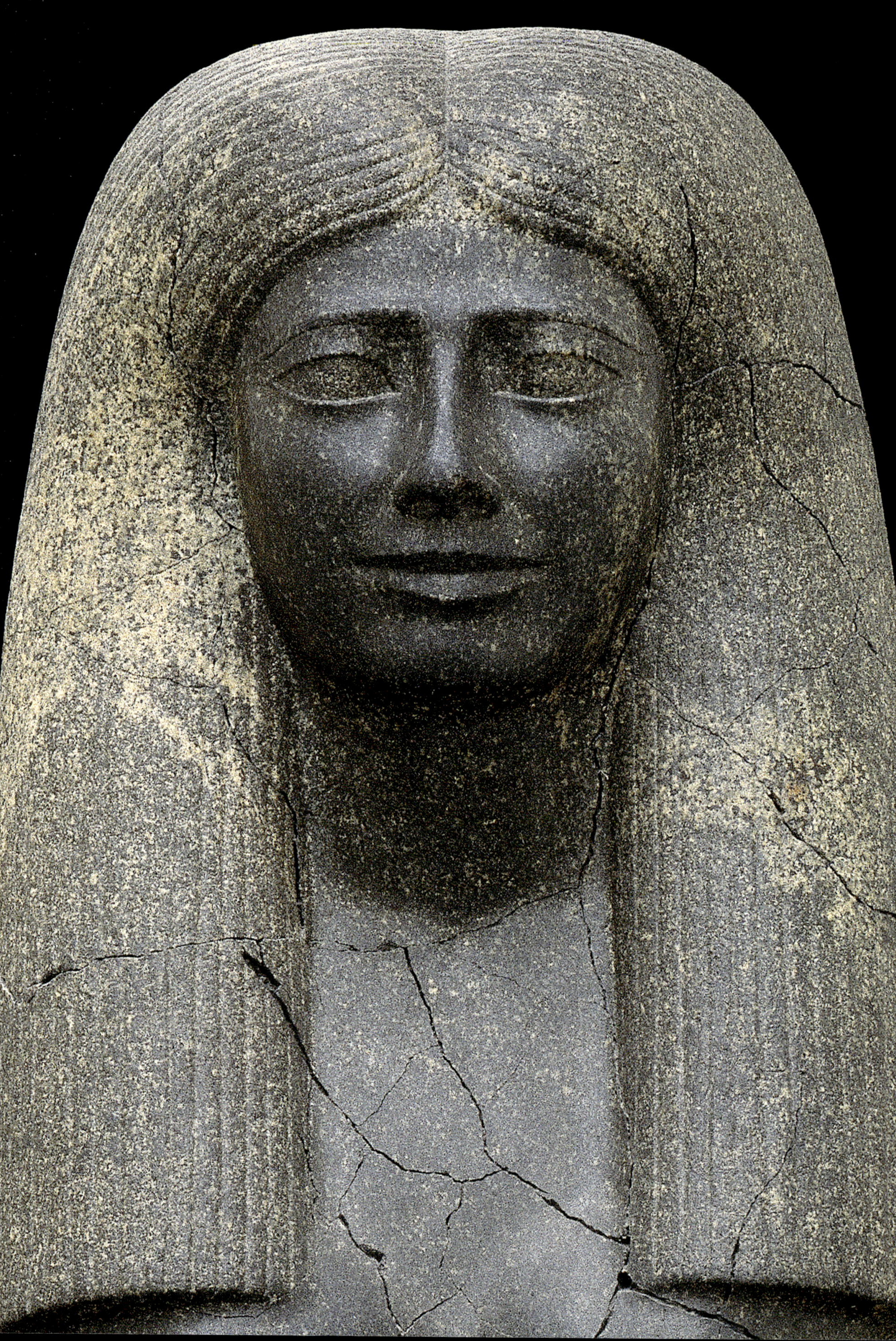

THREE

Renaissances and Revivals

The ancient Egyptians were acutely aware of their ancient past: they were surrounded by it. At the start of a new period or dynasty, rulers often looked back to earlier times for inspiration. Amenemhat I, the founder of the Twelfth Dynasty, who assumed the throne in 1991 BCE, took as one of his royal names the epithet "Repeating of Births," or renaissance, proclaiming a period of rebirth and renewal. The monuments of the Old Kingdom, with their connotations of strength, stability, and strict central control, provided the template for the art and architecture of the new dynasty. Pyramids were built, temples were founded, and statues were produced in great number. Their forms are simple, classic, and technically superb. These qualities are exemplified by the statue of Lady Sennuwy, arguably the most beautiful Middle Kingdom female portrait in existence—complete and life-size.

Lady Sennuwy was the wife of Djefaihapi I, governor of the province of Asyut in Upper Egypt in the reign of Senwosret I (1971–1962 BCE). Djefaihapi was a very wealthy man, the possessor of a considerable private income in addition to the benefits accruing to him through his offices. We know this from ten contracts with funerary priests carved on the walls of Djefaihapi's tomb, arranging for the upkeep of his funerary cult, including the care and feeding of his statues.[1] The tomb itself, excavated in the hillside overlooking the town at Asyut, is one of the largest rock-cut tombs ever built for a nonroyal personage.[2] Lady Sennuwy's statue, expertly carved of costly granodiorite from Aswan, compares well with the statuary produced for Senwosret I himself.[3]

Sennuwy has a broad smiling face, square jaw, and prominent cheekbones. She is elegantly made up, with beautifully contoured eyes and

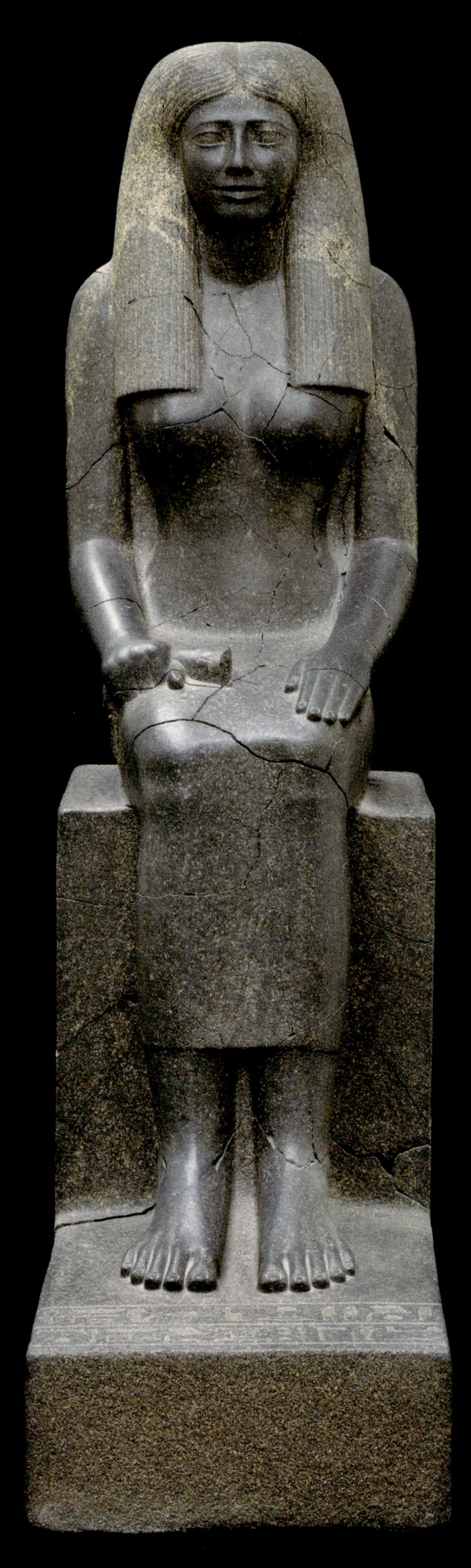

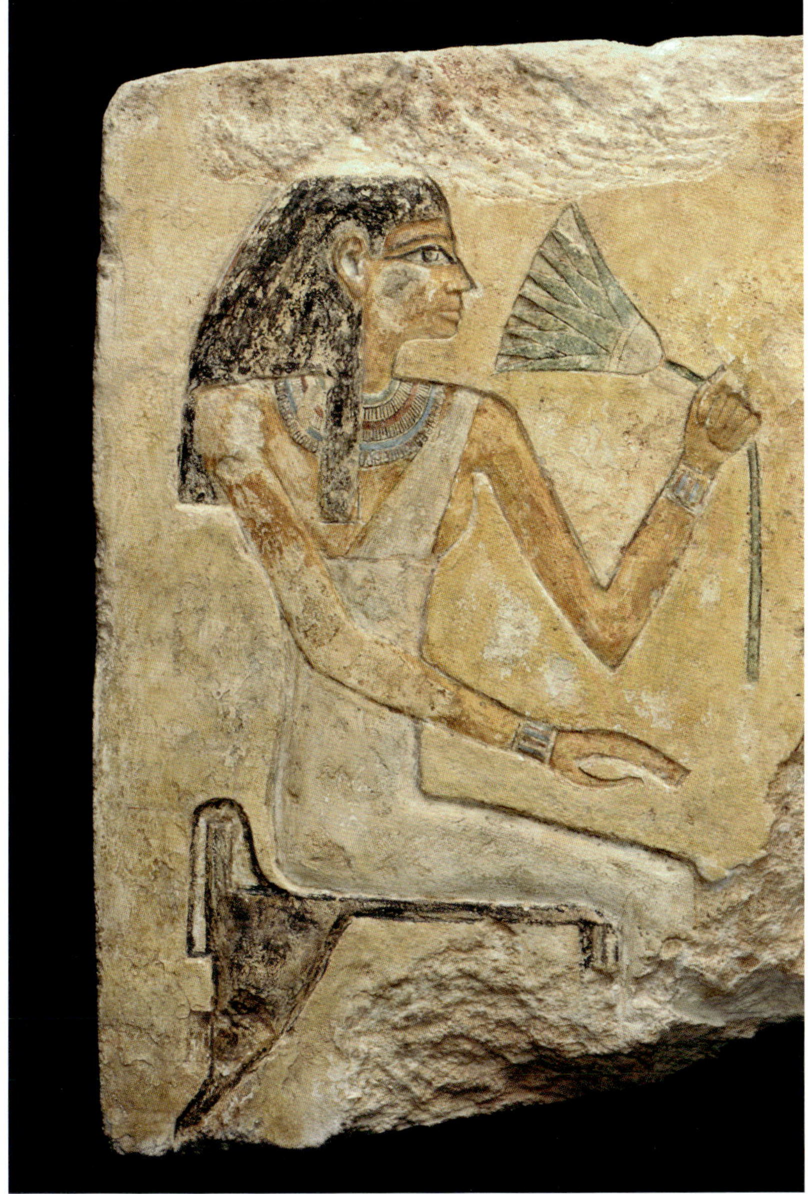

21 Relief of Lady Wadjkaues, 1971–1926 BCE (detail). Painted limestone, 59 × 37 cm (23¼ × 14⅝ in.)

eyebrows. The sculptor has left the surfaces of the eyes rougher than the rest of the face, a subtle effect. We cannot know how closely Sennuwy resembled her portrait, but it was how she saw herself and wanted to be seen (fig. 20).

Seated bolt upright on a cuboid seat, she is a model of composure. She has a slender waist, flat stomach, and firm, rounded breasts. Her long, striated wig is parted in the middle, its long tresses dividing over her shoulders. Her long sheath dress hugs her body, its hemline reaching to just above her ankles. She holds a blue lotus blossom, associated with rebirth, in her right hand, with its stem draped over her thigh. The stem of an actual lotus, of course, would not bend that way. Comparison with a relief shows how to interpret this staid pose. It shows Lady Wadjkaues—a contemporary of Lady Sennuwy's and, like her, the wife of a provincial governor—seated at an offering table laden with loaves of bread (fig. 21).

20 Statue of Lady Sennuwy, 1971–1926 BCE. Granodiorite, overall: 170.2 × 116.2 × 47 cm (67 × 45¾ × 18½ in.)

Her white shift with shoulder straps is the same garment that Sennuwy is supposed to be wearing. With one hand she holds a blue lotus blossom up to her nose; with the other hand she reaches toward the table of offerings. This is how we should envision Lady Sennuwy. Egyptian sculpture in the round is compact and avoids projecting limbs: the arms and any attributes they hold are kept close to the body. Likewise, the chair has been transformed into a cube, both to avoid breakage and in keeping with the tendency of sculptors to reduce objects to abstract forms. Relief carving entailed no such modifications. Like Ankhhaf with his plaster models, Lady Sennuwy is a recipient of offerings—no static presence, but a living image to engage with in tomb or temple. Indeed, one of the ancient Egyptian words for statue is *shesepu*, "one who receives," from the verb *shesep*, "to receive," alluding to this very function of statuary.[4]

Two lines of beautifully cut hieroglyphs at the statue's feet read: "The one honored with Osiris, lord of the living land; may he give libations and incense to the *ka* (vital spirit) of the lady of the house, Sennuwy." The sides of the seat are inscribed with columns of hieroglyphs, five on each side, each column beginning with the phrase "the one honored with" such and such a god or goddess, and ending with "the lady of the house, Sennuwy." To be honored with a deity certifies that an individual is worthy of the god's largesse in the form of offerings. Lady Sennuwy is provided for by a conclave of protective cosmic and funerary deities: Osiris, Ptah-Sokar, Tefnut, Nut, and Isis on one side, and Anubis, Nephthys, Hathor, Neith, and Selqet on the other. Osiris and Ptah-Sokar are gods of the underworld. Tefnut is the moisture that is in the air; Nut is the sky. Hathor is the all-embracing mother goddess. Isis, Nephthys, Neith, and Selqet are probably most familiar as the shapely guardians stationed along the four sides of Tutankhamen's golden canopic shrine.

All this divine protection did not save her statue from a bizarre fate. As Egypt grew weaker after the end of the Middle Kingdom in the mid-seventeenth century BCE, the kingdom of Kerma in northern Sudan conducted periodic raiding forays into Egypt, bringing home quantities of Egyptian sculpture as booty. The statue of Lady Sennuwy was probably seized in such a raid shortly before 1550 BCE. The four-hundred-year-old statue—now a prized trophy—was laboriously transported to Kerma and buried in the king's vast tumulus grave, a low mound of earth three hundred feet (ninety meters) across, encircled by a ring of stones. Inside was a honeycomb of mudbrick retaining walls defining chambers filled with grave goods and covered with sand, bisected by a central corridor spanning the full length east to west. That is where the Harvard-Boston expedition discovered her on December 16, 1913, as recounted in the expedition's diary for that day and captured in photographs on the spot: "I had just started breakfast when a man came running to say they had found a granite head—which later proved to be part of a life-sized seated female

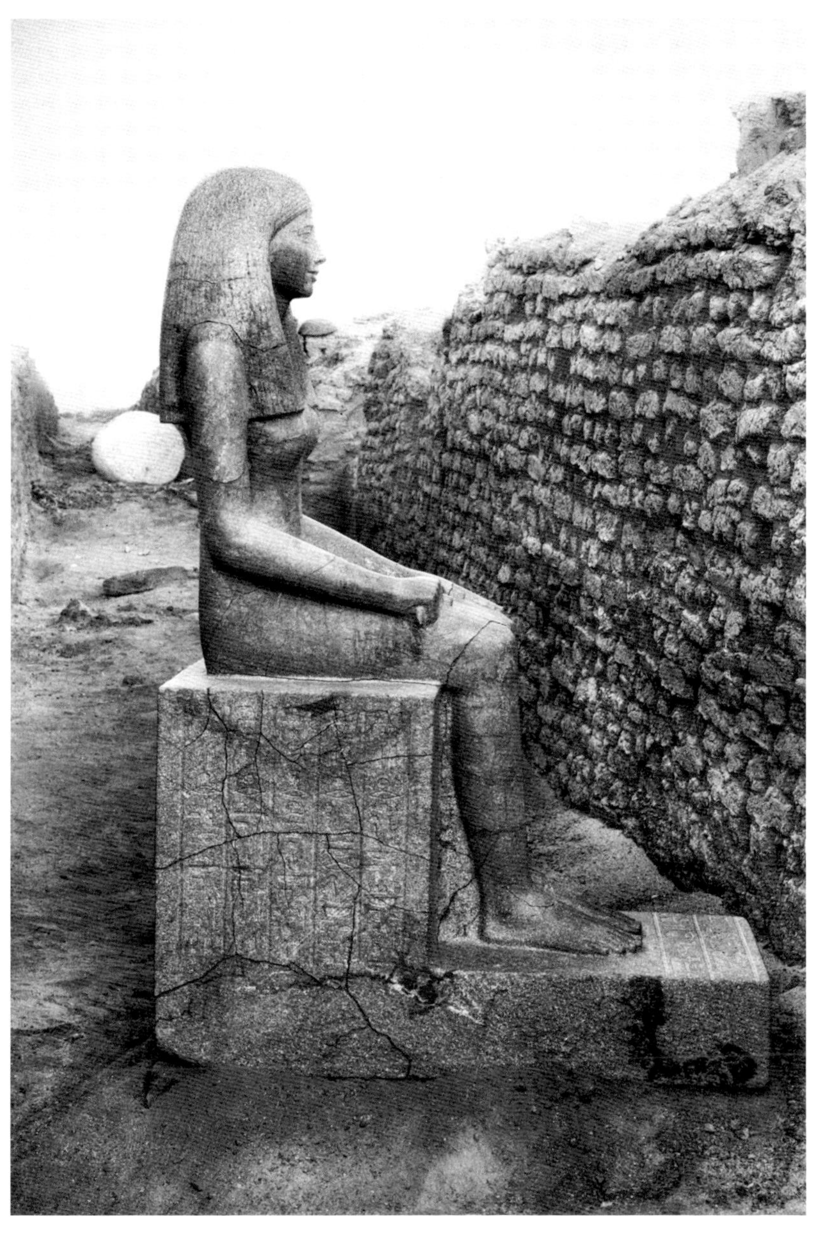

22 Lady Sennuwy as found, December 17, 1913

figure in absolute perfect condition except for surface cracks from the weather. It was standing in the long hall III a, but not in position"(fig. 22).[5]

One custom in particular distinguished the burial practices at Kerma from Egyptian funerary rites of the same period. At Kerma, the rulers and owners of the larger tombs were accompanied in death by sacrificial burials, sometimes in great numbers. The tumulus where the statue of Lady Sennuwy was found contained more than one hundred sacrificed Kermans.

In addition to Lady Sennuwy's statue there was a life-size statue of her husband, Governor Djefaihapi, of which only the knees and part of the seat remain.[6] The two statues were evidently made as a pair. They could have been brought from their tomb at Asyut, a distance of eight hundred miles; however, that site is much farther north than any attested Kerman foray into Egyptian territory. A likely alternative, well within the reach of the Kermans, is the shrine of Heqaib on Elephantine Island, near Aswan, where many Middle Kingdom dignitaries dedicated statues of themselves.[7] The statues of Lady Sennuwy and Djefaihapi were the largest but by no means the only Egyptian statues found at Kerma. Tumulus III alone contained thirty-seven Egyptian statues, and the remaining royal tumuli yielded at least sixty-four others.[8] This wholesale removal of Egyptian statuary to Kerma is one of the earliest examples in history of the large-scale transportation of heavy monuments from enemy territory to the land of the victors, comparable to the capture and removal to Susa of ancient Mesopotamian sculptures like the stele of Naram-Sin and the Code of Hammurabi by the Elamites in the twelfth century BCE.[9]

Partly because of this history, Lady Sennuwy's statue was the cause of one of the biggest misconceptions in Nile Valley archaeology. Reisner went to Sudan partly out of a longstanding interest in Egyptian-Nubian relations and partly to fill gaps in the MFA's Egyptian collection. Although rich in monuments of the Old Kingdom from Giza, the Museum was relatively weak in the art of the Middle and New Kingdoms. As northern Sudan had been all or partly under Egyptian control during much of that time, it promised to be a likely source of Egyptian art of these periods.

Reisner succeeded only too well. At Kerma he found just what he was looking for. But he was misled by all the Middle Kingdom sculptures he found there. He mistook the royal Kerma tumuli for the graves of the Egyptians represented by the statuary, whom he assumed to be the Egyptian governors of Kerma during the Middle Kingdom. Reisner proposed that Djefaihapi had been sent to Kerma by Senwosret I, had died there, and was buried there (rather than in Asyut) with Lady Sennuwy, having adopted local burial customs, including human sacrifice. In fact, there were no Egyptian governors of Kerma in the Middle Kingdom. Egyptian control of Nubia at that time did not extend beyond the Second Cataract of the Nile, not far from the present-day border between Egypt and Sudan. Kerma, rather than being the Egyptian colonial outpost that Reisner imagined, was the capital of an independent and powerful Nubian kingdom, and the Egyptian statues found in the royal tumuli were war booty the Nubians plundered from Egyptian sites. Such a state of affairs would have been inconceivable to Reisner, so thoroughly imbued was he with the Egyptians' own negative depictions of the Nubians, their traditional enemies, and by engrained prejudice.

A century after Lady Sennuwy was carved, a new and influential style of portraiture emerged during the reign of Senwosret III (1878–1841 BCE). In place of her smooth, unruffled calm, we have faces with complex, highly animated surfaces full of bumps, folds, and depressions, as seen in over a hundred surviving portraits of this king, including a colossal quartzite head in Kansas City (fig. 23). As this was Senwosret's own image, the directive to change the style must have come from the king himself. The features must have their basis in his own, but what to make of the expression, and what was the ruler trying to project? It has been described variously as grim, sad, forbidding, imperious, or intimidating.

We know much more about Senwosret III than we do about Menkaura or any Old Kingdom ruler. Senwosret III was a great and powerful monarch. He built two tombs: a pyramid complex at Dahshur, and a second mortuary complex at Abydos, where he was probably buried.[10] Under his rule, administration became more centralized, and the power of the provincial governors was reduced and eventually phased out. The conquest of Lower Nubia was completed, with the southern border firmly established below the Second Cataract of the Nile at Semna, about 65 kilometers (40 miles) south of the modern border between Egypt and the Sudan. There, the king erected a magnificent sandstone stele some five feet tall. His stirring address to his troops guarding the border gives us perhaps the best idea of the king's self-image:

> *I am a king who speaks and acts,*
> *What my heart plans is done by my arm.*
> *One who attacks to conquer, who is swift to succeed,*
> *In whose heart a plan does not slumber.*
> *Considerate to clients, steady in mercy,*
> *Merciless to the foe who attacks him.*
> *[. . .]*
> *As for any son of mine who shall maintain this border which my majesty has made, he is my son, born to my majesty. The true son is he who champions his father, who guards the border of his begetter. But he who abandons it, who fails to fight for it, he is not my son, he was not born to me. Now my majesty has had an image made of my majesty, at this border which my majesty has made, in order that you maintain it, in order that you fight for it.*[11]

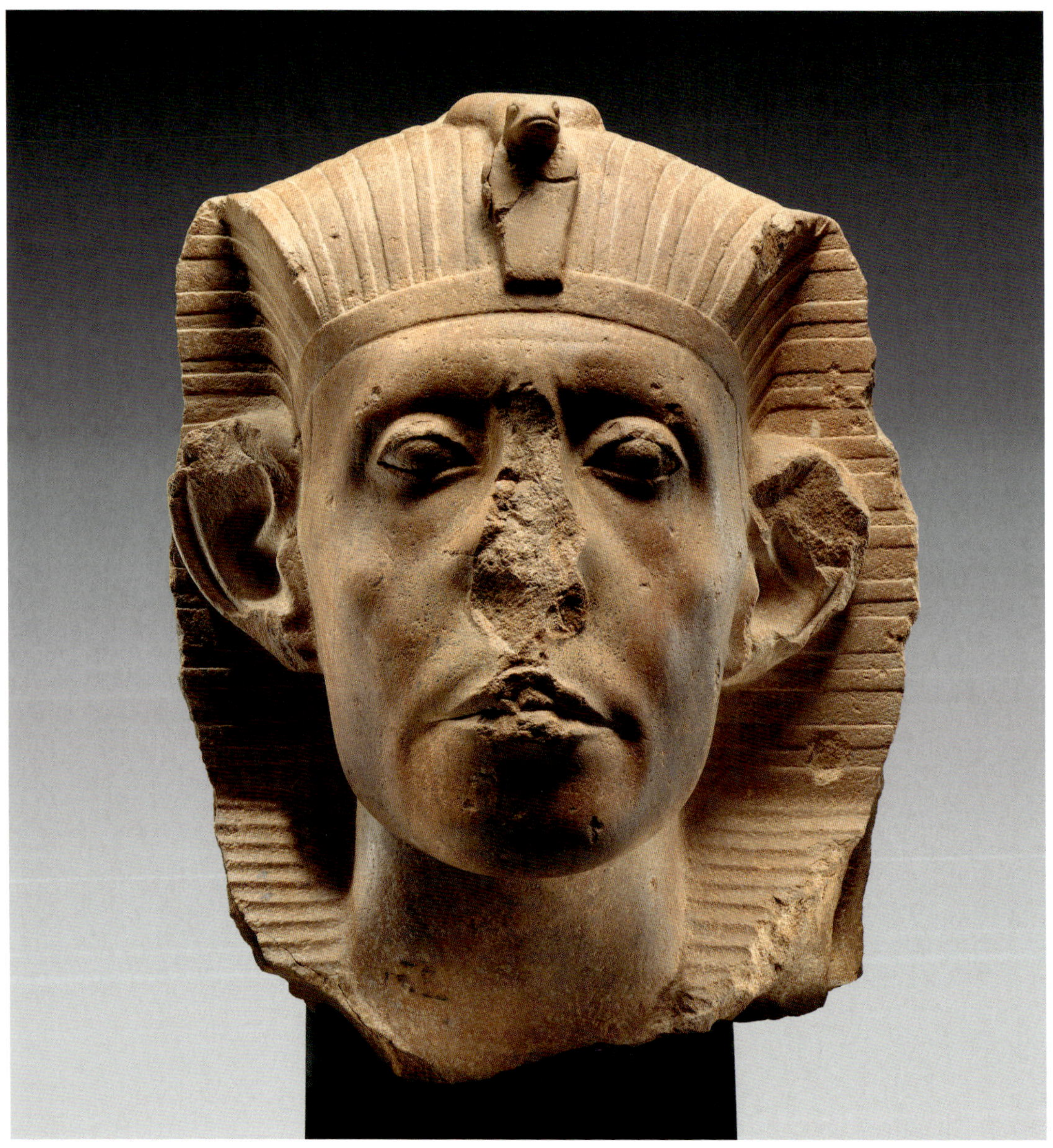

23 Head of Senwosret III, 1878–1841 BCE. Yellow quartzite, 45.1 × 34.3 × 43.2 cm (17 3/4 × 13 1/2 × 17 in.)

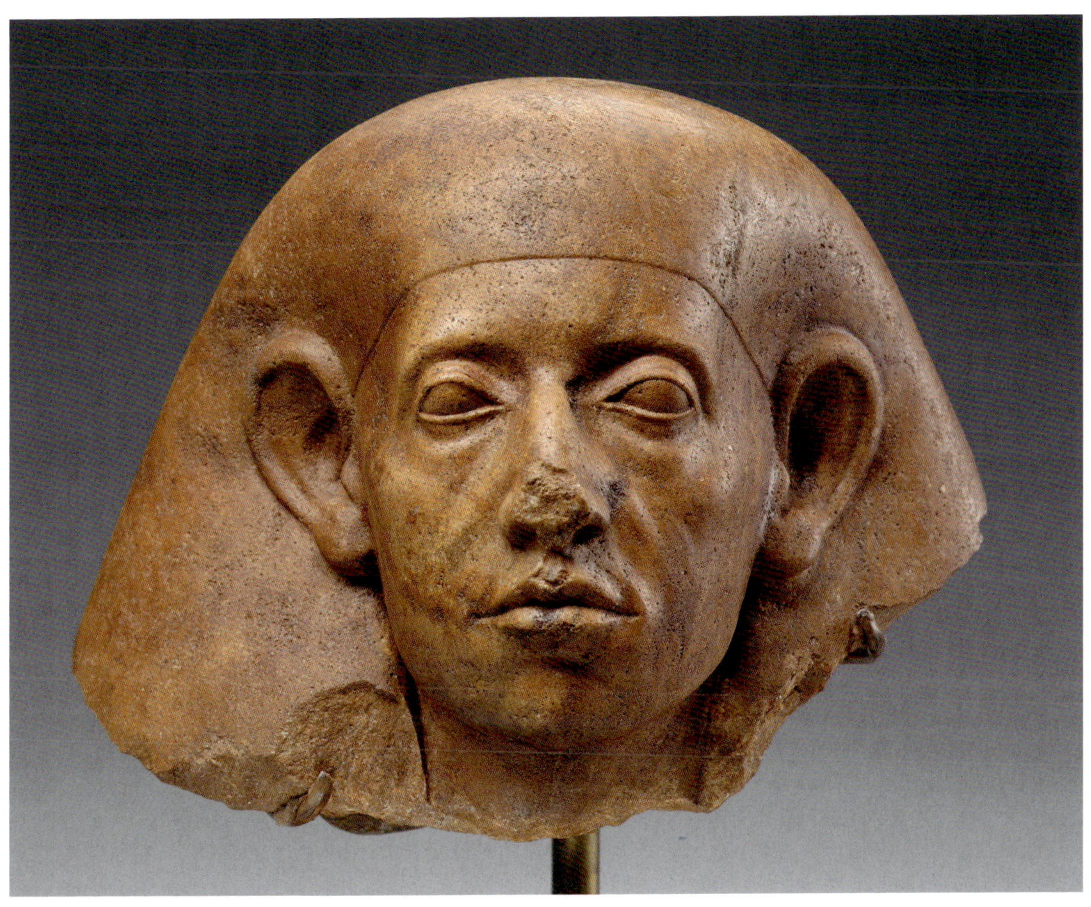

24 Head of an official (The Josephson Head), 1878–1841 BCE. Quartzite, 18.5 × 24 × 21 cm (7¼ × 9½ × 8¼ in.)

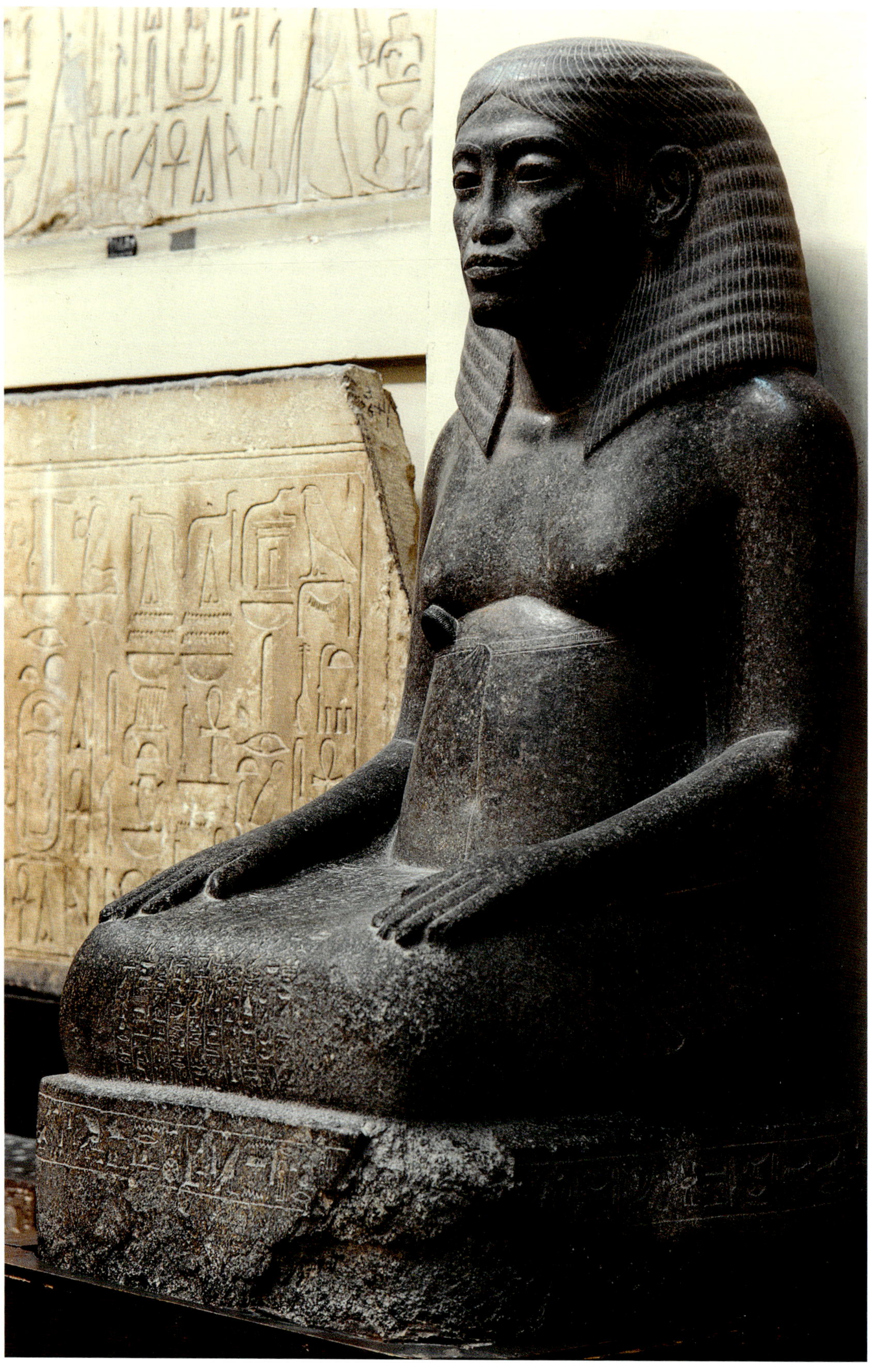

The image the king refers to is the stele itself, emblazoned with the king's names.

Senwosret III's features are as distinctive and individual as Menkaura's, but whereas Menkaura's features occur only on statues of the king, queen, and deities, the features of Senwosret III are grafted onto his subjects as well. A magnificent portrait of an official, known as the Josephson Head after its previous owner, has features so closely resembling his sovereign's they could almost be the same person (fig. 24). The one discordant note, characteristic of the king's statues as well, is his unnaturally large ears. There must be a reason for making them so big—the artist who modeled such a face was clearly capable of carving correctly proportioned features. The *Instruction of Ptahhotep*, a collection of maxims purporting to be the advice of an Old Kingdom vizier to his son that was composed in the Middle Kingdom, may provide an answer:

If you are a man who leads,
Listen calmly to the speech of one who pleads;
Don't stop him from purging his body
Of that which he planned to tell.
A man in distress wants to pour out his heart
More than that his case be won.
[. . .]
Not all one pleads for can be granted,
But a good hearing soothes the heart.[12]

The head first appeared in the art market in the 1940s and is without an archaeological context or any indication of where it originally came from. As it is detached from its body, there is no identifying inscription. It is tempting to see in him one of the highest officials of the realm—a vizier, treasurer, or high steward, a man highly favored with the king—but unfortunately the subject of this masterpiece must remain anonymous.

In Egyptian art, lines, pouches, and other signs of age are equated with wisdom. Four centuries later, Amenhotep son of Hapu, overseer of all royal building projects under Amenhotep III, the man who brought the Colossi of Memnon to Thebes, clearly availed himself of Middle Kingdom models when he commissioned a statue of himself as an old man seated on the ground (fig. 25). The inscription tells us he has already reached the age of eighty—extremely old by ancient standards—and hopes to live to 110.[13] So successfully has the artist evoked the style of the late Middle Kingdom, it has even been suggested that Amenhotep's statue was actually a reworked Middle Kingdom statue rather than an Eighteenth Dynasty original. That is probably going too far, but that it could be proposed at all is telling.[14] Not only the age-marked face but also the wig style, costume, and pose—seated on the ground, with hands laid flat on the thighs—follow

25 Statue of Amenhotep son of Hapu as an old man, 1390–1352 BCE. Granodiorite, h. 117 cm (46⅛ in.)

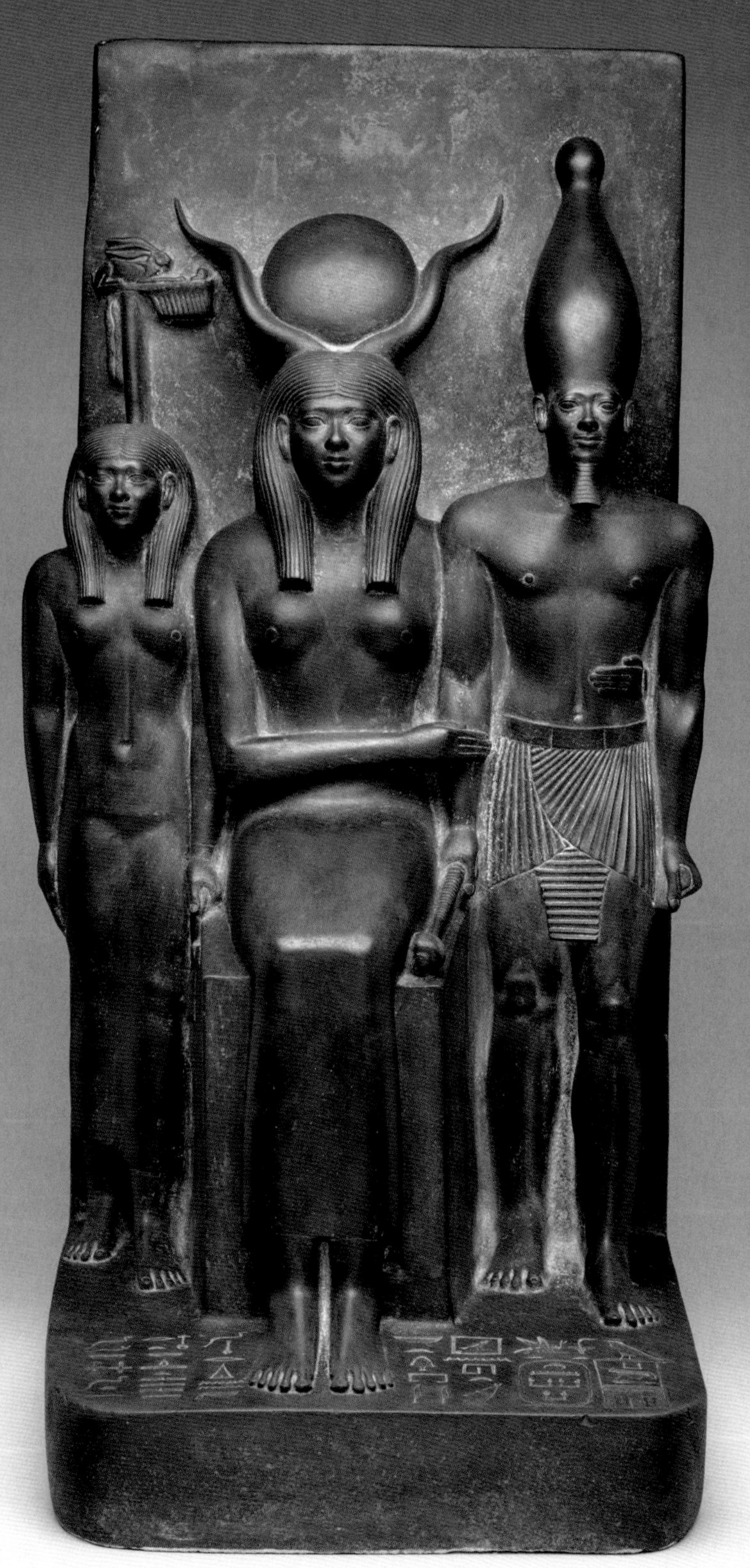

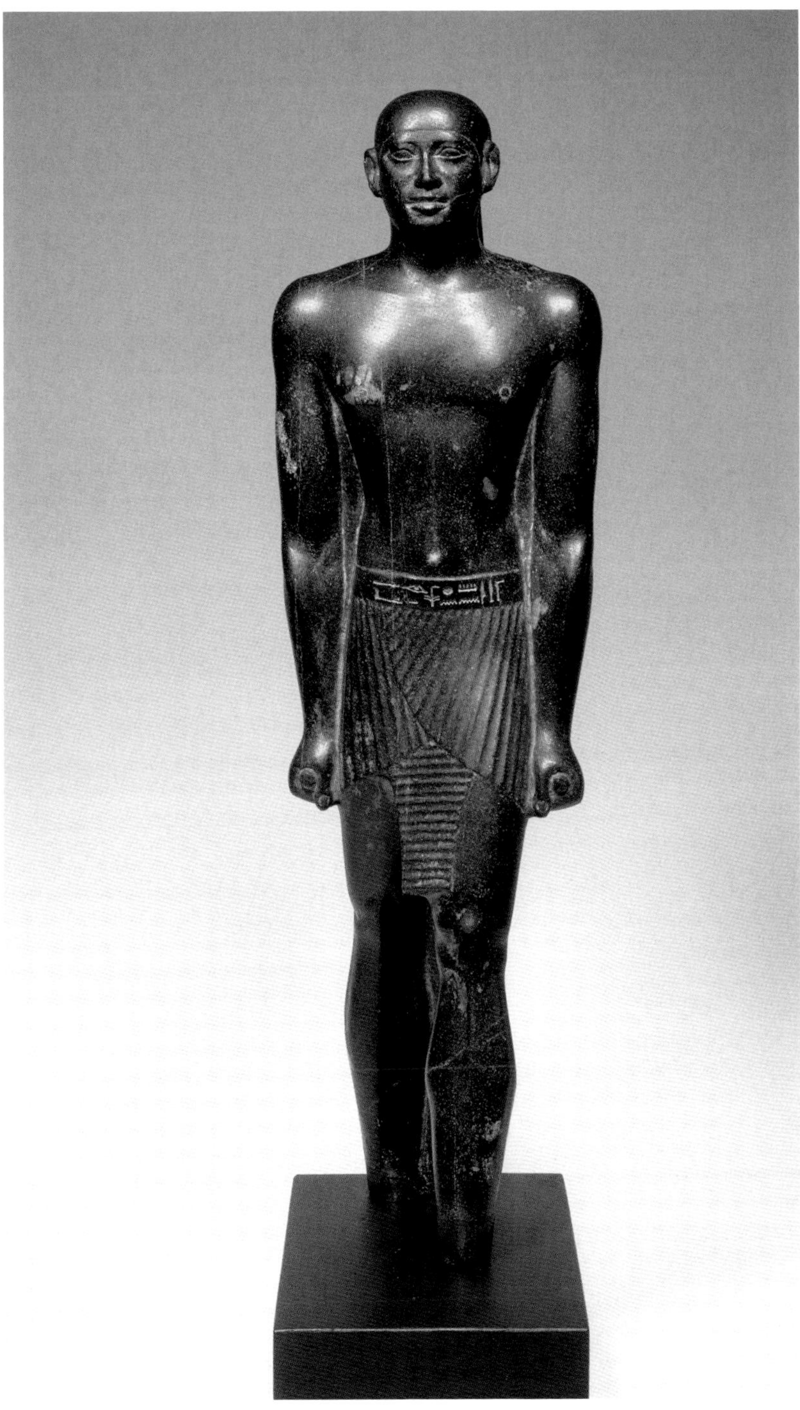

26 Triad of Menkaura, the goddess Hathor, and the deified Hare nome, 2490–2472 BCE. Graywacke, 84.5 × 43.5 × 49 cm (33¼ × 17⅛ × 19¼ in.)

27 Statue of Khonsuiraa, 760–660 BCE. Black stone, 43.5 × 12.6 × 13.5 cm (17⅛ × 5 × 5⅜ in.)

Middle Kingdom prototypes. Amenhotep son of Hapu prided himself on his antiquarianism. By eschewing the elegant, youthful style of his own time and harking back to an earlier era, he was showing off his erudition and making a personal statement. In later times, this remarkable individual was worshipped as a god of wisdom and healing alongside Imhotep, the architect of Djoser's Step Pyramid, who was credited with inventing the art of building in stone.[15]

Archaism—the deliberate harking back to the past—although a recurring feature of ancient Egyptian art, reached its heyday in the seventh century BCE, under the Twenty-fifth and Twenty-sixth dynasties.[16] By that time artists, and those who commissioned them, had two thousand years' worth of art to look back on. They could choose from Old Kingdom robustness, Middle Kingdom sobriety, and New Kingdom glamour. Monuments were studiously copied, and the ancient sites of Giza and Saqqara experienced a revival. The pyramid of Menkaura was restored and the royal mummy provided with a new wooden coffin, and the venerable cemetery once again became a burial place of choice for the elite.[17]

The evocation of past styles is so successful that it can be difficult to tell an archaizing work of the seventh century BCE from an original work of the Old or Middle Kingdom. The reverse is true as well. It is hard to believe nowadays, but even such iconic Old Kingdom works as the Khafra and Menkaura statues, when first discovered, were thought to date to the seventh century BCE, because their style was already familiar from later copies, and comparatively few Old Kingdom sites had been systematically excavated (fig. 26). Even experienced archaeologists dated the Menkaura triads to the Twenty-sixth Dynasty, though Reisner himself believed them to be Fourth Dynasty.[18]

Three portraits dating to roughly the same period illustrate the sophistication and learned eclecticism of Late Period archaism. The statue of Khonsuiraa, a priest of Amen, harks back to the Pyramid Age (fig. 27). The statue is broken above the ankles, and the belt is inscribed with his name and title. The figural proportions show a return to the ideal male form seen in the Menkaura statues. Khonsuiraa has what we might call a swimmer's build, with broad shoulders, long arms, a V-shaped torso, slim waist, and narrow hips—like Menkaura, but sleeker. The head is small in relation to the body, and the outline of the hair, like a close-fitting cap, recalls the limestone portrait heads from Giza. Although the facial features are not individualized, the workmanship is superb, with the hard, dark stone polished to a glossy sheen.

Late Period archaism is by no means limited to art production; the trend is also apparent in inscriptions. These developments reflect changes in religion and ideology. Khonsuiraa lived toward the end of the Twenty-fifth, or Kushite, Dynasty. The Kushites were Nubians from northern Sudan, who invaded Egypt around 730 BCE and ruled over both Egypt and

Nubia until 664 BCE, when they were expelled from Egypt by the Assyrians. The Kushite invasion was not a cataclysm, but a spur. Although they were foreigners, the Kushites considered themselves defenders of tradition, more orthodox than the Egyptians themselves. One of the most important religious documents of the period is the Shabaka Stone, named after the second Kushite pharaoh. It is a black slab inscribed with a hieroglyphic text expounding the role of the Memphite god Ptah as the creator, which the pious king claimed to have had copied from a worm-eaten old papyrus—a well-established trope. Even today scholars disagree whether the text is as old as it purports to be or is an invention of the Twenty-fifth Dynasty masquerading in old clothes.

The second of these archaizing portraits, a head of a man in a bag-shaped wig, subtly evokes the late Middle Kingdom (fig. 28). Although the subject's name is not preserved, the inscription on the back pillar mentions Khentykhety, god of Athribis in the Nile Delta, suggesting that was where he lived. It is an extremely accomplished and sensitive portrait, with what one writer has called a "Mona Lisa air of ambiguity."[19] Here the full wig, the bumps and shallows of the face, and the overall serious expression recall the earlier period. Although the features are individualized, the man from Athribis is far more restrained in expression than the Josephson Head, and was given a glossy finish to appeal to Late Period taste.

The third example is the head of Ankhkhonsu, a priest of Montu, which in its cool elegance looks back to the early New Kingdom. The face is youthful and serene, without line or blemish, with beautifully shaped eyebrows outlined in relief (fig. 29). The nose, for once unbroken, is fine and straight. It is a beautiful work, the polish of the stone matte and velvety smooth.

The carefully carved but fragmentary inscription on the back pillar does not suffice to give us the man's name. We know it because of a brilliant discovery by the Egyptologist Bernard V. Bothmer. Suspecting he had identified the body, he placed a plaster cast of the head on a headless statue in the Cairo Museum. The experiment was a success: the two fit perfectly, showing that they were originally joined (fig. 30).[20] The complete statue portrays Ankhkhonsu seated with his knees drawn up to his chest and his arms folded over them, a type known as a block statue. The inscription gives the names and titles of Ankhhonsu's father, grandfather, great-grandfather, and great-great-grandfather on his father's side, as well as his mother's name and that of her father. These lengthy genealogies reaching back several generations are characteristic of the overall archaizing tendencies of the time. We also learn that the statue was dedicated by Ankhkhonsu's son Hor, presumably after his father's death. This same Hor also dedicated a block statue of his grandfather—another Hor, father of Ankhkhonsu—also in Cairo, intact and in near perfect condition.[21] Both Cairo pieces were found in 1905 in the temple of Karnak; the head in Boston, purchased in 1903 from a Luxor antiquities dealer, must

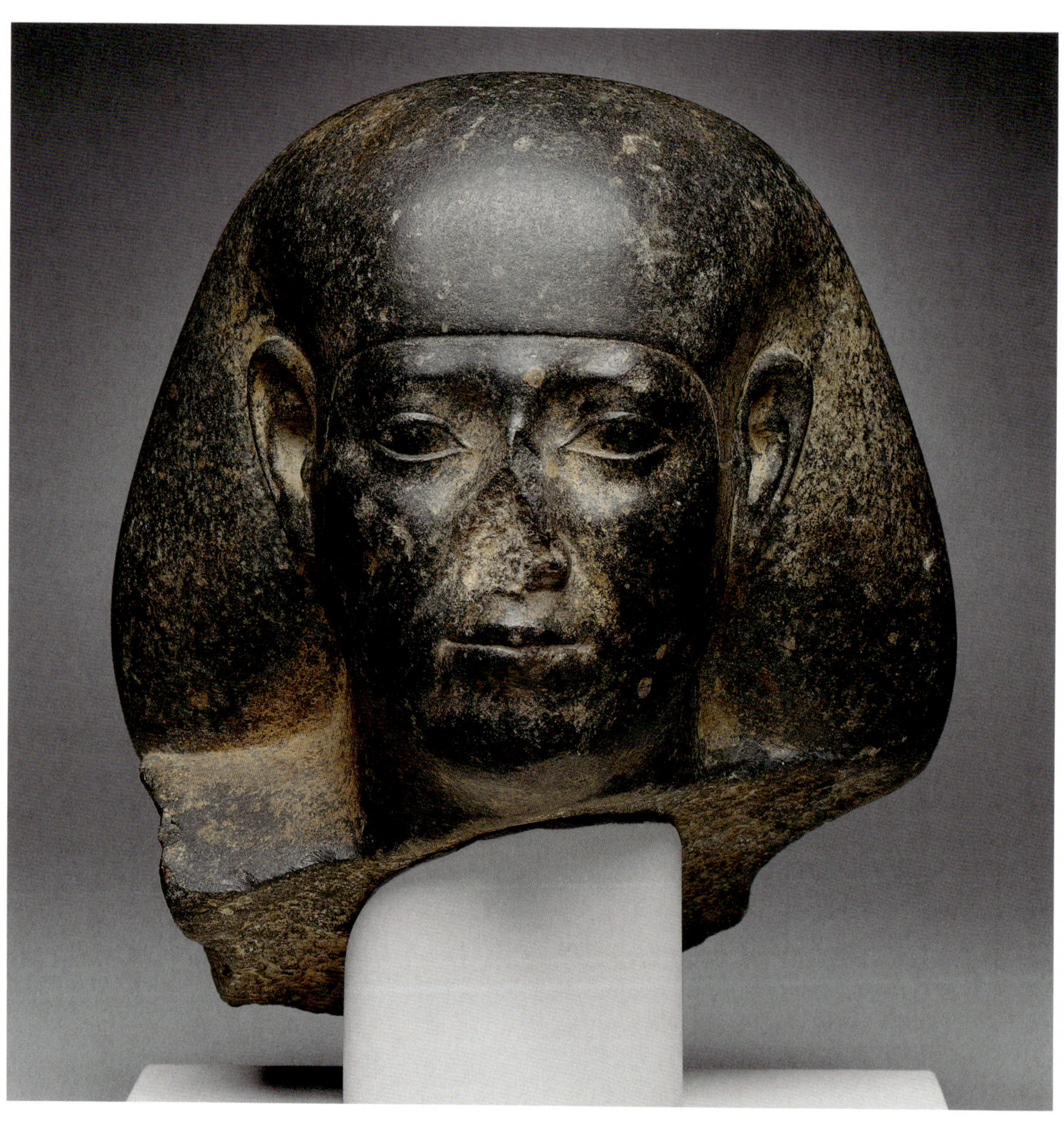

28 Head of a man in a bag wig, 664–525 BCE. Granodiorite, 22.8 × 18 cm (9 × 7 1/8 in.)

29 Head of Ankhkhonsu, 664–525 BCE. Graywacke, 19.5 × 18.5 × 15 cm (7 5/8 × 7 1/4 × 5 7/8 in.)

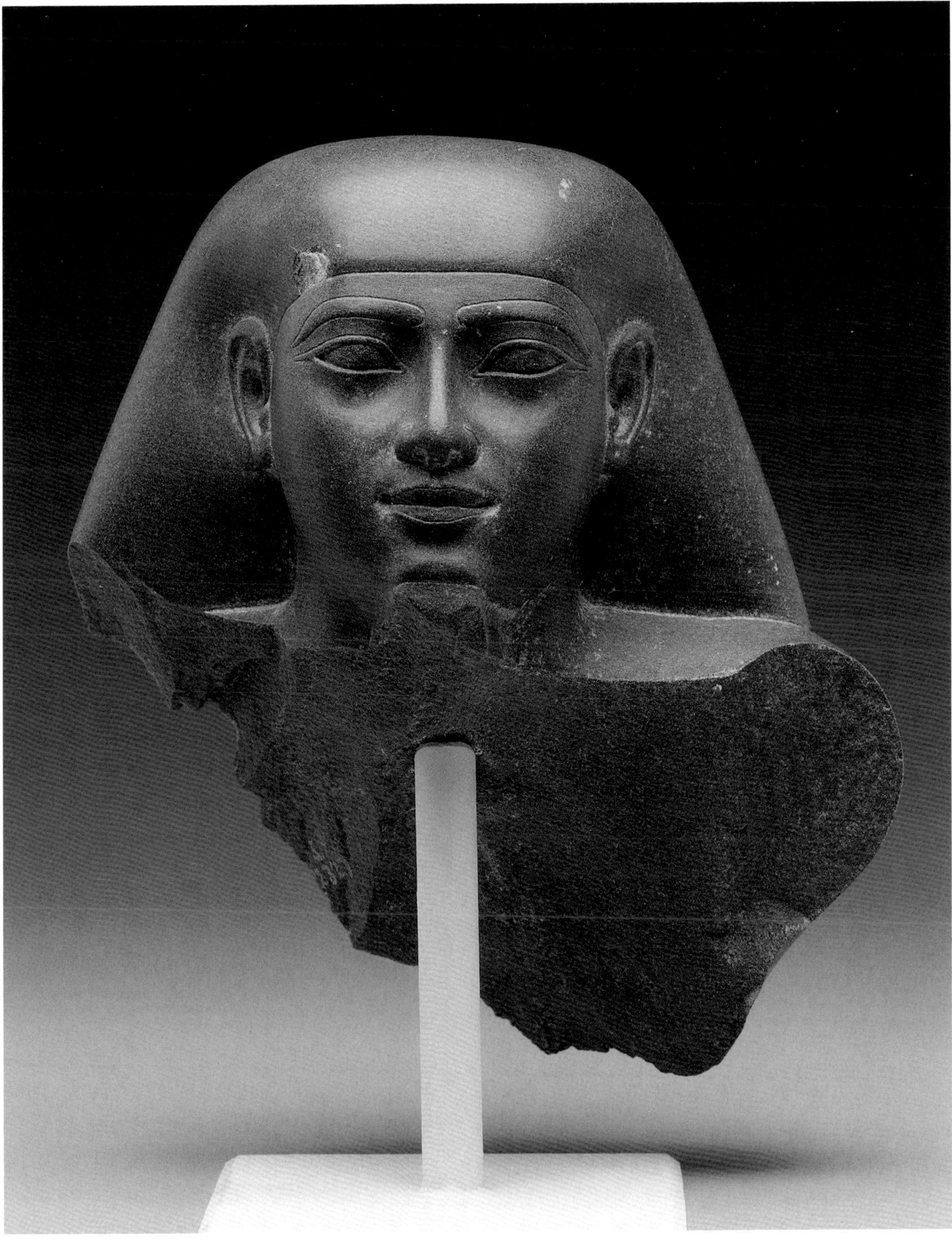

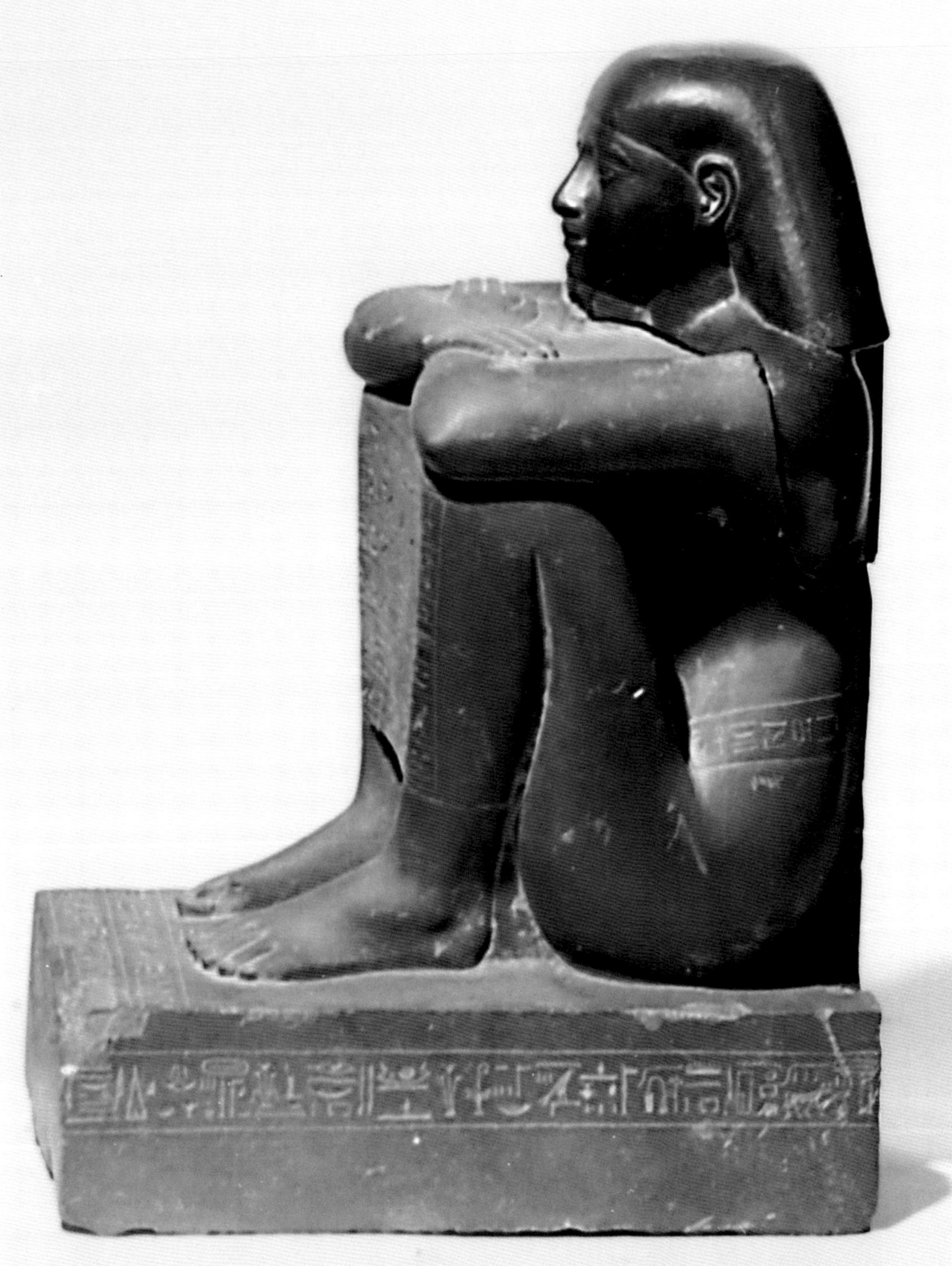

therefore also come from Karnak. Joining these two pieces shows how much information goes missing when a statue loses its head.

Father and grandfather have nearly identical features. The two statues are so similar in style, workmanship, material, and size that Hor must have commissioned them at the same time from the same sculptor's workshop. In that case, there can be no question of individual physical likeness. It is a portrait of an ideal. Some find it cold and impersonal, and—especially in its Late Period manifestation—academic. For the Egyptians, however, this was, as one scholar has put it, "the most satisfactory and successful idealism ever created, the most perfect expression of what they considered essential and important in the human image."[22] That ideal mode of representation goes back to the early Eighteenth Dynasty, the time of Hatshepsut.

30 Cast of head of Ankh-khonsu joined to body

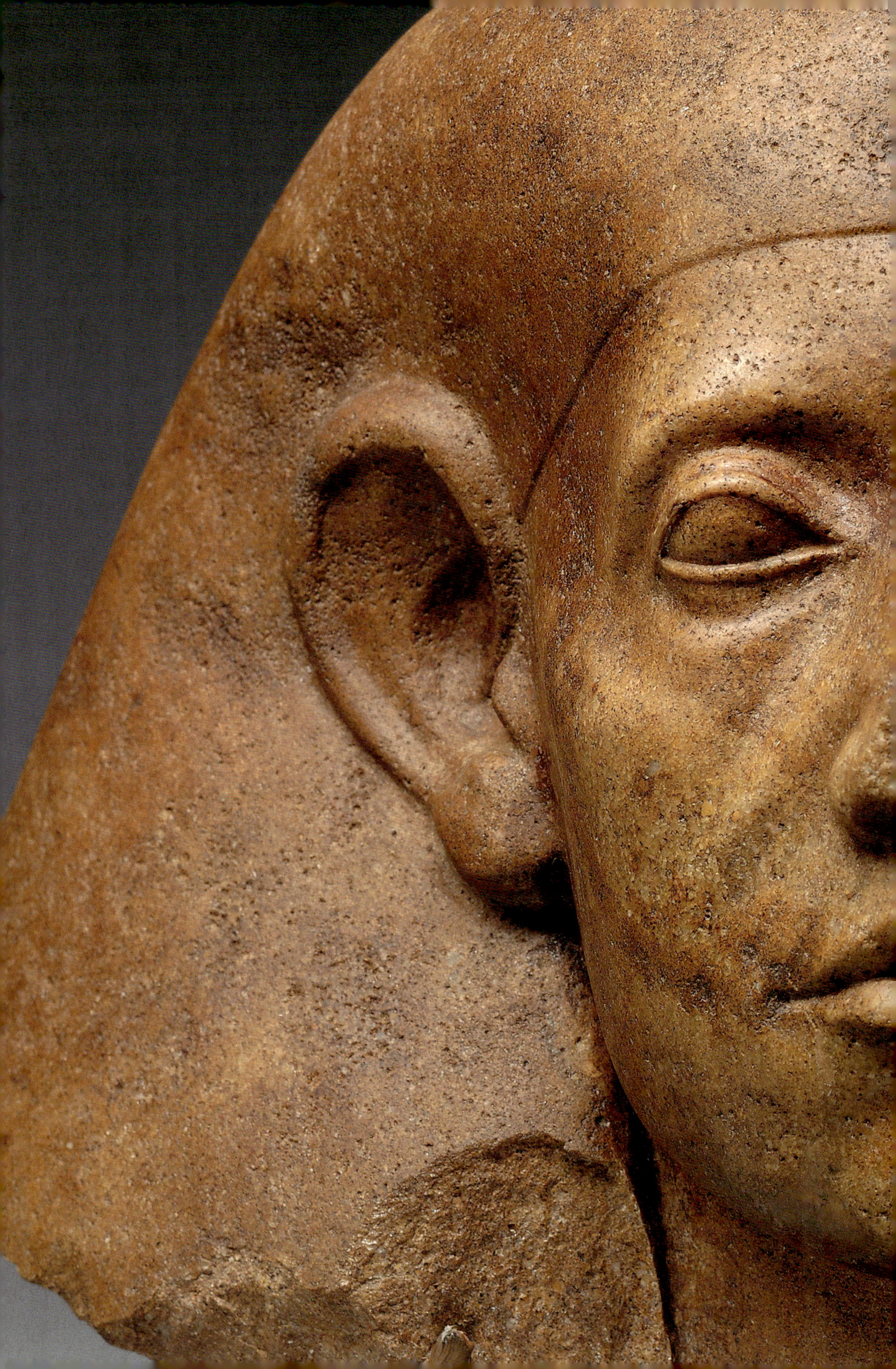

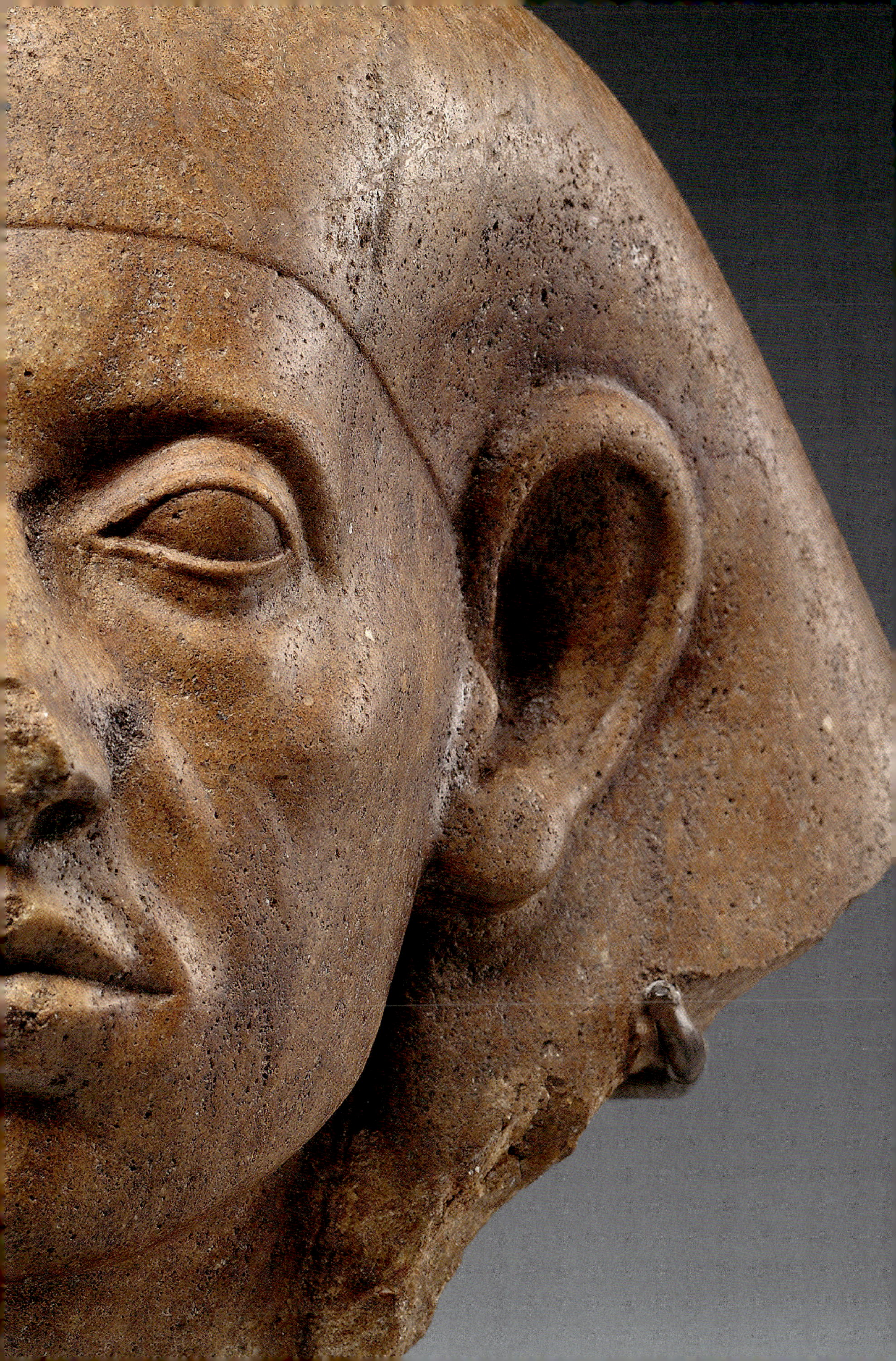

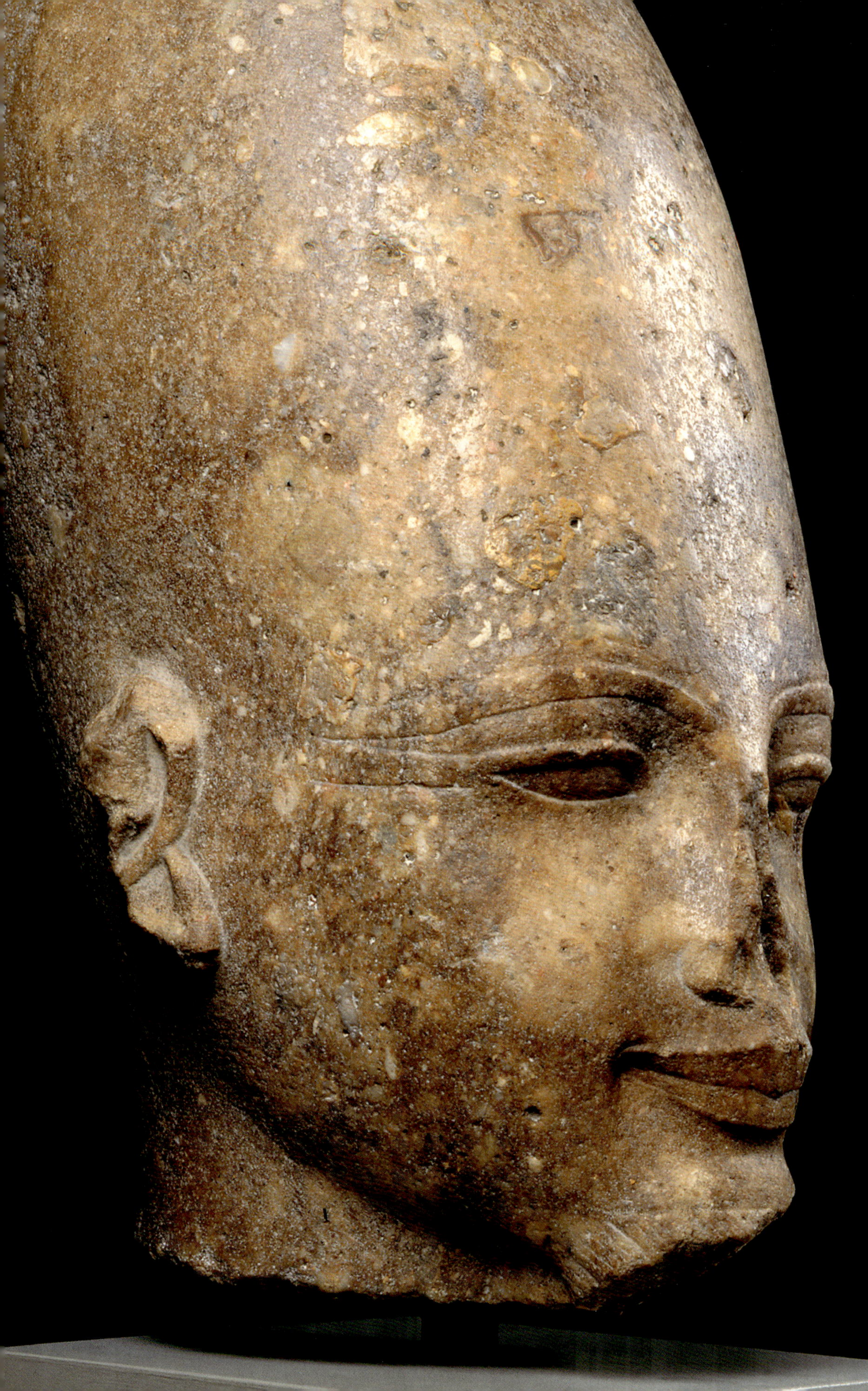

FOUR

Mavericks and Glamour Kings

Of the handful of women who attained supreme power in ancient Egypt, Hatshepsut was by far the most successful (fig. 31). When her husband, Thutmose II, died unexpectedly after a short reign, leaving a young son by a minor wife as heir, Queen Hatshepsut assumed the reins of government—first as regent, then as full-fledged king beside the boy. Including her time as regent, Hatshepsut ruled over Egypt for twenty-two years (1479–1458 BCE).

How did she do this? Thutmose II and Hatshepsut were not just husband and wife but half-siblings, children of Thutmose I by different mothers. Hatshepsut had the claim to more royal blood, as her mother was Thutmose I's principal queen, whereas Thutmose II's mother was a secondary wife. He was a man, however, and kingship in ancient Egypt was a male role. (There was no concept of a ruling queen: the term we translate as "queen" literally means "king's wife.") In statuary and reliefs, therefore, Hatshepsut regularly appears as a bare-chested male pharaoh. It is only when you read the inscriptions identifying her as the "female Horus" and "daughter of Ra" that her gender is disclosed. But most people could not read. In scenes on temple walls showing the ruler interacting with the gods, it was important for everyone to be able to identify the figure of the king, and that figure looked like a man.[1]

Hatshepsut became one of the greatest builders and patrons of the arts in Egyptian history. In addition to her great memorial temple nestled in the cliffs of western Thebes at Deir el-Bahri, one of the architectural wonders of the ancient world, she made important additions to the temple of Amen-Ra at Karnak, including two pairs of obelisks. In fact, the accomplishments she was most proud of were these obelisks and a lucrative

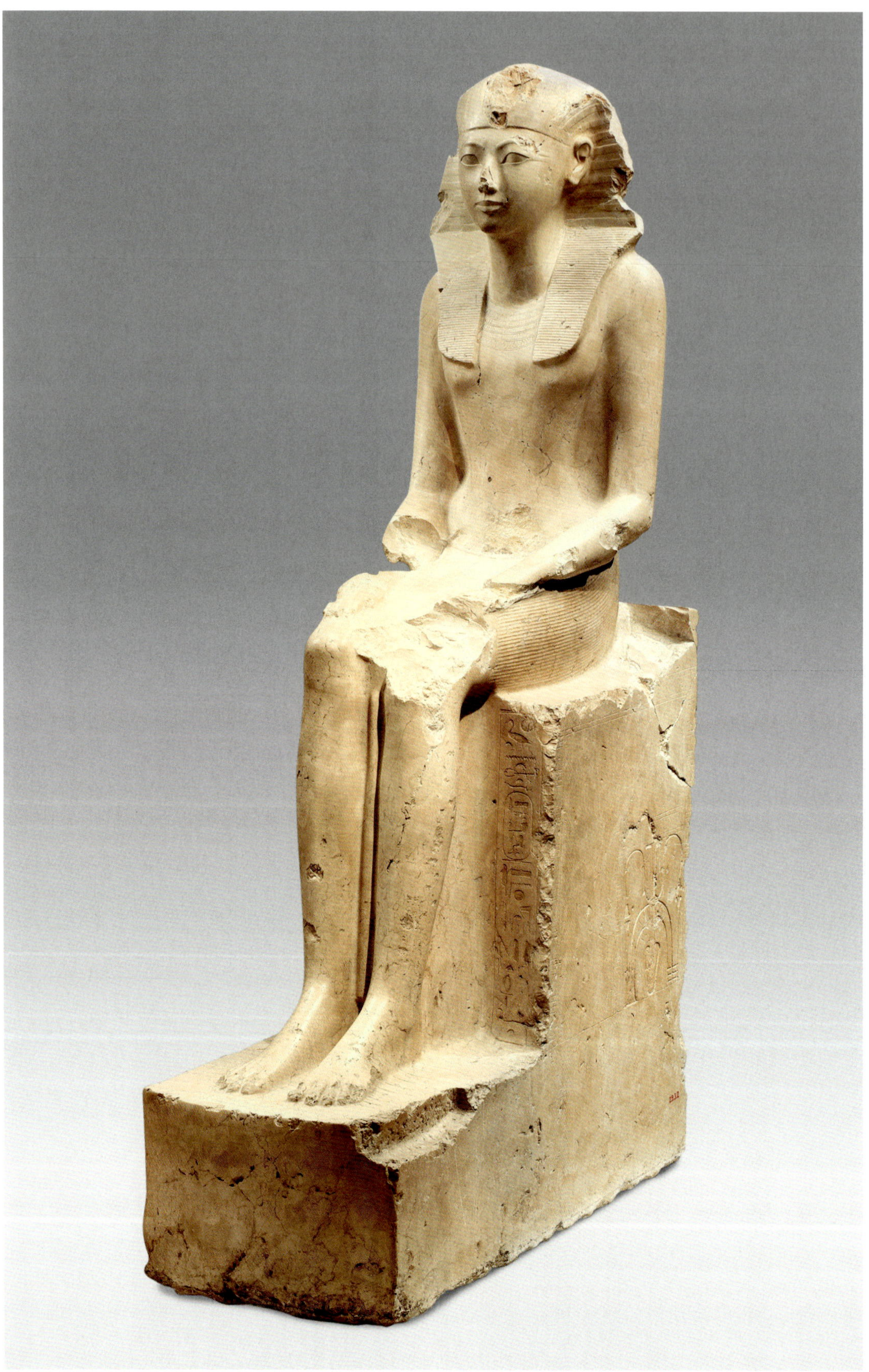

trading expedition she sent to the fabulous land of Punt, south of Egypt on the Red Sea coast—the source of exotic goods, especially incense used in temple ceremonies.

Only one of the obelisks still stands in its original position between the Fourth and Fifth Pylons in the temple of Amen-Ra. At more than 97 feet tall and weighing 323 tons, it is the tallest standing obelisk in Egypt, and the second-tallest in the world, surpassed only by the Lateran Obelisk in Rome (fig. 32).[2] Fragments of its shattered companion lie broken on the ground. The quarrying, transport, and erection of these granite monoliths demanded immense resources of skill and manpower. Made of solid granite, they had upper surfaces sheathed in electrum, a naturally occurring alloy of silver and gold much prized by the Egyptians. The effect of these skyscrapers gleaming in the sun must have been dazzling. As Hatshepsut herself proudly explains in the inscription on the base of the standing obelisk:

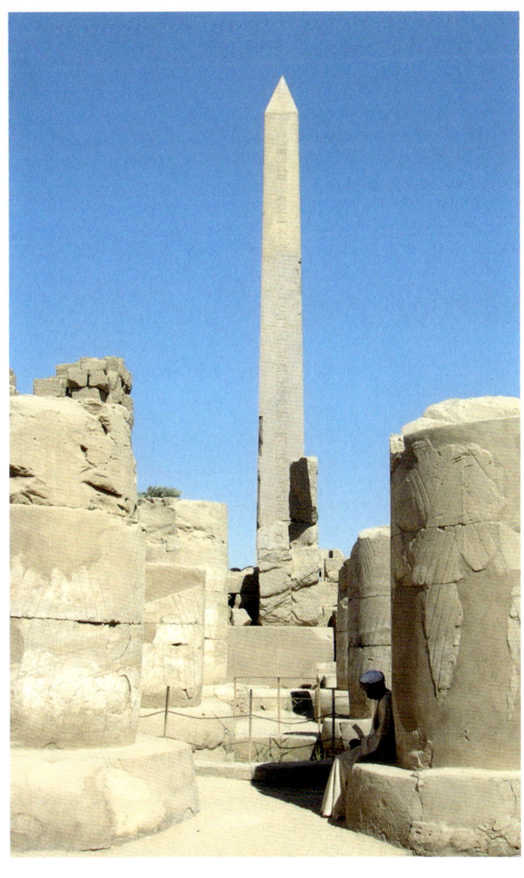

32 Standing obelisk of Hatshepsut, Karnak

> *She made it as her monument to her father Amen, Lord of Thrones-of-the-Two Lands, presiding over Ipet-sut, the making for him of two great obelisks of hard granite of the South, their upper side being of electrum, of the best of all foreign lands. Seen on both sides of the river, their rays flood the Two Lands when Aten dawns between them, as he rises in heaven's lightland. . . . They are each of one block of hard granite, without seam, without joining together!*
>
> *My Majesty began work on them in year 15, second month of winter, day 1, ending in year 16, fourth month of summer, last day, totally seven months of quarry work. . . . I gave for them of the finest electrum. I measured it by the gallon like sacks of grain. My majesty summoned a quantity beyond what the Two Lands had yet seen.*[3]

These are the most elaborately decorated of all known obelisks. A long hieroglyphic inscription runs down the center of each face of the shaft. On the upper part of each side are scenes showing the ruler offering to Amen, with the king and the god facing each other across the column of inscription. The pointed top of the obelisk, or pyramidion, shows Hatshepsut

31 Seated statue of Hatshepsut, 1473–1458 BCE. Indurated limestone, paint, 213 × 50 × 119 cm (83⅞ × 19⅝ × 46⅞ in.)

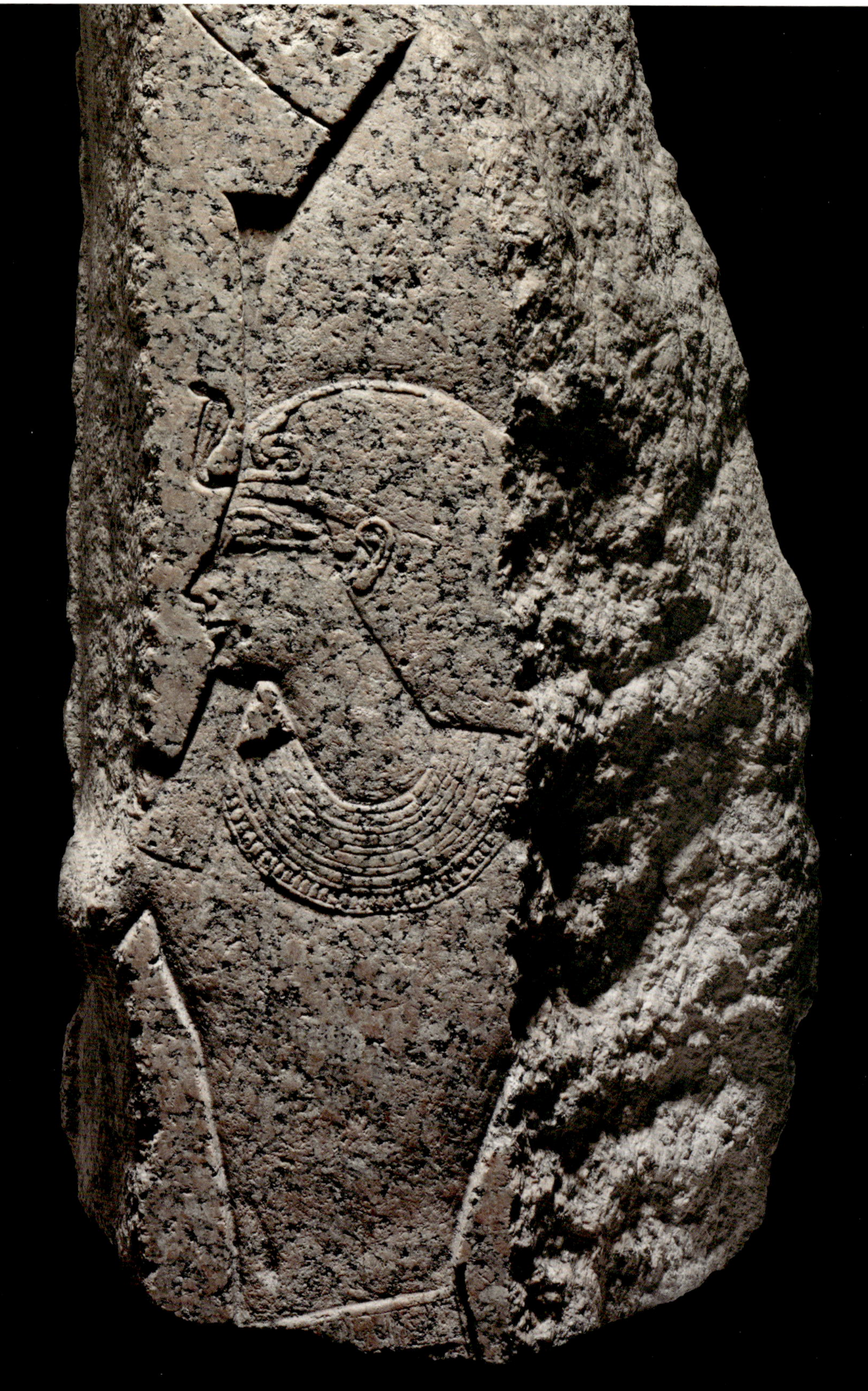

crowned by Amen-Ra. The upper part of the fallen obelisk has now been propped up on its side near the Sacred Lake outside the temple proper, where the superb carving may be admired up close.

Two sizeable fragments of Hatshepsut's fallen obelisk, now in the MFA, were among the first monumental Egyptian sculptures to arrive in America.[4] They were sent over by John Lowell, Jr., a wealthy Bostonian who traveled up the Nile in 1835.[5] The smaller fragment depicts "King" Hatshepsut wearing a headcloth adorned with a rearing cobra, surmounted by the so-called Double Crown combining the crowns of Upper and Lower Egypt (fig. 33). She is bare-chested and wears a false beard. Enough of her torso remains to show that she wore a king's pleated kilt; the broad collar is unisex. Her nose is straight and pointed, her almond-shaped eye extended by lines of makeup and surmounted by an elegantly arched eyebrow. The larger Boston fragment is a corner block with back-to-back scenes of the god Amen-Ra and part of the central inscription. It is possible that the right-facing image of the god belongs to the same scene as the left-facing figure of the queen on the smaller fragment.[6]

A ruler who commanded the resources to erect two pairs of obelisks brought the same ambition to her other commissions.[7] An innovator in this as in so many other things, Hatshepsut was the first Eighteenth Dynasty ruler to have a sarcophagus of stone. Not content with just one, she ordered three. She commissioned the first one while she was still "great king's wife" of Thutmose II, and had it placed in the tomb prepared for her in western Thebes. After assuming control as pharaoh, Hatshepsut relocated her tomb to the Valley of the Kings, the new royal cemetery inaugurated by her father, and had a new sarcophagus made for that tomb. At some point, she decided to transfer her father's mummy from his tomb into hers, and this second sarcophagus was retrofitted for Thutmose I.[8] Hatshepsut then commissioned a third sarcophagus. Hatshepsut's tomb in the Valley of the Kings was excavated in 1903 by Howard Carter, then at the beginning of his career (in 1922 he was to discover the tomb of Tutankhamen). He found both sarcophagi lying open and empty in the burial chamber.[9] The excavation was financed by Theodore M. Davis, a retired American businessman from New York, who generously gave his share of the finds awarded him by the Egyptian government to the MFA, including the sarcophagus Hatshepsut recut for her father (fig. 34).

The whole decorative scheme of the sarcophagus is designed to assist the king's passage to the afterlife. Even the material, quartzite, aids the king's journey, as the stone's ruddy color (here intensified by a red wash) associated it with the sun, the ultimate symbol of rebirth. Protective funerary deities surround him on all sides. The figures have the same svelte proportions and elegant lines as the carvings on the obelisk, and have similar facial features.[10]

33 Fragment from Hatshepsut's fallen obelisk at Karnak, 1473–1458 BCE (detail). Granite, 106 × 45.7 × 22.9 cm (41¾ × 18 × 9 in.)

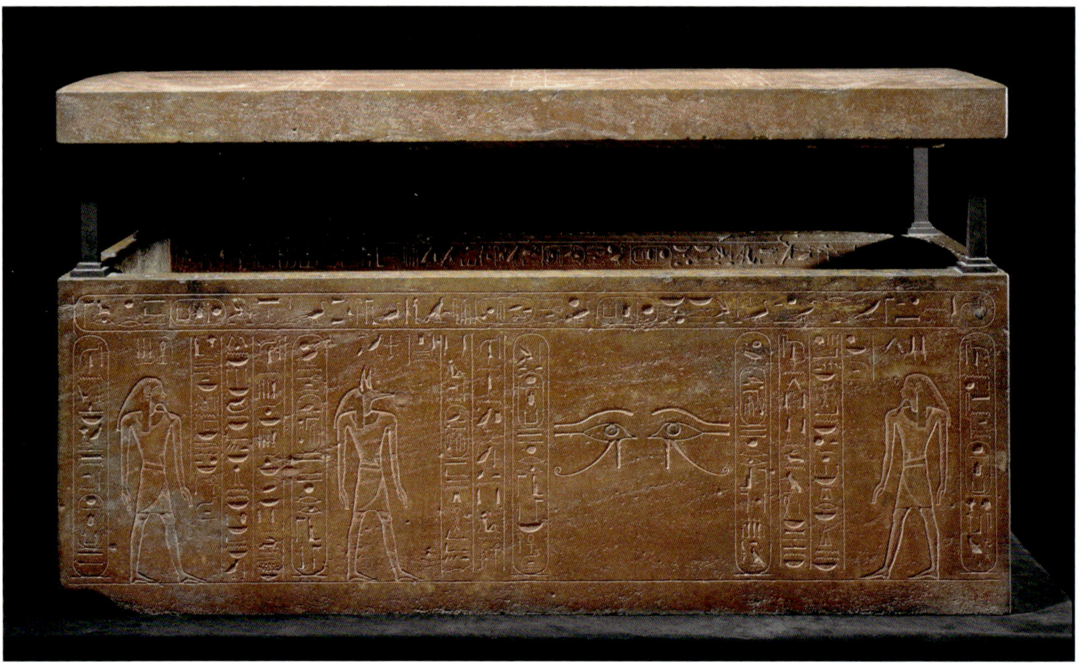

34 Sarcophagus of Hatshepsut, recut for her father, Thutmose I, 1473–1458 BCE. Painted quartzite, 82 × 225 × 87 cm (32¼ × 88⅝ × 34¼ in.)

Twenty years after Hatshepsut's death, for reasons still not fully understood, Thutmose III ordered her statues shattered and her name expunged from the monuments. He even had the lower parts of her obelisks encased by stone walls, so that from ground level no one could see her work. In modern times her reputation has suffered at the hands of Victorian-era Egyptologists and their successors, who seem more alarmed by the idea of a female pharaoh than the ancient Egyptians were.[11] It was claimed she usurped the throne and maintained her position through liaisons with powerful men at court, suffering the same bad press as strong female rulers from Cleopatra to Catherine the Great. It is only recently that Hatshepsut has been given her due as one of the greatest of the pharaohs.

During the thirty-eight-year reign of Amenhotep III (1390–1352 BCE), Egypt reached its acme of wealth and power. Like Hatshepsut's reign one hundred years earlier, Amenhotep's is distinguished by a strong economy and pioneering construction projects rather than military conquests. He inherited a great empire with borders stretching from Syria to Sudan; an abundant supply of gold from the Eastern Desert and northern Sudan gave the Egyptians the advantage in trade relations with the other great powers. Clay tablets found at el-Amarna preserve part of the diplomatic correspondence between Amenhotep III and foreign rulers. The kings of Assyria and Mittani (in northern Syria) wrote regularly to Egypt begging for gold: "Gold in your country is dirt," wrote the king of Assyria, "one simply gathers it up." In return, they sent their sisters and daughters as wives for Amenhotep III. But when the king of Babylon asked for an Egyptian princess in marriage, the answer was "From time immemorial no daughter of the king of Egypt is given to anyone," leaving no doubt who had the upper hand.[12]

Amenhotep III may well have been the greatest patron of the arts in Egypt's history. "His Majesty's heart was pleased with making very many great monuments, the like of which never existed before since the primeval time of the Two Lands," proclaims a stele from Thebes.[13] He would not be the last king of Egypt to make such a boast, but in Amenhotep's case the claim is justified.[14] In a way, Amenhotep III picked up where Hatshepsut left off. With her memorial temple at Deir el-Bahri and new southern entrance to Karnak, Hatshepsut transformed the ritual landscape of Thebes. Amenhotep built an even larger memorial temple on the west bank, its entrance flanked by the sixty-foot-tall Colossi of Memnon, and further developed the southern axis at Karnak. There he added another mighty pylon gateway along the processional way to the temple of Mut and thence to Luxor, where he erected the major part of the great edifice that stands there today.[15]

Amenhotep III's sculptors crafted for him a royal image that embodies the elegance and sophistication of the age. An over-life-size quartzite head of the king wearing the tall, conical crown of Upper Egypt shows these features to perfection (fig. 35). The king's almond-shaped eyes, extended by makeup lines, are paralleled by the sweeping curves of his eyebrows. The eyes are angled so they appear to be looking down. His mouth is wide and voluptuous, the upper lip thicker than the lower. Not a care or wrinkle disturbs the serenity of his expression. In fact, the king appears here in the guise of a god, as indicated by the remains of a plaited beard of the kind worn by deities. In the full statue, the ruler probably stood, arms crossed, feet together, in the pose commonly associated with Osiris, the resurrected king. Indeed there is a very fine line between images of kings and images of gods. Amenhotep III carries this concept to an extreme at Soleb Temple in the Sudan, where he appears in the act of worshiping his own deified self.[16]

Amenhotep III was depicted in so many statues, and his facial features are so consistent, that it is easy to identify heads like this one as his even without an identifying inscription. But they are hardly realistic: for instance, it is impossible to smile so broadly without making a crease in the cheeks. Instead this is an elegant mask. Amenhotep III's statuary translates very well into relief, as seen in a block from Memphis (fig. 36).[17] The ruler's elongated eyes, snub nose, and thick lips are if anything even more salient in a portrait that respects the conventions of Egyptian art in two dimensions by showing the eyes frontal, and the nose and lips in profile.

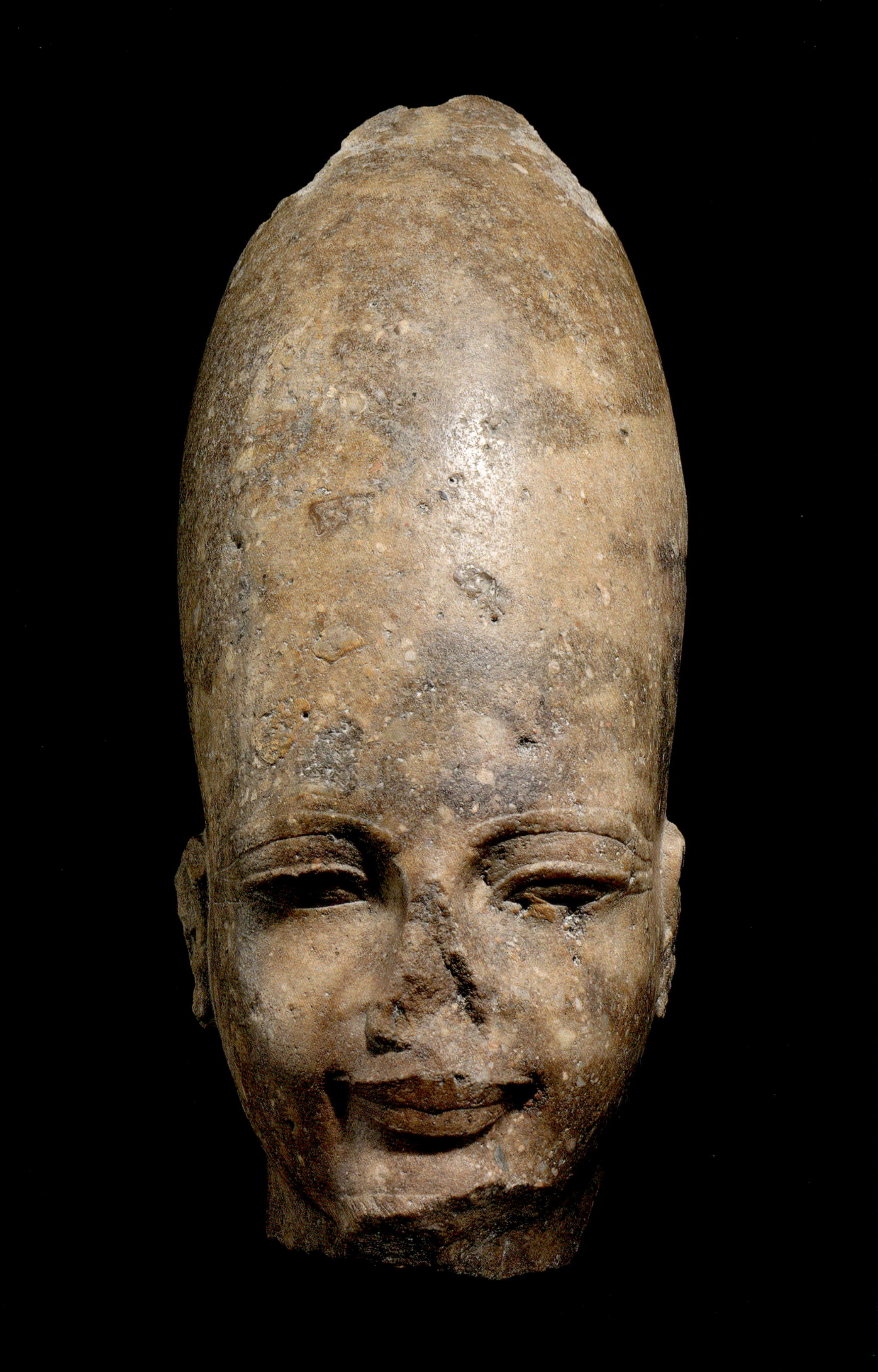

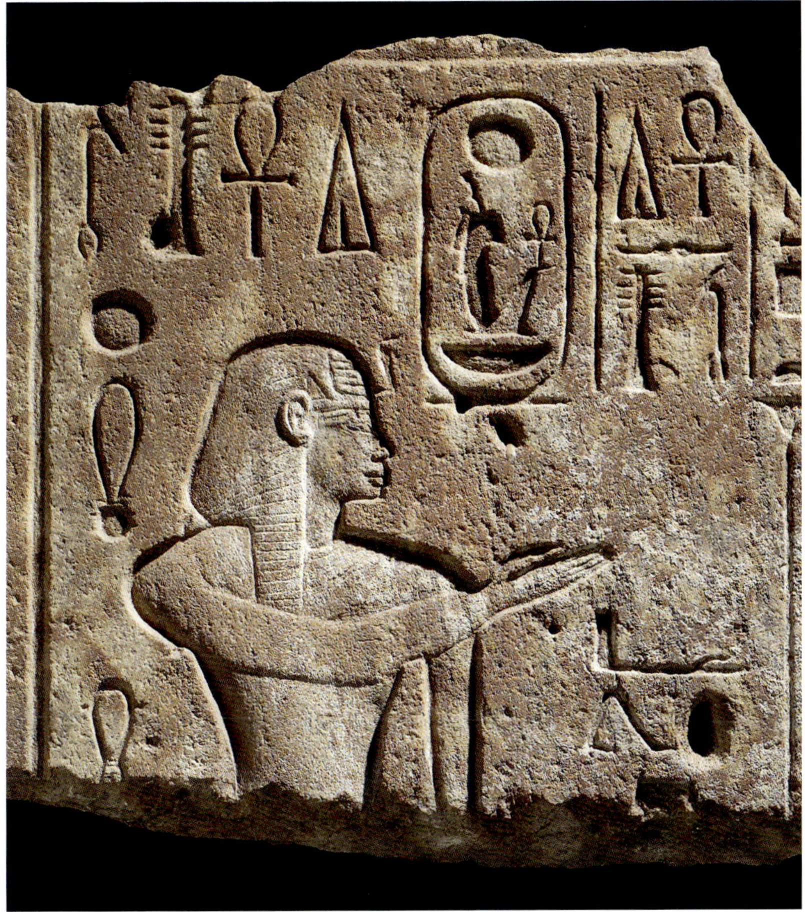

36 Relief of Amenhotep III and Sekhmet, 1390–1352 BCE (detail). Quartzite, 41 × 65 cm (16⅛ × 25⅝ in.)

Although best known from large-scale works, Amenhotep III is also portrayed in a number of smaller statues and statuettes, many of them produced on the occasion of his Sed-festival, or jubilee after thirty years of rule.[18] A glazed steatite statuette in Boston shows the king kneeling and holding a now-damaged offering, perhaps a vessel (fig. 37). Although Amenhotep must have been in his forties at the time, he has a baby face and a pudgy body like a child's. His elaborate headdress—the Double Crown of Upper and Lower Egypt over a round, curly wig—associates him with the child-god Neferhotep, "perfect of appeasement." Implicit in any child-god is the prospect of a new beginning, full of promise. Even the color added to the symbolism, for the statuette originally was glazed a lustrous blue-green. A glazed steatite statuette of Queen Tiye, Amenhotep's principal wife, originally from a family group (you can see the king's arm), gives an idea of its original color (fig. 38).

35 Head of Amenhotep III, 1390–1352 BCE. Quartzite, 52.5 × 21.2 × 26.2 cm (20⅝ × 8⅜ × 10⅜ in.)

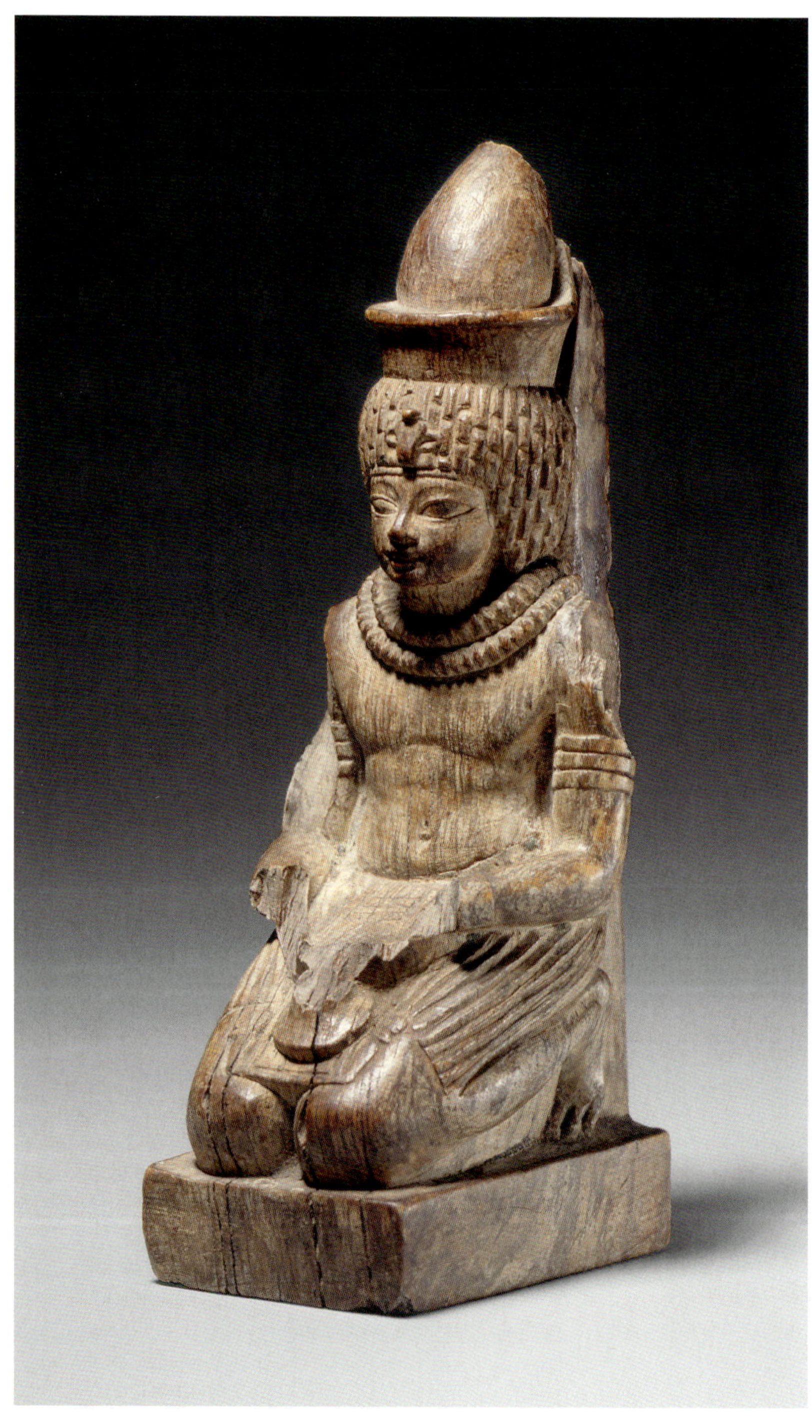

37 Statuette of Amenhotep III as the god Neferhotep, 1390–1352 BCE. Glazed steatite, 13 × 3.8 × 5.3 cm (5 1/8 × 1 1/2 × 2 1/8 in.)

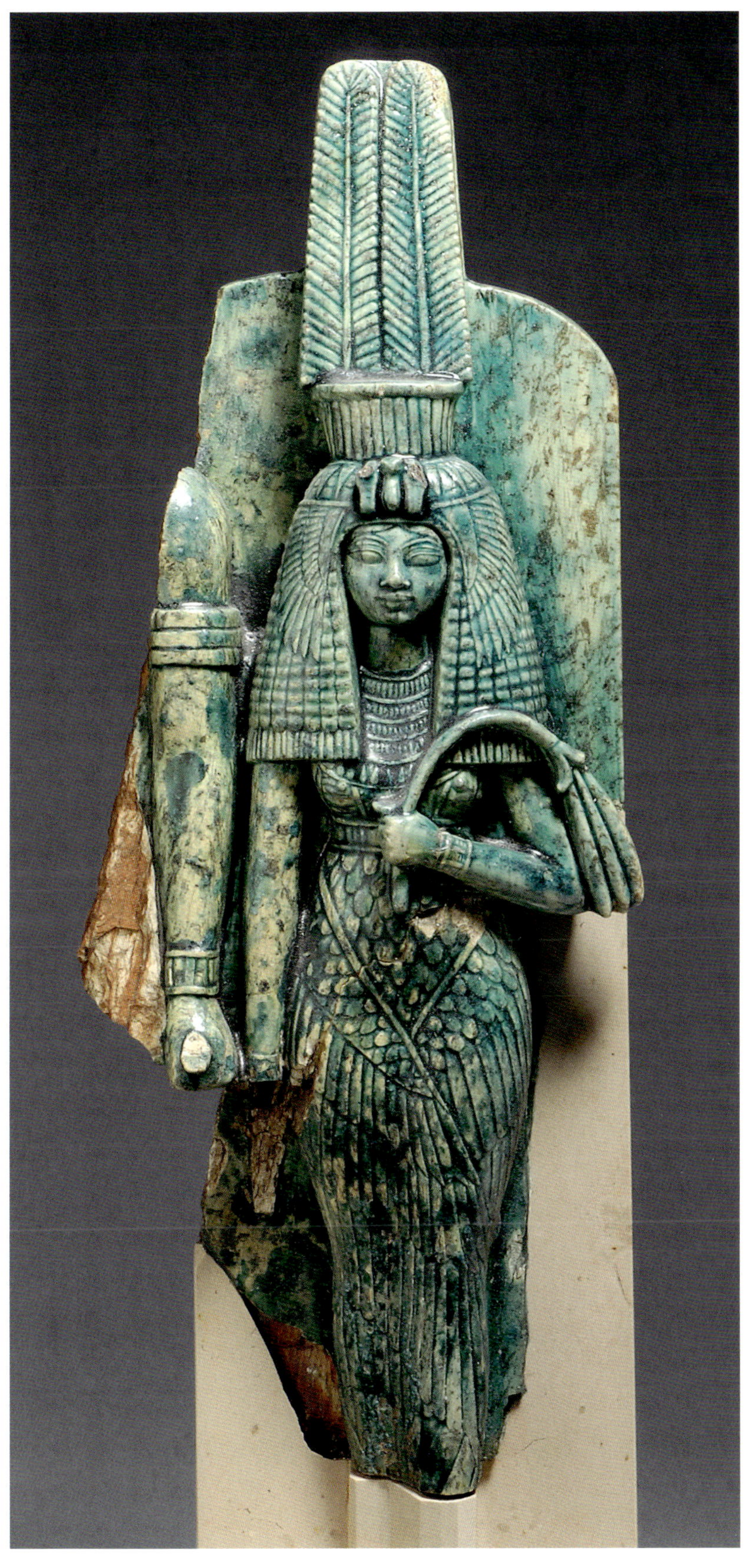

38 Statuette of Tiye from a family group, 1390–1352 BCE. Glazed steatite, h. 30 cm (11¾ in.)

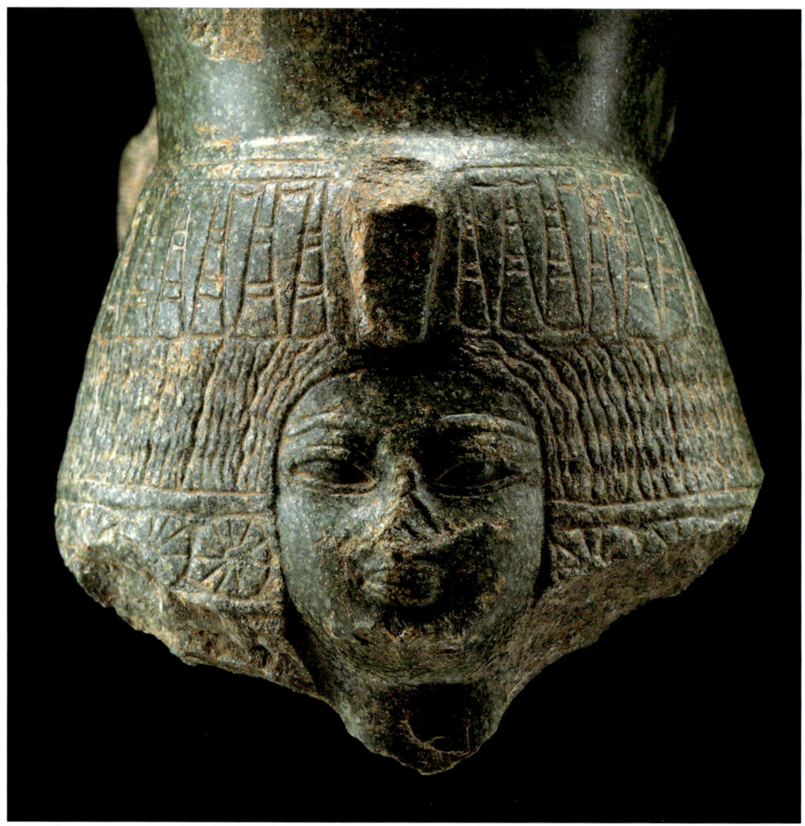

39 Head of Tiye, 1390–1352 BCE. Peridotite, 20.3 × 11.5 × 12 cm (8 × 4½ × 4¾ in.)

In ancient Egypt as today, to be green meant to be young; in ancient Egyptian, the same triconsonantal root, *rnp*, makes "fresh greens," *renput*, and "young," *renpy*. Additional symbolism is provided by the word for glazed material: *tjehenet*, "dazzling, luminous," like the sun. And we have not yet exhausted the statuette's symbolism. The king's magnificent set of ornaments—a double-strand necklace of gold disk beads and matching armbands—is worn by the ruler only after his Sed-festival in regnal year 30, when the king was rejuvenated as the young sun god.[19] In this image of himself as the youthful Neferhotep, Amenhotep III, who liked to call himself the "dazzling sun-disk of all lands," found the perfect form of self-expression.

Queen Tiye, Amenhotep III's "great royal wife," was one of the most prominent women in Egyptian history. No previous queen was so visible in her husband's lifetime.[20] Images of Queen Tiye are recognizable by her round, chubby face; long, almond-shaped eyes with heavy eyeliner; and pursed lips. In short, she looks just like her husband. Just as many images of Amenhotep III show him as a god, Tiye can appear as a goddess. On her

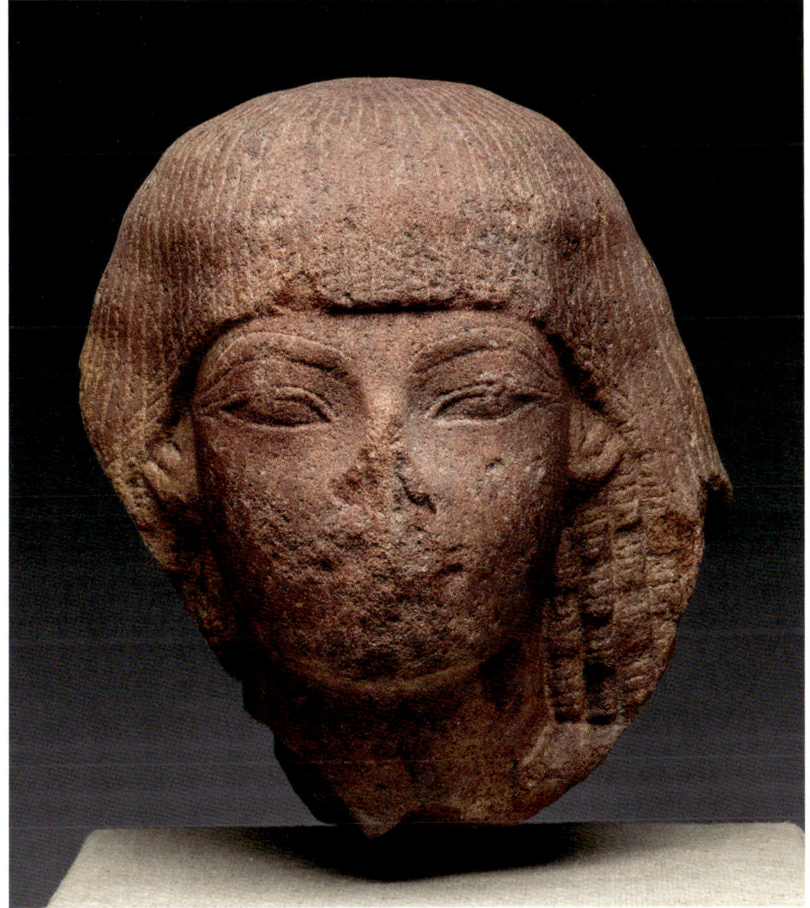

40 Head of an official, 1390–1352 BCE. Quartzite, h. 20 cm (7⁷⁄₈ in.)

head are remains of a sun disk and cow horns. These elements—attributes of the goddess Hathor—emphasize her role as the king's divine as well as earthly partner. Yet the large, enveloping wig, encircled by a floral wreath and a band of rosettes, is not a conventional goddess's hairdo but that of a contemporary lady of fashion. The combination of divine and queenly attributes intentionally blurs the lines between deity and mortal ruler (fig. 39).

Amenhotep III could not have achieved what he did without a dependable coterie of officials, who saw to it that his plans were fulfilled.[21] These men (and they were all men) were amply rewarded for their services in life as well as in death, with sumptuously furnished tombs and statues of the finest workmanship in the temples where they might share in the offerings made to the gods. They would be recognized not by their individual features, however, but by those of the king they served: every one of them is stamped with the king's own image. These people were not self-effacing, as lengthy inscriptions attest. There was no greater glory or distinction, however, than to be visually recognizable as the king's intimate.[22]

An excellent example is the head of an official in striking, deep purplish-red quartzite (fig. 40). Despite the damage to the lower part of the face, enough remains to show that it was a masterpiece. The almond-shaped eyes are surmounted by elegant arched eyebrows tapering to a point. The texture of quartzite encourages different surface treatments, as the smoothness of the skin contrasts with the elaborate wig fashionable among Amenhotep III's courtiers. Strands of hair radiate from the crown of the head, making bangs across the forehead and cascading in layers of corkscrew curls on the sides that bare the earlobes.

Doubtless the subject was an important official, but as the head has been separated from its body and has no inscription, we are not able to identify him. The head has an interesting modern history. It was purchased, along with five other fragmentary sculptures, in 1864 during the American Civil War at the Customs House in New Orleans by John Milton Grosvenor Parker of Lowell, Massachusetts. In 1909 Mr. Parker's grandson, while at boarding school, wrote on behalf of his mother to the director of the MFA offering to sell the statues, explaining: "Somebody got them in Egypt, and was bringing them into this country, and the officials seized them. My grandfather was postmaster there at the time, and with the help of my cousin the late Gen. B. F. Butler bought them at a very low price. When the war was over he brought them to his home on Tenth Street, Lowell, and had them placed on the front lawn around the piazza, where they have been ever since."[23] Snapshots show the statues, some still in their crates, looking forlorn after sitting out on the lawn for sixty years. In 1929 the MFA purchased the whole lot for $1500.[24]

Amenhotep III's son and successor, Akhenaten (ruled 1352–1336 BCE), rejected the pantheon of traditional Egyptian gods in favor of the one god, the Aten, worshipped in the form of a sun disk radiating beams of light. In his fifth regnal year, he changed his name from Amenhotep ("Amen Is Satisfied") to Akhenaten ("Serviceable to the Aten") and moved to a new capital at el-Amarna, which he called Akhetaten ("Horizon of the Aten"), dedicated exclusively to the worship of the Aten. The other gods effectively ceased to exist. Up and down the Nile, the name of Amen, formerly king of the gods, was erased from the monuments, and his images were destroyed—even the word "gods" was expunged, as there was now no god but Aten.

Akhenaten's religious reforms mandated a new artistic program. Gone were the animal-headed deities of tradition. Akhenaten himself, however, was not averse to being depicted in hybrid form: he remained fond of the sphinx, and often had himself depicted as that fantastic creature, part man, part lion. Back in the Pyramid Age, the Great Sphinx at Giza represented the king presenting offerings to the sun god.[25] So, in a relief from el-Amarna, Akhenaten appears as a sphinx with human arms and hands offering to the deity (fig. 41).[26] Aten shines at the upper left, with his rays ending in hands, some reaching out to the offerings below, some holding *ankh*-signs to bestow life to the royal worshipper. Akhenaten's face is one of the most fantastic creations in the history of art. Despite the damage, one can still discern his characteristic slanted eyes, long nose, hollow cheeks, drooping lower lip, and pendulous chin.

Akhenaten's chief queen was the famous Nefertiti ("The Beautiful One Has Come"). Nefertiti was, if anything, even more visible than Tiye had been. Those familiar with her only from her painted bust in Berlin will be surprised at how she looks in a relief carving from a column. It shows Akhenaten, Nefertiti, and their eldest daughter, Meretaten ("Beloved of the Aten"), at worship, one of the most frequent subjects in Amarna art (fig. 42). The Aten's rays caress the royal couple and extend the sign of life to the queen's nose. Although the king's face is missing, enough remains to show he was wearing a short wig with streamers. Nefertiti, entitled "Lady of the Two Lands," wears her customary tall crown and holds what appears to be a floral bouquet; her pleated dress and shawl of sheer linen cling to her figure. The queen has a drooping lower lip and a pendulous chin. Her nose is impossibly long, and the entire lower part of her face is distended like a muzzle.

Both Akhenaten and Nefertiti have long, gangly necks, high waists, large hips and thighs, and spindly arms. Out of context or without distinguishing attributes it can be difficult or impossible to tell them apart. Their appearance is outlandish, and purposefully so. Although some of these features may be based on the king's actual appearance, they have

41 Relief of Akhenaten as a sphinx, 1349–1336 BCE. Limestone, 51 × 105.5 cm (20⅛ × 41½ in.)

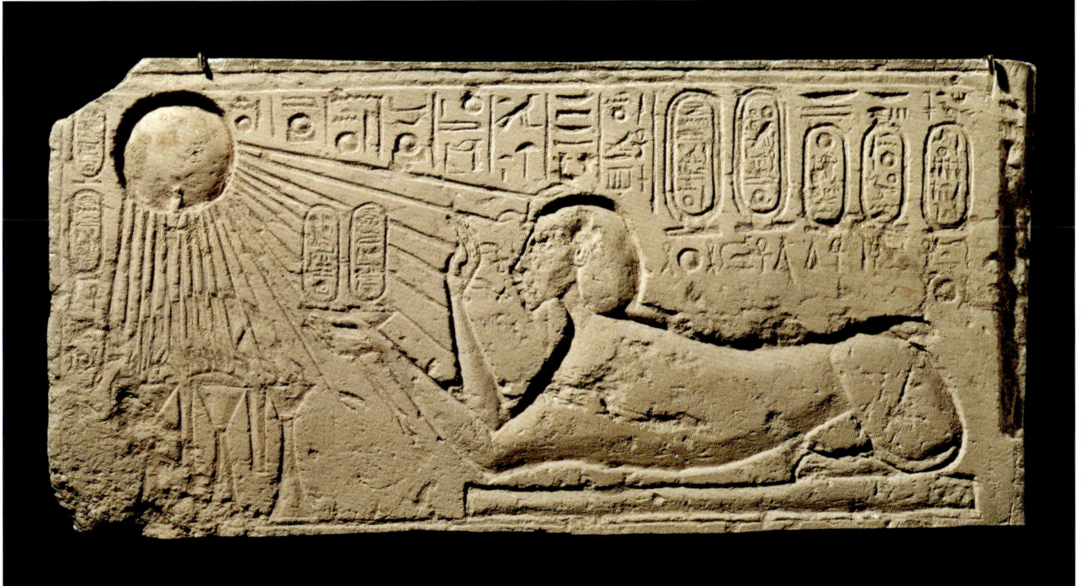

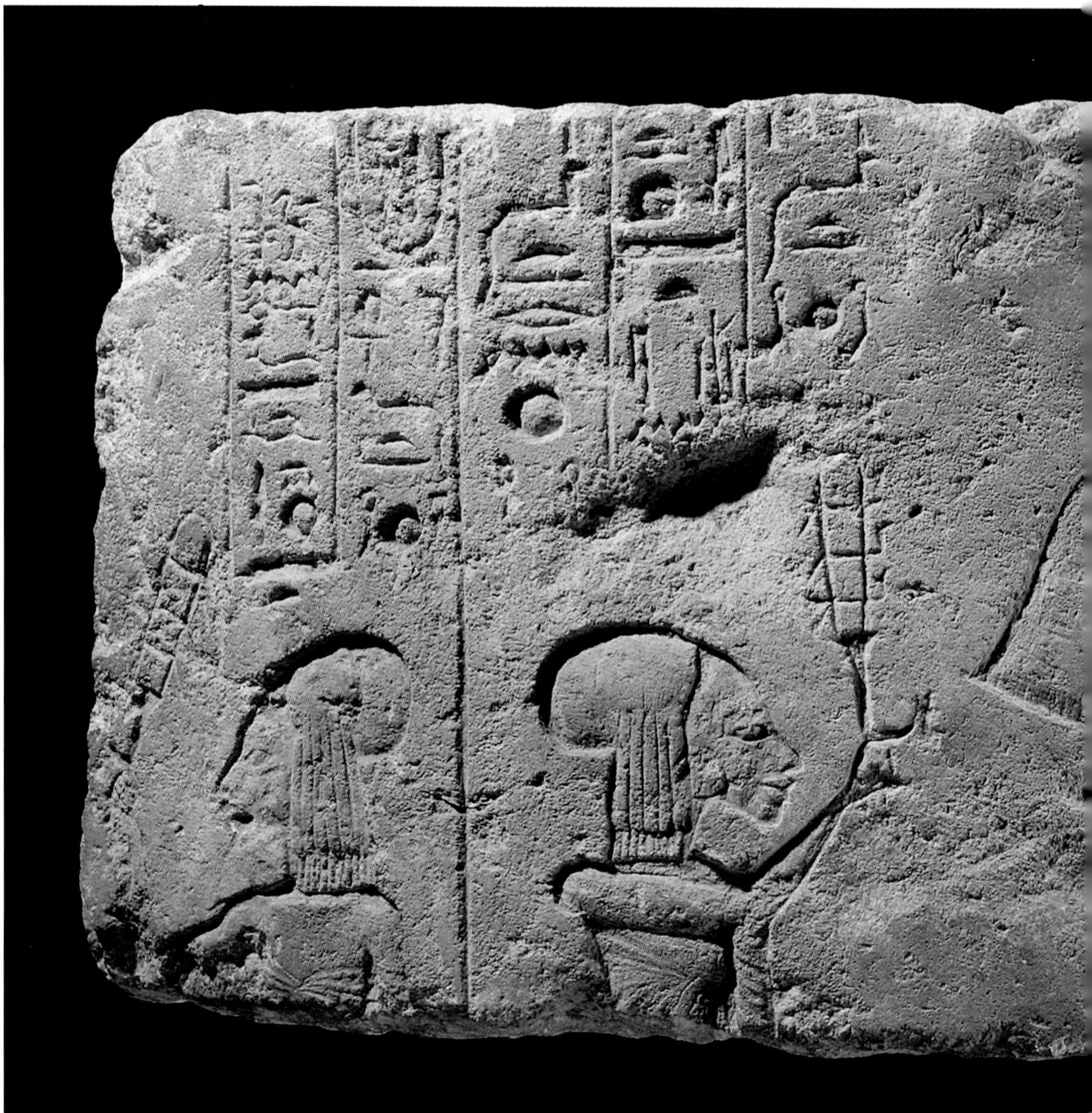

42 Fragment of a column drum featuring the royal family worshipping, 1349–1336 BCE. Limestone, 22.4 × 52.5 cm (8⅞ × 20⅝ in.)

been exaggerated for effect, to distinguish the royal family from ordinary humans. Some of the artistic vocabulary for communicating this already existed. Gaunt, emaciated features, deep creases, and folds of flesh had traditionally been used in Egyptian art to portray foreigners, venerable sages, people on the fringes of society. They are now applied to the royal family to set them apart from the common run of humanity and to characterize them as "extraordinary beings."[27] The body proportions emphasize the fertility of the royal couple as embodying the male and female principles of creation.

Princess Meretaten appears twice, back-to-back, indicating that the scene was repeated facing in the opposite direction. The princess wears a thick sidelock with multiple braids and holds a sistrum, a kind of rattle used in religious ceremonies that was supposed to have a calming effect on the gods, particularly the goddess Hathor. Evidently the Aten liked it

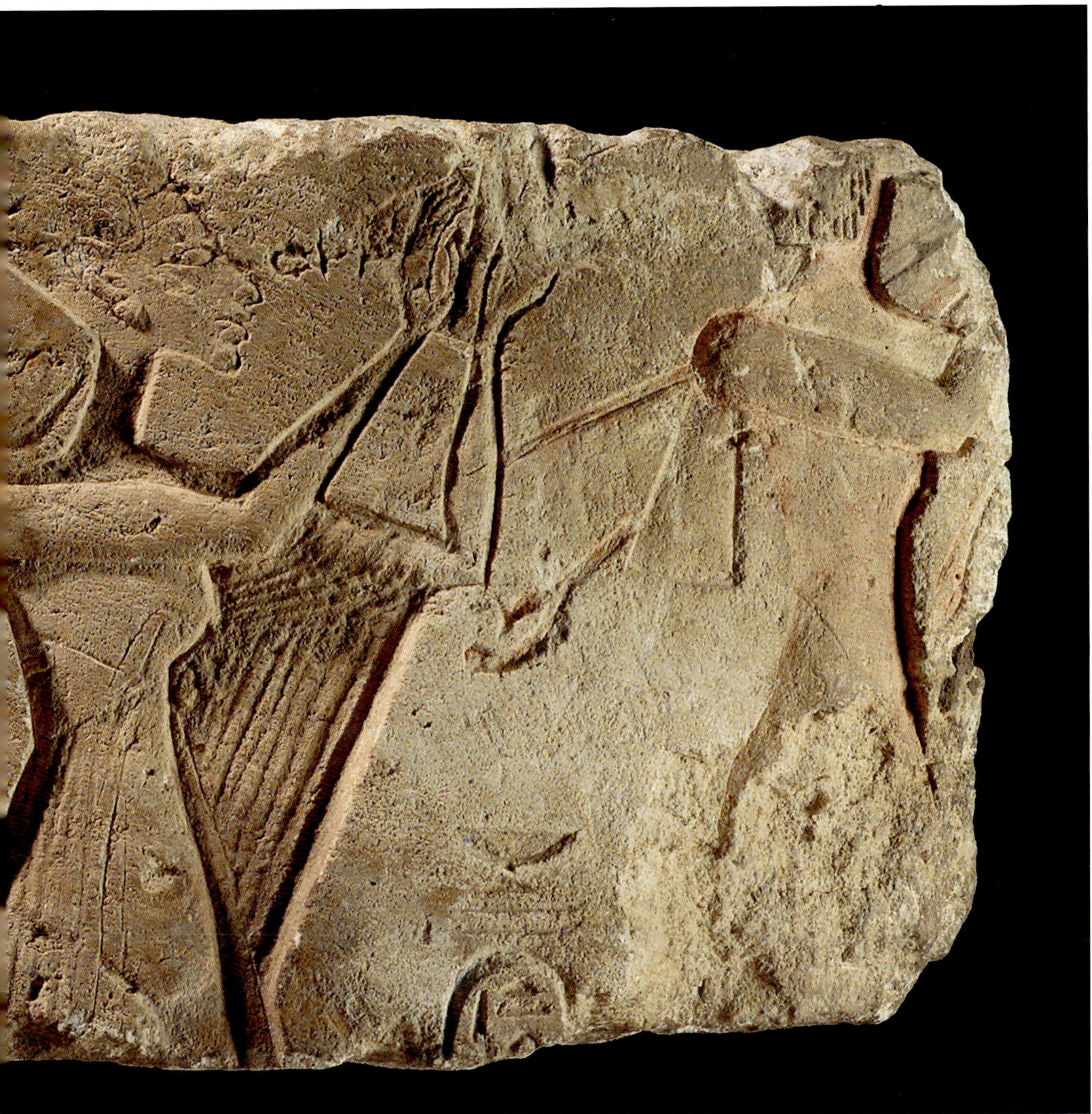

too. While her face resembles Nefertiti's, the most distinctive aspect of her appearance is her grossly elongated cranium. This feature is typical of the Amarna princesses, and is even more striking in sculpture in the round. Although some scholars have suggested that the princesses' heads were compressed by head-binding in infancy, this does not appear to have been the case.[28] It is best not to take Amarna art too literally.

Inscriptions tell us that the king personally instructed his chief sculptor in the new mode of representation, but all the same it was not easy to adjust so quickly, and numerous trial pieces show artists trying to get hold of the radical new style (fig. 43).[29] With time, however, the gawkiness of early Amarna art yields to a lyrical grace, as seen in a relief of a princess, probably Meretaten, standing behind the king as she offers a cone of scented fat to the Aten (fig. 44). Her seemingly elastic fingers undulate gracefully around the base of the cone.

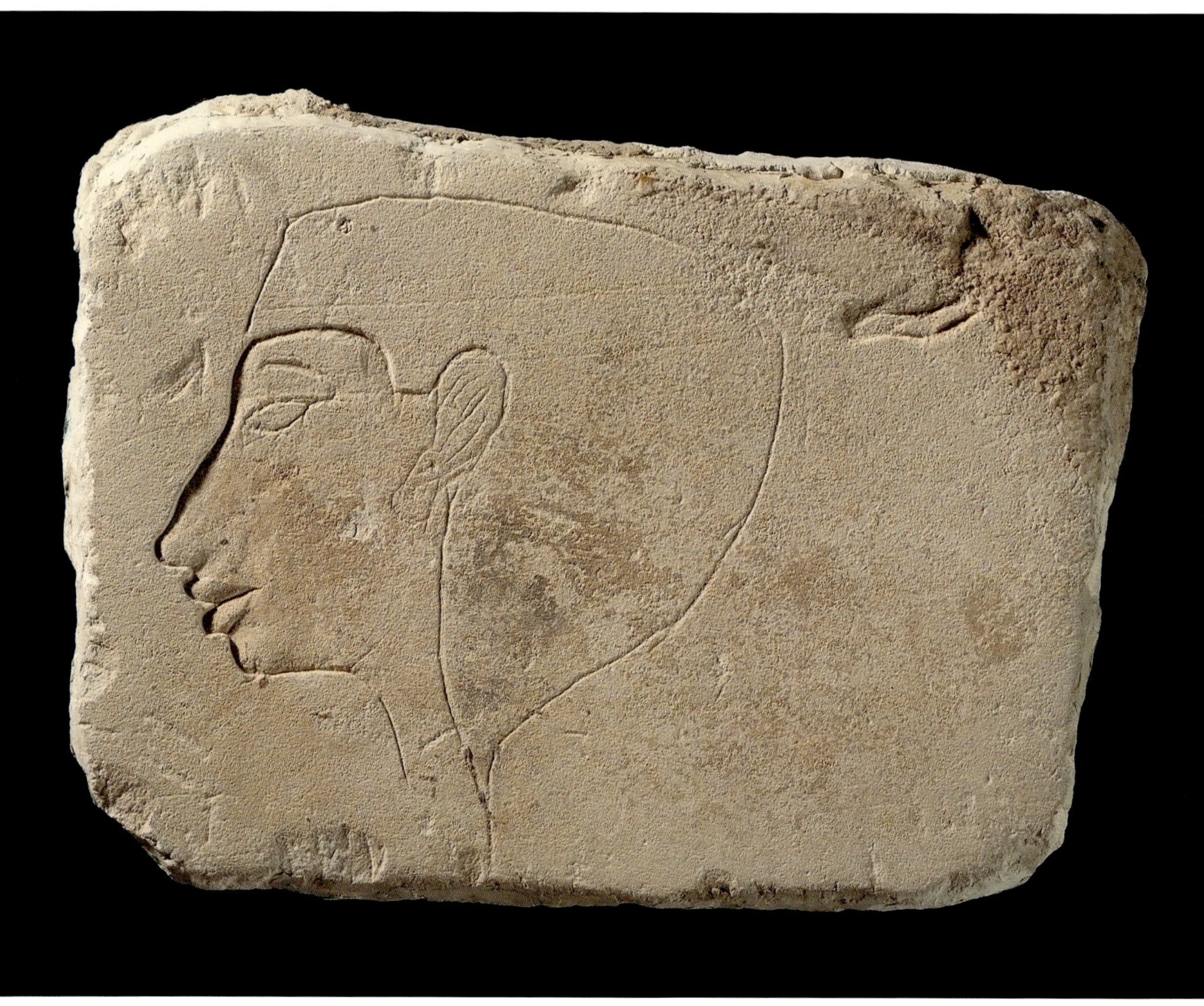

43 Trial carving of head, 1349–1336 BCE. Limestone, w. 22 cm (8⅝ in.)

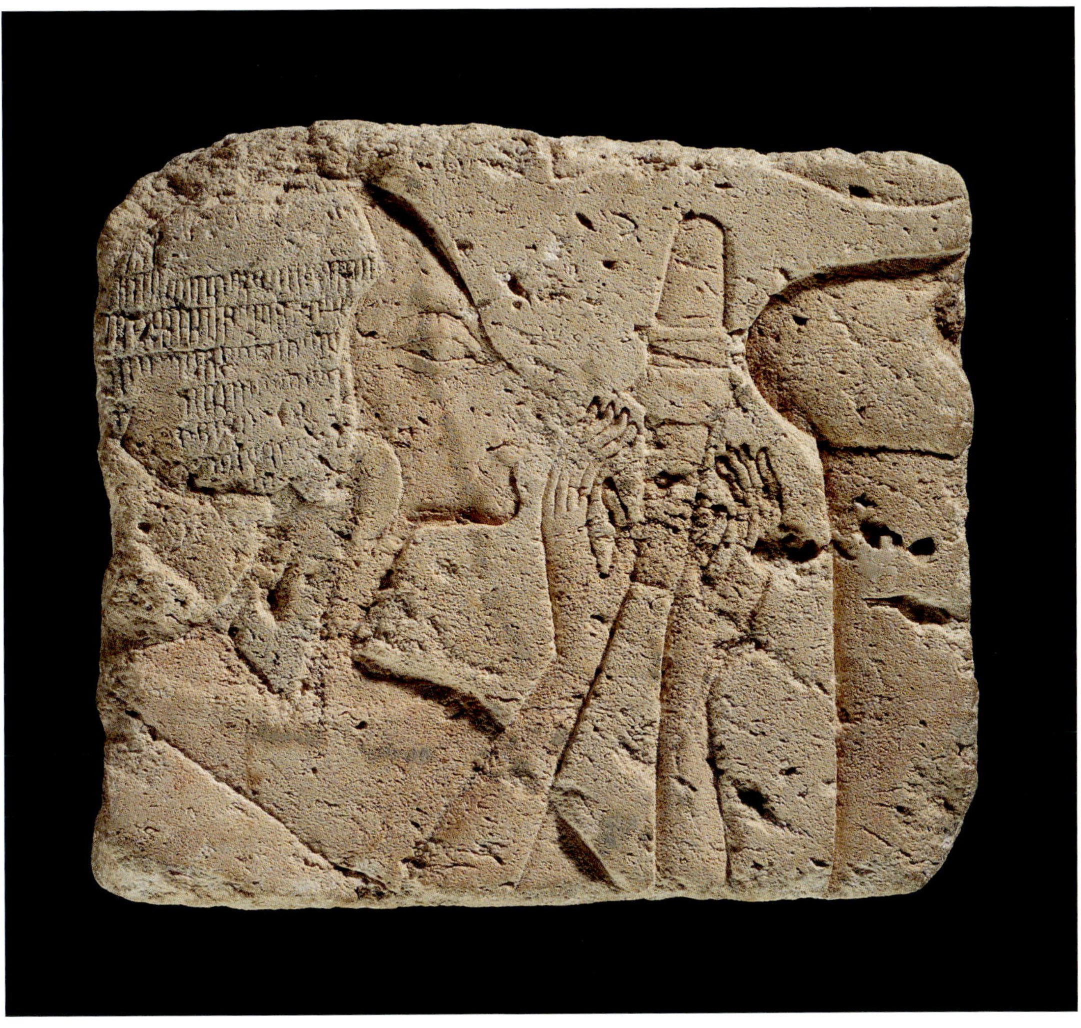

44 Relief of princess offering to the Aten, 1349–1336 BCE. Limestone, 23 × 27 cm (9 × 10⅝ in.)

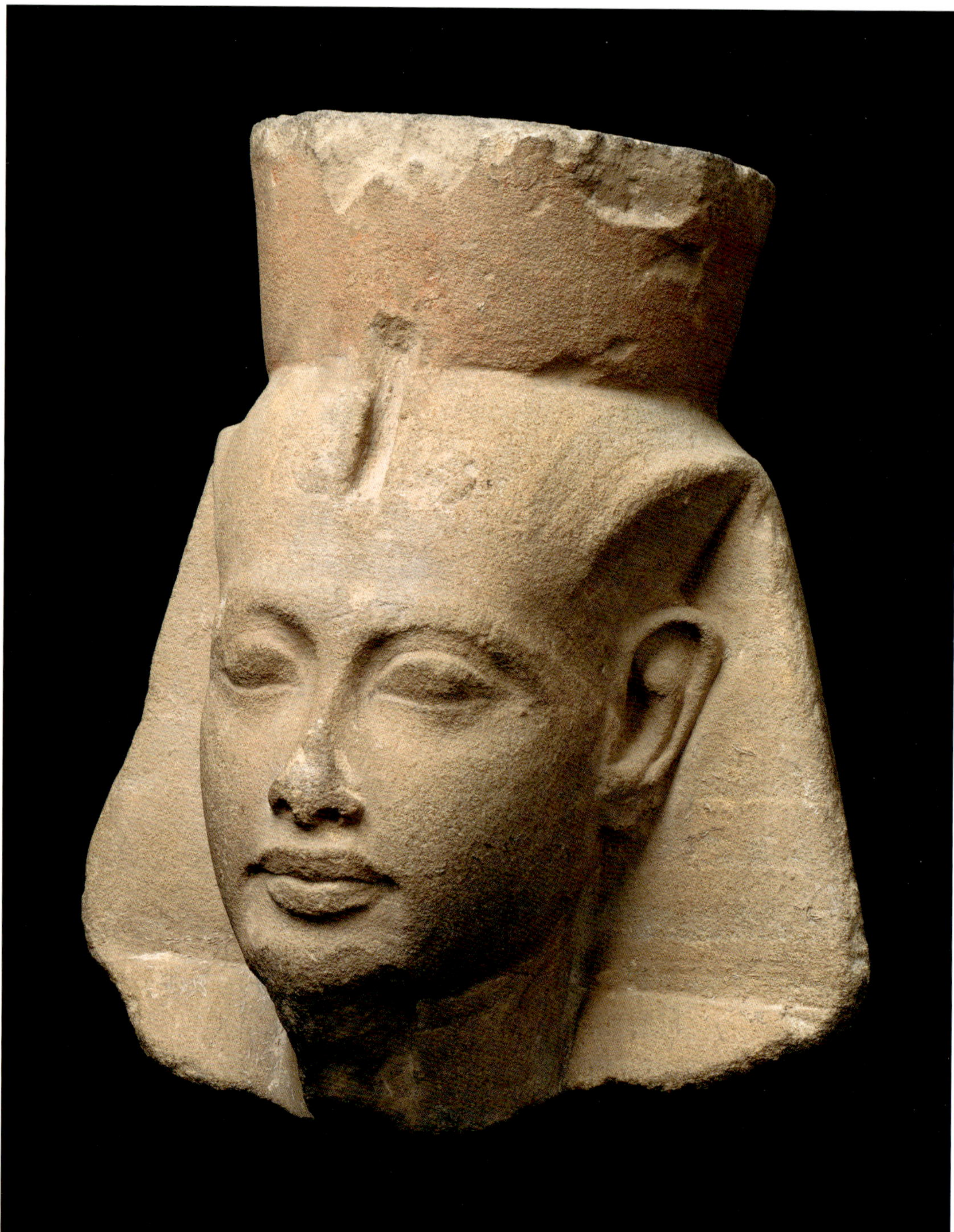

A close look reveals that alterations have been made to the princess's hairstyle. Comparison with other examples suggests that the relief started out depicting another woman. Akhenaten had a second wife, by the name of Kiya. Little is known about her, and Egyptologists were not even aware of her existence until the 1960s. Nefertiti may have been the "great king's wife," but Kiya was his "great beloved wife." Like Nefertiti, Kiya appears with Akhenaten in offering scenes, although the two queens never appear together. After Kiya's death toward the end of the reign, her name was erased and her portraits were changed into images of Meretaten simply by altering her hairstyle from the short, curly wig favored by Kiya to the thick sidelock more suitable for a princess.[30] Smoothed over with plaster and painted, the change would have been hardly noticeable.

Akhenaten ruled for seventeen years. After his death, his young successor restored the cults of the old gods and changed his name from Tutankhaten ("Living Image of the Aten") to Tutankhamen ("Living Image of Amen"). Yet the boy king received little thanks for his piety: later rulers still associated him with the heretic Akhenaten. History forgot him until the discovery of his treasure-filled tomb in 1922 catapulted him to worldwide fame. In a statue head that is not from the tomb, the king's face is so familiar that his portrait is immediately recognizable, even if it lacks an archaeological context and an identifying inscription (fig. 45). The sandstone it is made of is by nature coarse and does not take a high polish. Originally, the king's face was painted red with the eyes outlined in black, and the headdress was striped alternately blue and yellow, the same as the famous gold mask from the king's tomb. The loss of paint fortuitously enhances the king's dreamy, otherworldly expression, a survival from the art of Amarna.

Hatshepsut, Amenhotep III, and Akhenaten were visionary pharaohs with the means to turn their ambitions into reality. Each invented a new portrait style that distinguished them from their predecessors and materialized their self-image. Hatshepsut, the woman who ruled as king, defined the elegant art style of the early Eighteenth Dynasty. Amenhotep III, under whose rule Egypt was more powerful than it had ever been before or would be again, fashioned an image that has become a byword for glamour and opulence. Akhenaten, whose radical form of expression was suppressed after his religious reforms failed to take root, has returned with a vengeance to imprint his features indelibly on the modern mind.

45 Head of Tutankhamen, 1336–1327 BCE. Sandstone, 29.6 × 26.5 cm (11 5/8 × 10 3/8 in.)

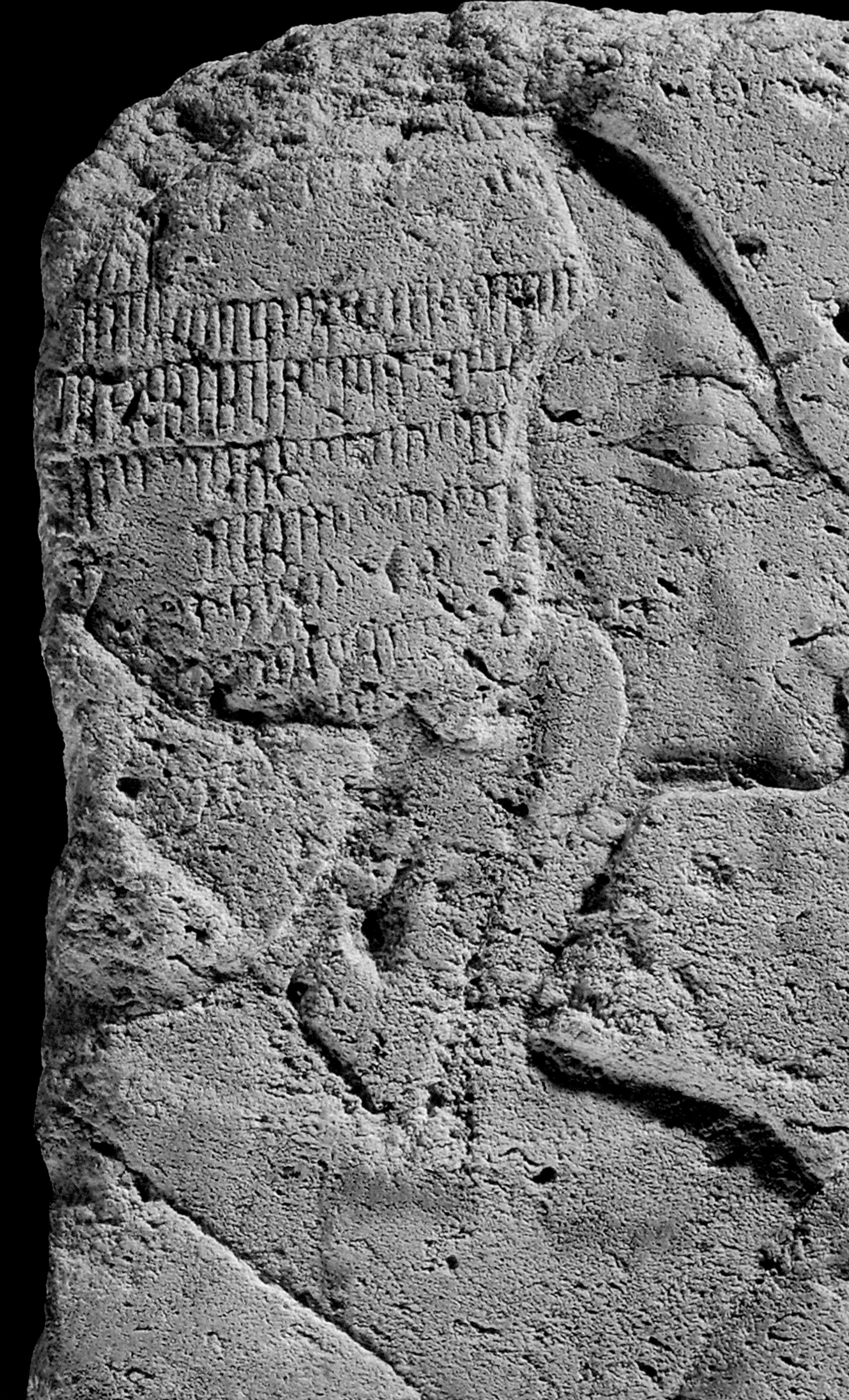

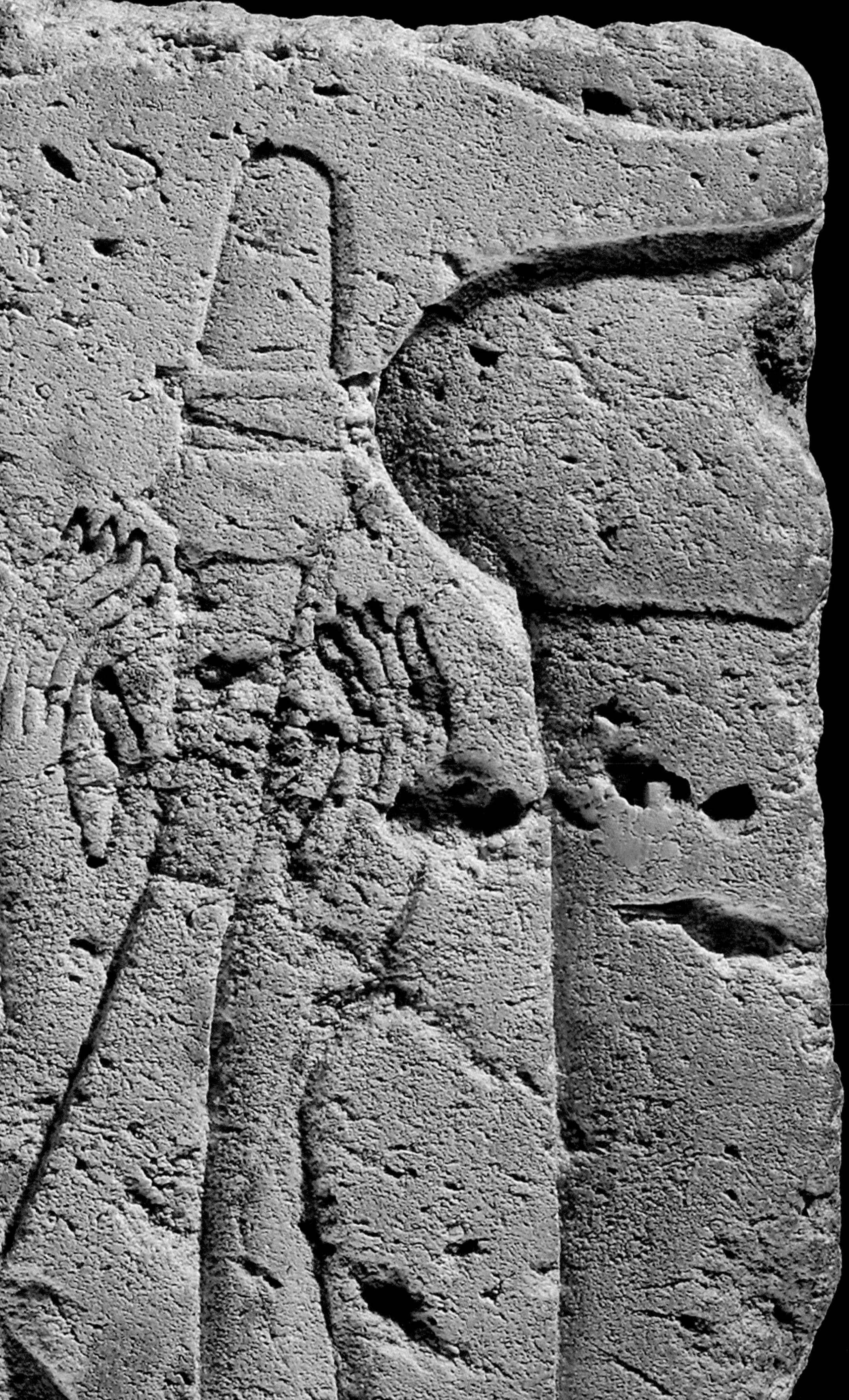

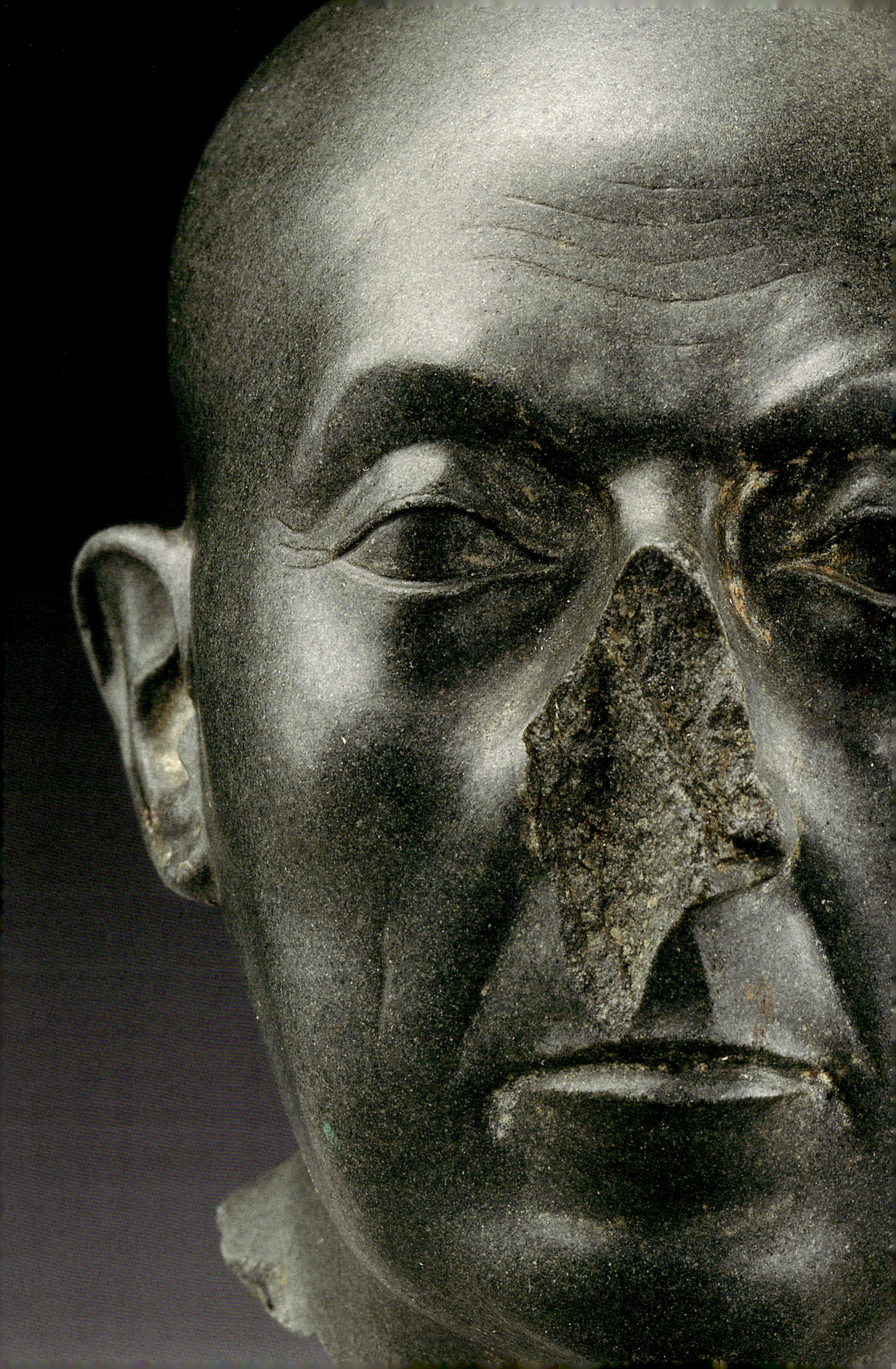

FIVE

Back to the Future

The most naturalistic portraits in Egyptian art are the earliest ones and the latest. If the bust of Ankhhaf is the greatest masterpiece of Old Kingdom portraiture, the head of a priest, known as the Boston Green Head, is the finest portrait of the Late Period, some two thousand years later (fig. 46). The sculptor has demonstrated a complete mastery of his medium. First, there is the bony structure of the skull, the bumps and shallows of the shaved head, brow ridges, and cheekbones. Second, the softness of the fleshy jowls. And third, the furrows of the brow, crow's feet around the eyes, and lines between the nose and mouth.

Although only a little over four inches high, the head makes a monumental impression. When complete, the figure was probably standing or kneeling, most likely holding an attribute such as a statue of a deity or a *naos* (shrine) containing the image of a god, a very common statue type from the seventh century through the first century BCE. If standing, the figure would have been about 28 inches high; if kneeling, about 17½ inches, plus a few more inches for the integral base.[1]

The top of the back pillar preserves the name of the Memphite funerary deity Ptah-Sokar. When complete, the inscription running down to the base would have included, at the very least, the subject's name and occupation. Lacking identification, this piece is known worldwide as the Boston Green Head, after the color of the stone and the place where it now resides.

If the Green Head and Ankhhaf are alike in quality, each representing the very best of the art of their times, their stories are very different. Ankhhaf was found in 1925 in the course of carefully conducted and methodically recorded scientific excavations in the mastaba chapel it was made

46 Head of a priest (The Boston Green Head), 380–332 BCE. Graywacke, 10.5 × 8.5 × 11.3 cm (4⅛ × 3⅜ × 4½ in.)

for. Two years later it was in Boston, where it remains. The Green Head's history is a lot more complicated.

The Green Head was discovered in 1857–58 at the Saqqara Serapeum, the catacombs of the sacred Apis bulls, by the French Egyptologist Auguste Mariette, who was soon to be appointed Egypt's first director of antiquities. The head was then presented by Said Pasha, viceroy of Egypt, to Prince Napoleon, known as Plon-Plon, the cousin of Emperor Napoleon III. Displayed in the Prince's newly built Pompeiian House in Paris, it appeared in the very first issue of the *Gazette des beaux-arts*, the prestigious French art journal.[2] After the dispersal of the Prince's collection in the 1860s, the head was acquired sometime later by the Boston collector Edward Perry Warren, the man who transformed the MFA's department of classical art from an assembly of plaster casts to America's premier collection of Greek and Roman originals, and he sold it to the MFA in 1904.[3]

Warren did not ordinarily collect Egyptian art. His taste in ancient portraiture was based on images of noble Romans of the late Republican period, noted for their brutal realism, which began to appear perhaps as early as the second century BCE (fig. 47). The Green Head would have appealed to Warren because it looked so Roman. Previous efforts at dating the Green Head have been unduly influenced by the portrait's supposed relationship to Greek and Roman art. Bernard V. Bothmer, the great scholar of late Egyptian sculpture, saw a causal connection between the Green Head and Roman Republican portraits and dated the head to the second century BCE.[4] Considering the evidence objectively rather than through the lens of Greek and Roman art, the most satisfactory date is the fourth century BCE, probably during the brief period of Egyptian independence between the ouster of the Persians in 404 BCE and their return in 348 BCE.[5] The Green Head then appears as the crowning statement of a tradition of realistic portraiture in Egyptian art as old as the pyramids.

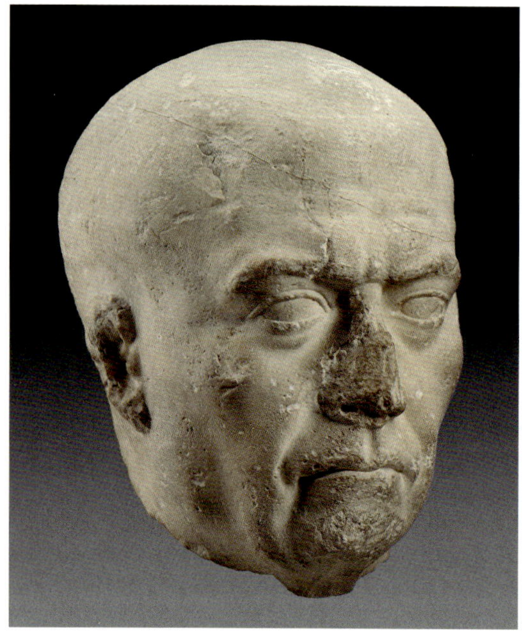

47 Head of an older man, possibly a priest, about 60–30 BCE. Marble, 31.8 × 25 × 22.9 cm (12½ × 9⅞ × 9 in.)

Mariette never published the details of his excavations of 1857–58. That same season Mariette worked simultaneously at Giza, Saqqara, Abydos, Thebes, and Elephantine.[6] That was his method: Mariette was always (and particularly at this stage of his career) racing against time, working at many sites at once, afraid that any time the Pasha might withdraw his support. Consequently, all the information about the Green Head's excavation comes to us secondhand. From those sources, and from knowledge

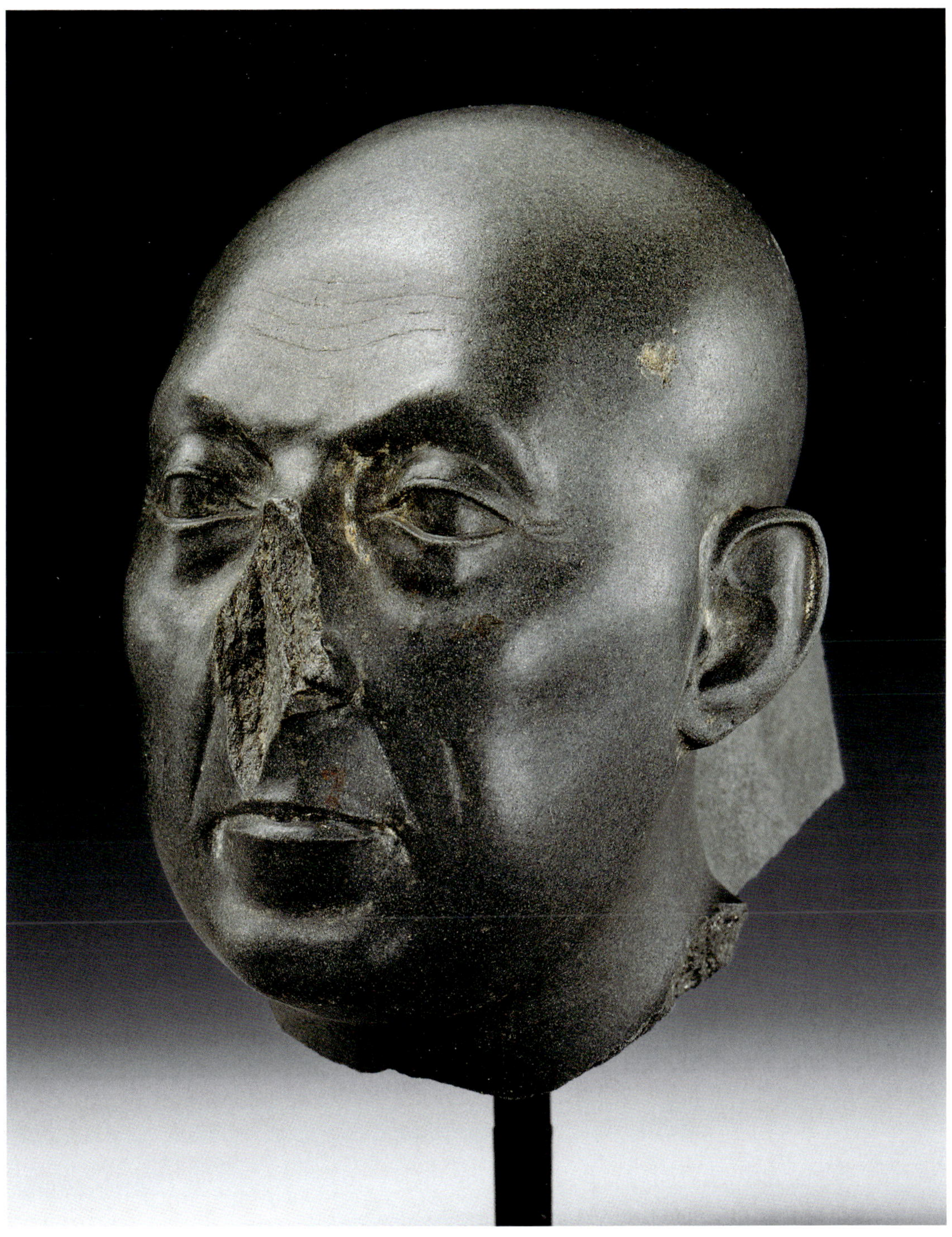

of the site since gained from well-documented excavations in the vicinity of the Serapeum, we can reconstruct the following scenario. The statue of a priest was set up in one of the temples of ancient Memphis, very likely during the reign of Nectanebo II (360–343 BCE), a brilliant period of heightened cultural and artistic achievement. (Although it could have been a tomb statue, it was more likely a temple statue, which far outnumber tomb statues in the Late Period.) The head was broken off during the Persian invasion of 343 BCE. Various sources report that great damage was inflicted at that time: city walls were demolished and the temples sacked. In 332 BCE Alexander the Great defeated the Persians and added Egypt to his burgeoning empire. Alexander and his successors resumed the building projects initiated by Nectanebo II and undertook the repair of buildings damaged by the Persians. The Green Head was salvaged and buried as part of the massive reconstruction work carried out under Alexander and his successors at the Serapeum, probably in a cache under the pavement where damaged or redundant temple and ritual objects, which could not be otherwise disposed of, were deposited for safekeeping out of respect for their sacred nature.[7]

The only clue to the subject's identity is his coiffure—or rather, the lack of one. Egyptian priests were required to shave their heads (indeed, their entire bodies) for reasons of ritual purity. They also had to wear only linen garments and papyrus sandals, to bathe twice daily, and to avoid certain foods (such as fish and beans).[8] Although not all priests appear shaven-headed in Egyptian sculpture, most statues of shaven-headed men represent priests. Our priest was probably a citizen of Memphis, attached to one of the gods of that great city.

A rare statuette in wood of a standing shaven-headed priest holding a *naos* not only illustrates the sort of statue to which the Green Head would have belonged but also is a masterpiece in its own right (fig. 48). The quality of the carving shines through despite damage to the surface. The facial features are hauntingly lifelike and individual. The face is long and gaunt, with hollow cheeks. The eyes were animated by covering them with a translucent inlay resembling glass. The pupils were painted black directly on the wood. The figure wears a calf-length wraparound skirt secured at chest level, the voluminous garment tied in the center like a bath towel, one end covering the left breast, the other hanging down below the right breast.

The *naos* originally contained a figure of a god, now lost; the mortise into which the deity was inserted is visible toward the back of the floor of the shrine. The man holds the *naos*, supported from below by a wooden strut, between his palms. Even made of wood, a shrine such as this would have been a heavy load. Reliefs in the temple of Dendara show priests using straps around their necks to carry the shrines up and down the stairs to the roof of the temple for the ceremony of the Union with

48 Statuette of priest holding a *naos*, 525–404 BCE. Wood, 40.5 × 12 × 27 cm (16 × 4¾ × 10⅝ in.)

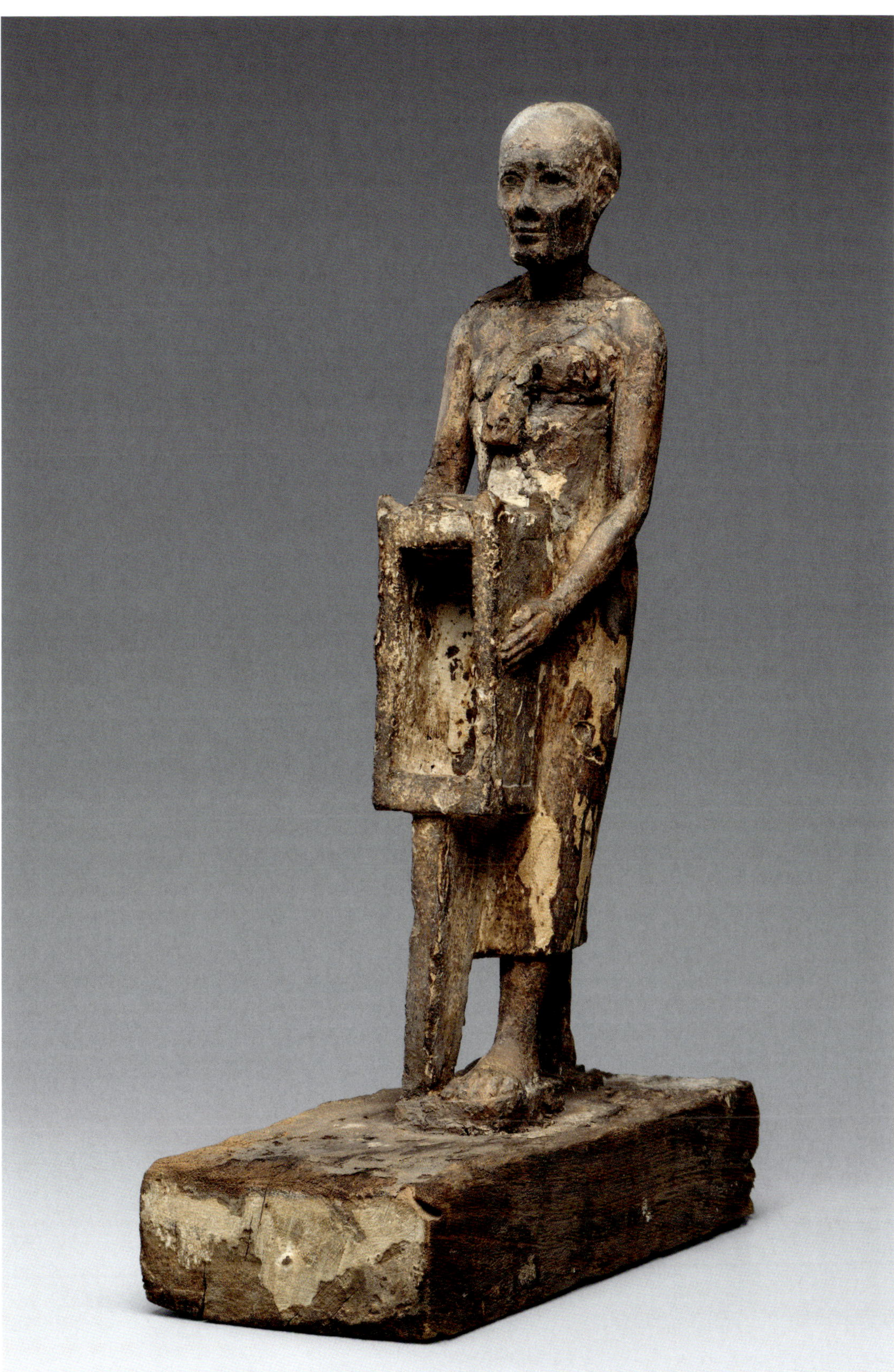

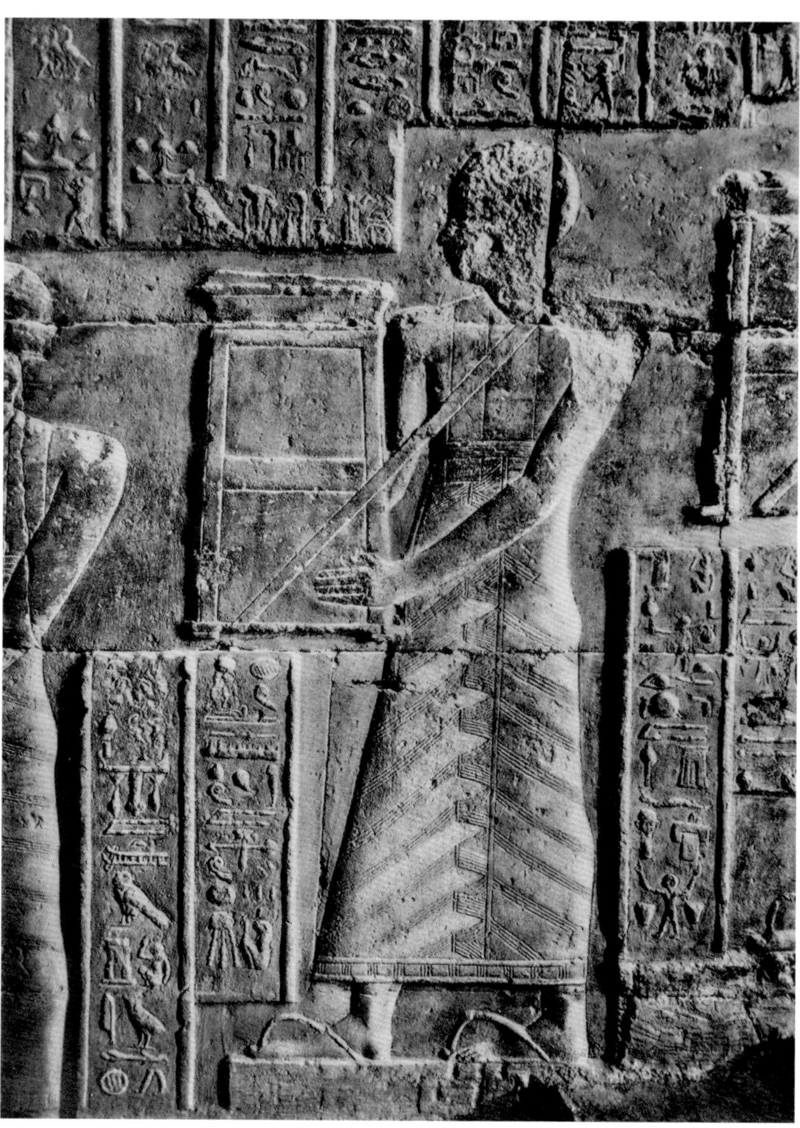

49 Relief of priest carrying a shrine, Dendara

the Sun, when the images of the gods were exposed to the sun's rays and magically "recharged" (fig. 49).[9]

There were many classes of priest in ancient Egypt. The most common were called *hemu-netjer*, literally "god's servants" (usually translated as "prophets"), and *wabu*, "pure ones." An ancient Egyptian temple was literally the god's house (in Egyptian, *hut-netjer*). The deity, incarnate in his cult statue of precious metal, rested in the furthermost recess of the temple, concealed within a *naos* with wooden doors bolted shut. Every morning the priests entered the holy of holies to perform the god's daily ritual, waiting on the divine image like privileged courtiers at the levee of a king. First, they burned incense and sprinkled water and natron to purify the room. Then, to the accompaniment of hymns and prayers, they opened the doors of the shrine, served the god his meal, washed him, and changed his clothes. Finally, they closed up the shrine until the next ceremony. Only the priests (and the king) ever had direct contact with the deity, and only they had access to his private chamber. Small wonder then that Egyptian priests were credited with secret knowledge and special wisdom.

The statue of a man holding a *naos* is not just to be taken literally as a representation of a priest performing his duty. It also operates on a higher plane, showing the officiant in the role of Shu, the god of air, who separated the earth from the sky (fig. 50).[10] This act created the world as the Egyptians pictured it, a bubble of air in the primeval ocean, around which the sun god circled across the sky by day and through the underworld by night. The image of the god Shu standing with his uplifted hands holding up the sky with the sun god sailing across was a fixture in Book of the Dead papyri and in the Underworld Books painted on the ceilings of tombs in the Valley of the Kings. In carrying the *naos* with the divine statue in procession, the priest is emulating Shu holding up the sky, in which the sun god sails in his boat from the eastern to the western horizons.[11]

As the wooden statue is uninscribed, we do not know the man's identity. The piece is said to come from Hermopolis Magna (modern el-Ashmunein) in Middle Egypt, a center of priestly learning since the Middle Kingdom (about 2000 BCE), although there is no evidence to substantiate that.[12] Probably on account of the supposed Persian origin of the garment, the statue was previously dated to the first Persian period, known as Dynasty 27 (525–404 BCE).[13] The high-waisted wraparound skirt, however, already occurs in Egyptian art before the Persian invasion and continues to be represented well into the fourth century BCE.[14] In the developmental sequence of *naos*-bearing statues, this example could date from late Dynasty 26 to Dynasty 30 (380–332 BCE).[15] Thus, it could

50 Shu holds up the sky, Greenfield Papyrus, about 950–930 BCE. Papyrus, ink, 47 × 53.4 cm (18½ × 21 in.)

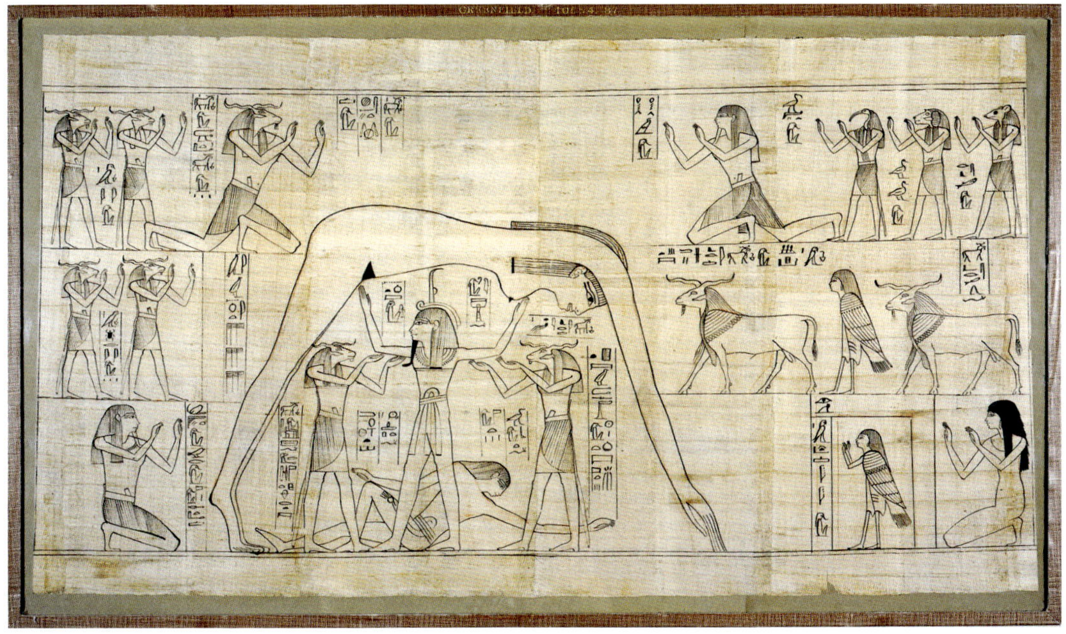

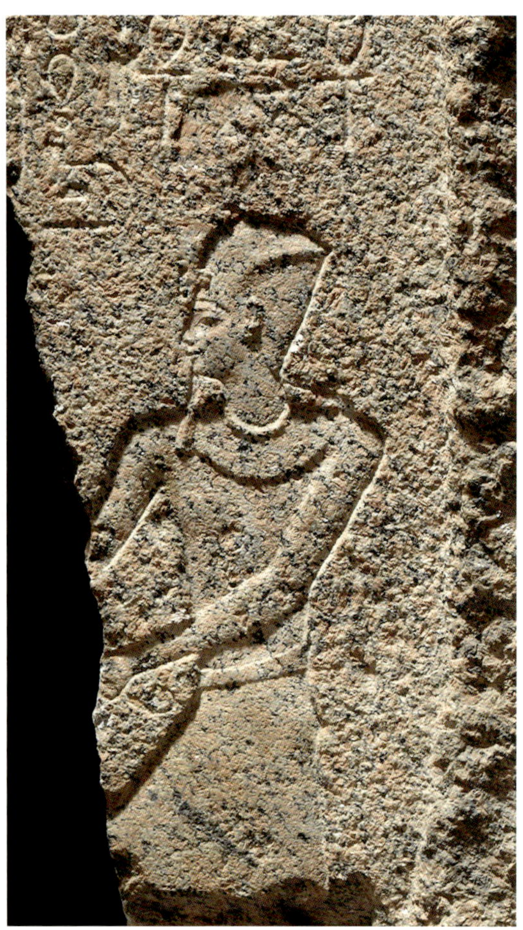

51 Relief of Philip Arrhidaeus, 332–316 BCE (detail). Granite, 166.5 × 74 × 94 cm (65½ × 29⅛ × 37 in.)

52 Head of Nectanebo II, 362–343 BCE. Granodiorite, 30 × 24.5 × 24 cm (11¾ × 9⅝ × 9½ in.)

be contemporary with the Green Head, or close to it. Because wood is so fragile, it might seem that its chances of survival would be greater in a tomb than in a temple; yet objects made of wood, including statues of fine quality, have been found in temple caches.

Alexander and his successors ruled the Nile as pharaohs for three hundred years. Egyptian art and architecture continued to flourish, and at first there was little change. The new rulers presented themselves as the legitimate successors of the last native pharaohs. In their sleek outlines and economy of form, images of Philip Arrhidaeus (323–315 BCE), Alexander's brother and successor, are scarcely distinguishable from those of Nectanebo II, the last native pharaoh (figs. 51, 52).[16]

In 305 BCE, Ptolemy, one of Alexander the Great's generals, declared himself king of Egypt. His descendants, the Ptolemaic Dynasty, ruled until 30 BCE. At its height in the third century BCE, the Ptolemaic kingdom extended well beyond Egypt's traditional borders to include Cyrenaica (Libya), Palestine, Cyprus, and the south Anatolian coast.

Gradually elements of Greek art began to appear in Egyptian statuary. Portraits of the Ptolemies as pharaoh now often show the rulers' natural hair emerging below the frontlet of the *nemes*-headdress in acknowledgment of their dual identity as Greek and Egyptian (fig. 53). Private statuary followed suit. In place of a traditional Egyptian wig or shaven head, the unidentified subject of an imposing, more than life-size portrait wears a diadem terminating in two lotus buds over his own, naturally styled "Greek" hair (fig. 54). It is an individual portrait, rugged and masculine, with two vertical furrows between the eyebrows, deep-set eyes, folds of flesh on the cheeks, and full lips. A sharp downward-curving line sets off the prominent chin. The contrast in surface treatment between the smooth face and rough hair is typical of statues of this period.[17] Although there is a back pillar, it was not inscribed so the identity of the sitter is unknown.

The statue probably dates to the reign of Cleopatra VII (51–30 BCE), the last of the Ptolemaic rulers of Egypt. A number of important nonroyal statues can be assigned to this period. Among them is the statue of Pakhom, governor of Dendara (fig. 55).[18] The statue is unfinished, lacking its

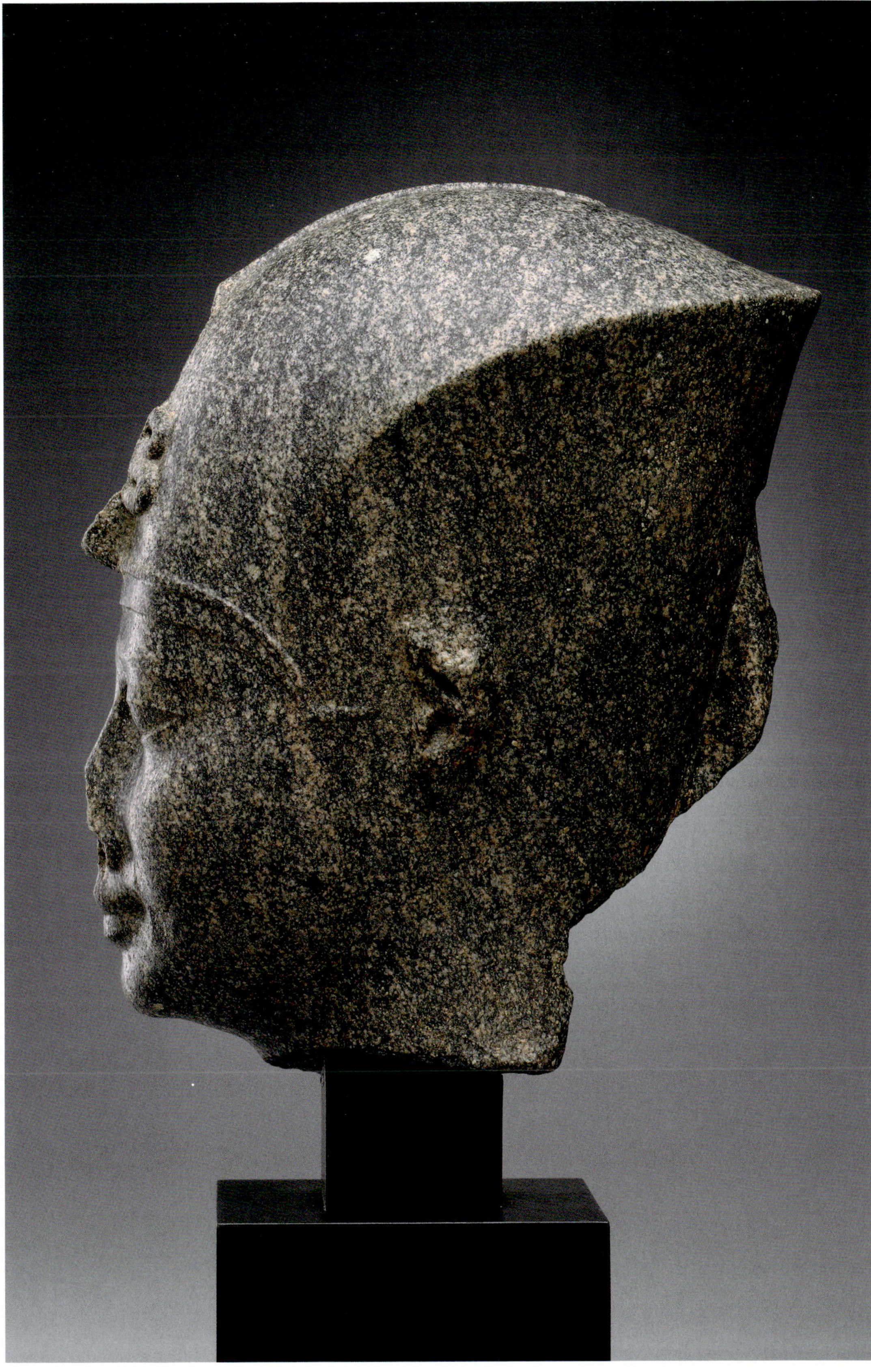

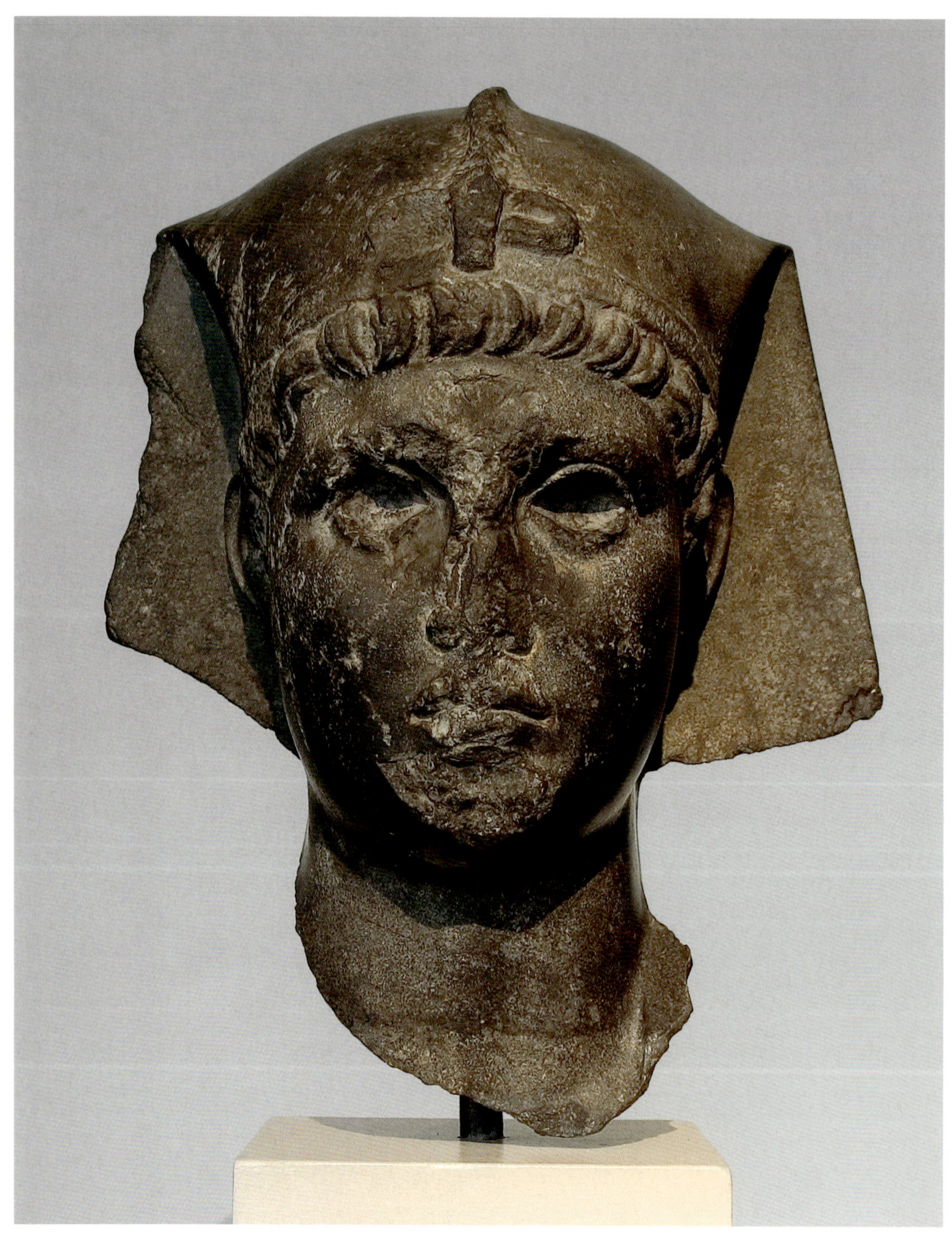

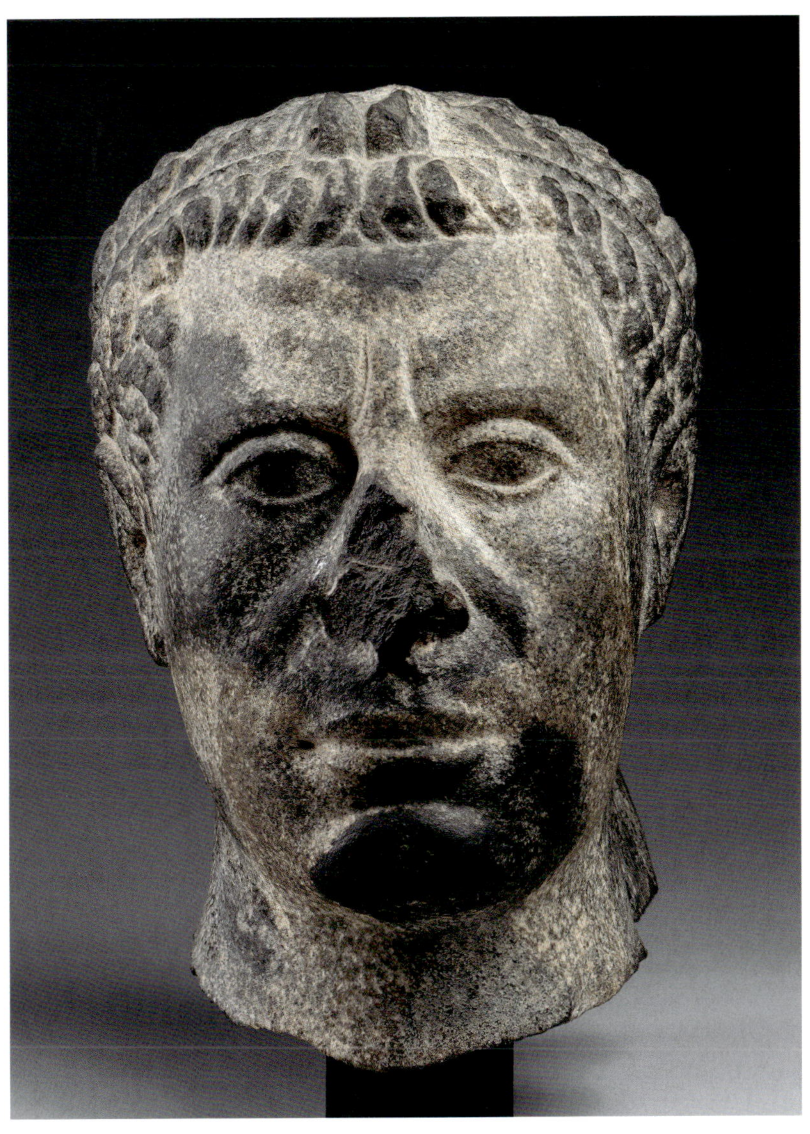

53 Head of a king, about 250–50 BCE. Dark gray schist, h. 37 cm (14 5/8 in.)

54 Head of a man with double lotus bud diadem, 1st century BCE. Granodiorite, 30 × 22 × 28 cm (11 3/4 × 8 5/8 × 11 in.)

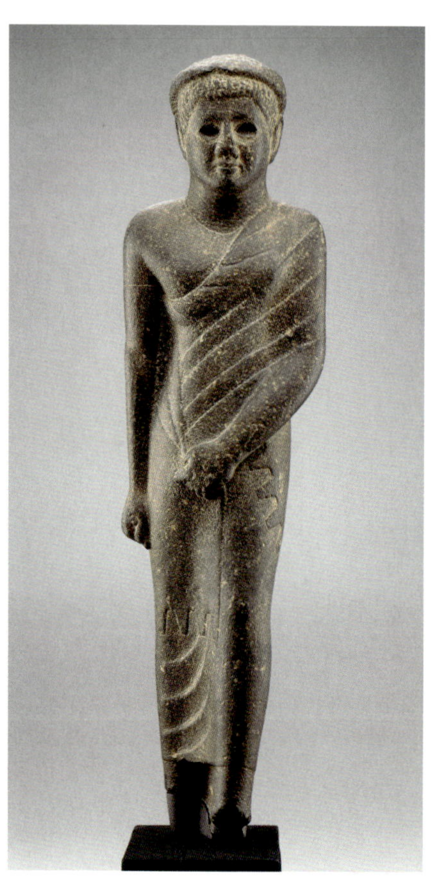

55 Statue of Pakhom, governor of Dendara, 50–30 BCE. Gray granite, 71.1 × 19.1 × 23.5 cm (28 × 7½ × 9¼ in.)

final polish, but as the head is still attached to the body, it provides a good indication of the type of body, pose, and costume that the man in the diadem would have had. The governor strides forward, left leg advanced, with his right arm at his side and his left arm bent at the elbow, his hand clasping the edge of his shawl. His naturally curly hair is encircled by a diadem carved in bold relief. He wears a three-piece outfit consisting of a T-shirt, wraparound skirt, and shawl. The three-piece costume is entirely Egyptian: it was the daily dress at the time. The diadem, however, is Greek. Very likely it indicates a rank in the Ptolemaic court. In addition to his administrative title of governor, Pakhom held the rank of *syggenes*, or "(royal) kinsman," rendered in Egyptian as *sn-nsw*, or "king's brother," the very highest rank at the Ptolemaic royal court. The lotus bud diadem may have a similar meaning.

The Egyptian sculptors of the Late Period could look back on thousands of years of artistic precedent, but today their portraits still pose challenges. Some scholars see even the Boston Green Head as a generic type—albeit a fine one—representing an older man. For others, this writer among them, it represents one of the most remarkable portraits from antiquity: a worthy successor to the great Old Kingdom portraits of Menkaura and Ankhhaf.

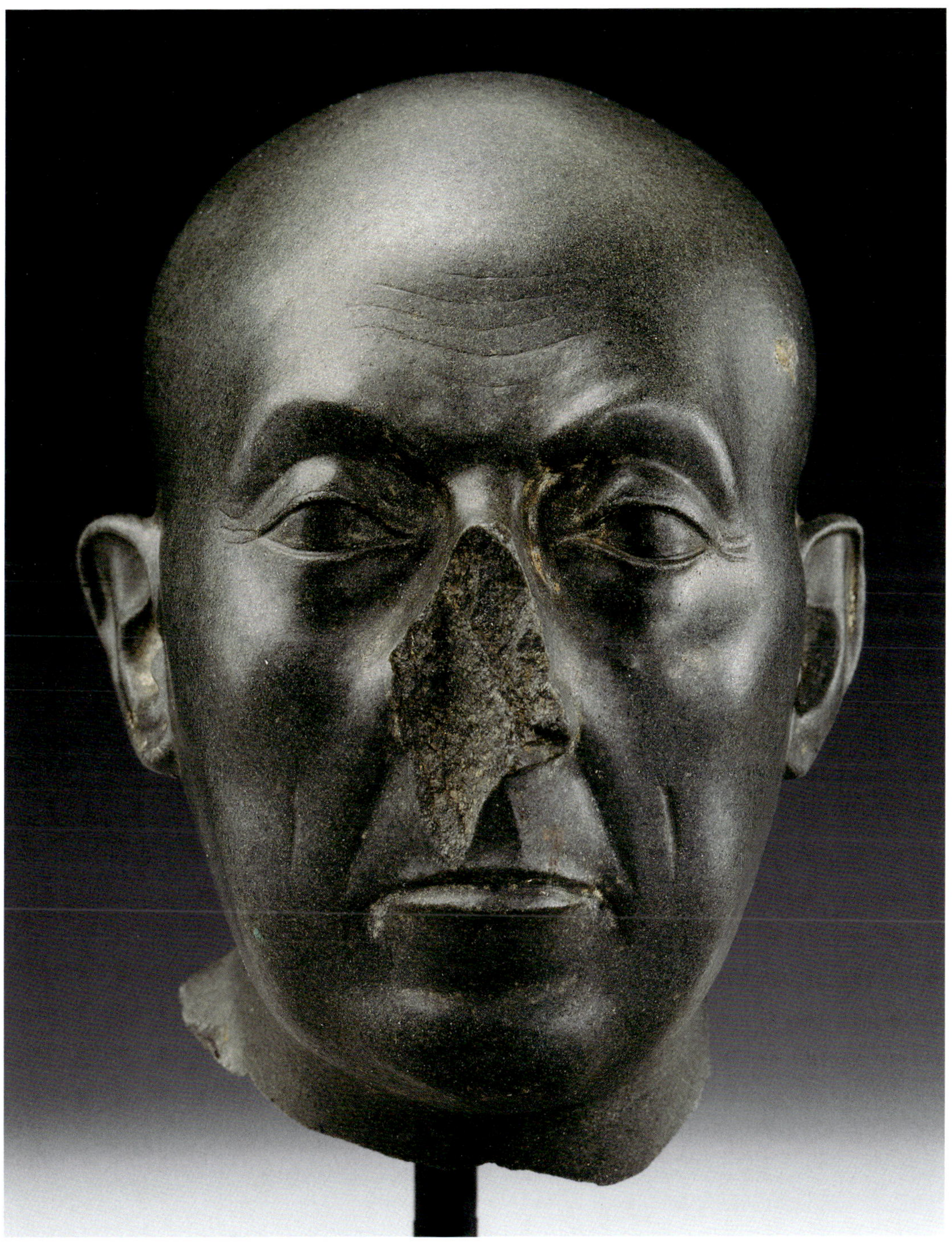

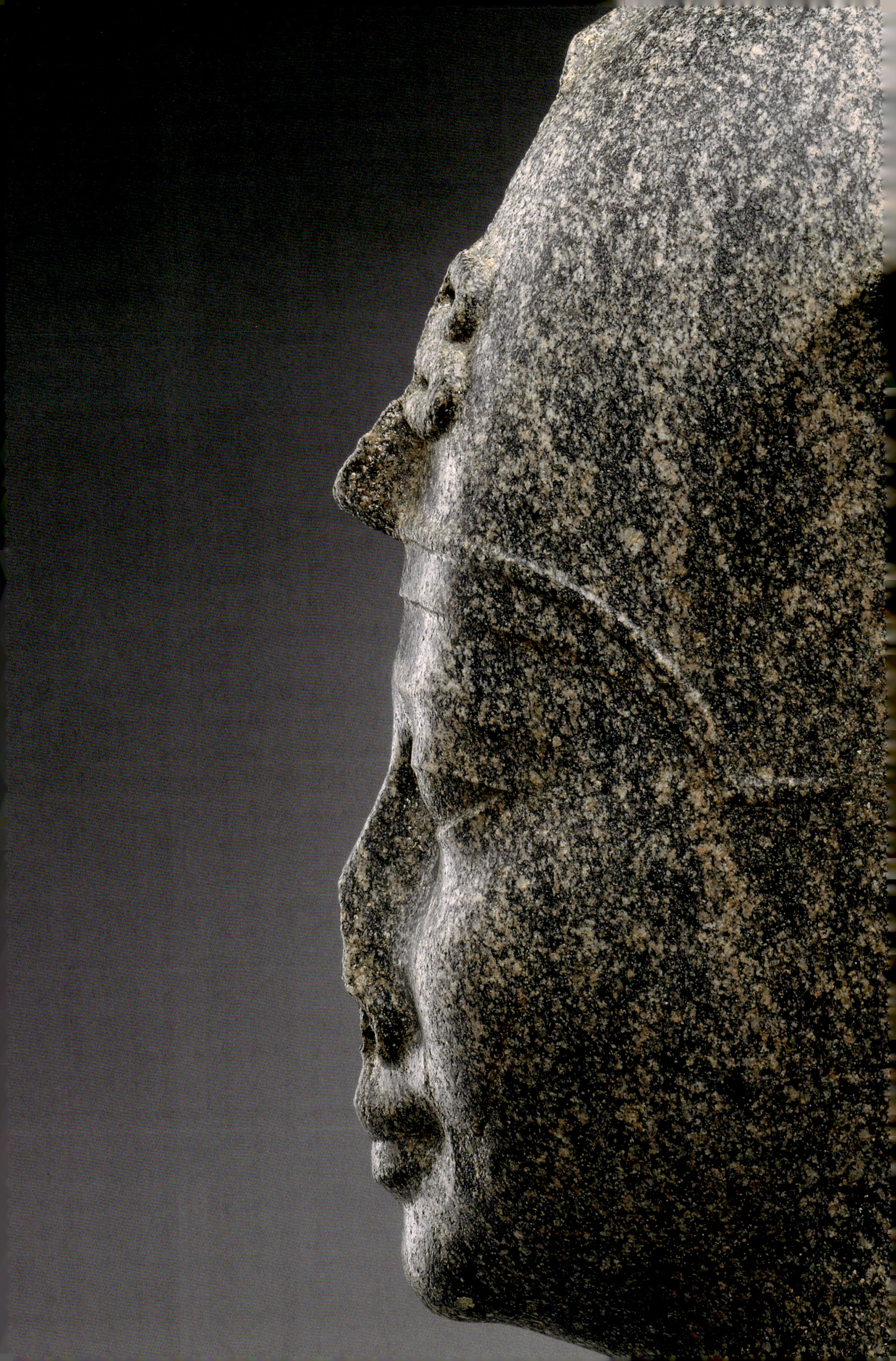

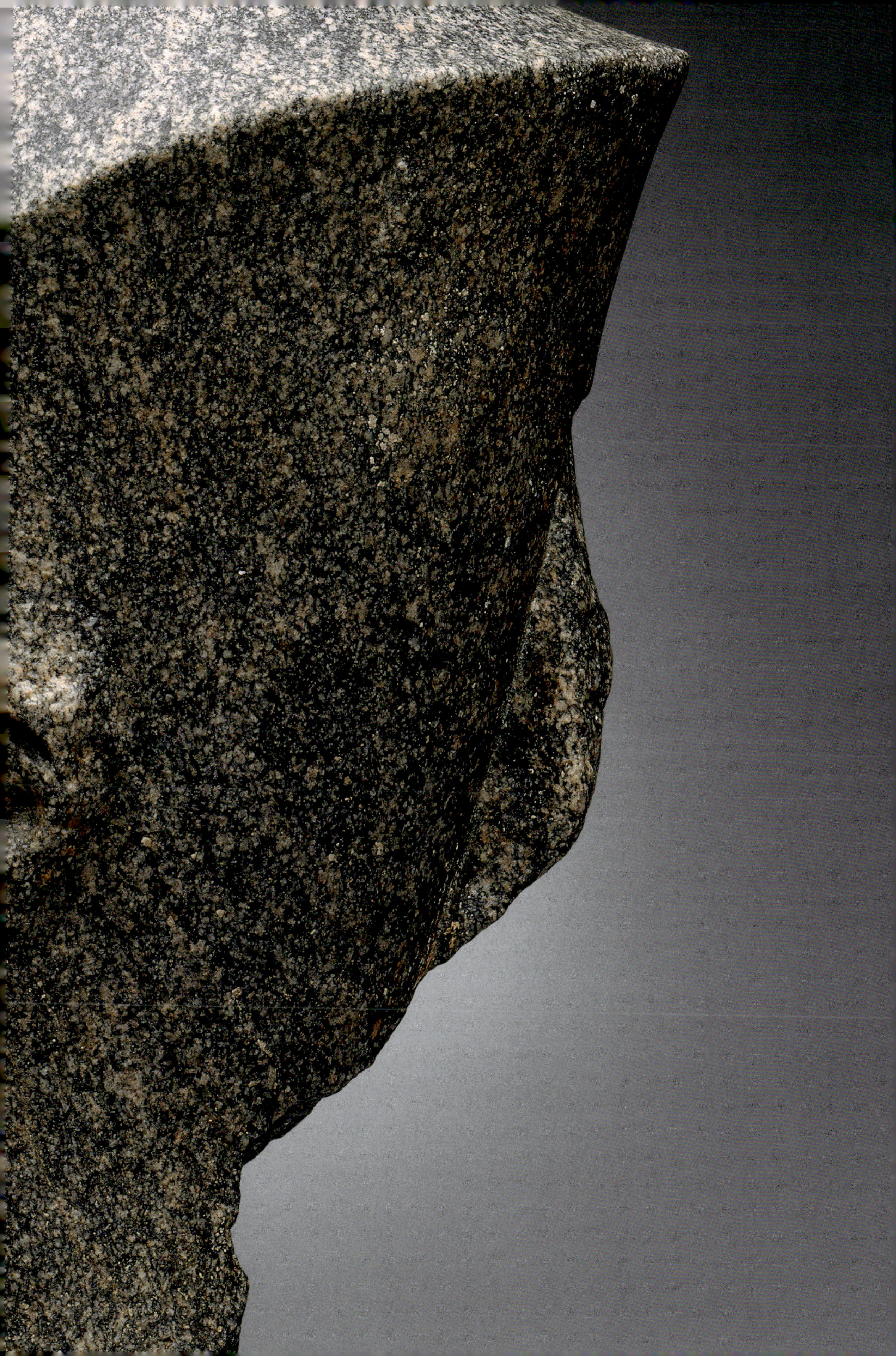

NOTES

The Case of Ankhhaf

1. Thomas Richard Duncan Greenlees, Expedition Diary, Sunday, February 8, 1925.
2. Mark Lehner and Zahi Hawass, *Giza and the Pyramids: The Definitive History* (Chicago: University of Chicago Press, 2017), pp. 29–30.
3. William Stevenson Smith, *A History of Egyptian Sculpture and Painting in the Old Kingdom* (London: Oxford University Press, 1946), pp. 107–8.
4. The modern restorer has been even more zealous, for he even painted over the gash in the forehead. One can only conclude that this was done to make the damage less distracting.
5. Expedition Diary entries for March 28, April 1, April 2, and April 8, 1925. Expedition records are available online, along with other resources, at *Digital Giza*, giza.fas.harvard.edu.
6. George Andrew Reisner, "Summary History of Excavations in Egypt, 1825–1927," unpublished manuscript, The George Andrew Reisner Collection, 1822–1983 (Bulk 1905–1947). EGP 13. Archives, Museum of Fine Arts, Boston.
7. In 1927, in recognition of his work for the Museum, Smith was appointed Honorary Curator of Egyptian Art. Museum of Fine Arts, Boston, *Annual Report for the Year 1927*, p. 73.
8. Only the proper left shoulder and upper arm have not been overpainted. For the treatment history of the bust, see Suzanne Gänsicke et al., "The Ancient Egyptian Collection at the Museum of Fine Arts, Boston," Part 2, "A Review of Former Treatments at the MFA and Their Consequences," *Journal of the American Institute for Conservation* 42 (2003): 207–9.
9. Joseph Lindon Smith, *Tombs, Temples, and Ancient Art*, ed. Corinna Lindon Smith (Norman: University of Oklahoma Press, 1956), p. 156.
10. See Smith, *Egyptian Sculpture and Painting*, pp. 38–39. An intriguing parallel from a much later age, worth mentioning if only to dismiss it, is Tutankhamen's "mannequin," a half-length wood figure of the king with arms cut off below the shoulder, of unknown use; Cairo T.16. See Edna R. Russmann and David Finn, *Egyptian Sculpture: Cairo and Luxor* (Austin: University of Texas Press, 1989), p. 125, no. 58; Nicholas Reeves, *The Complete Tutankhamen: The King, the Tomb, the Royal Treasure* (London: Thames and Hudson, 1990), p. 155.
11. See Andrey Bolshakov, "What Did the Bust of Ankh-haf Originally Look Like?" *Journal of the Museum of Fine Arts* 3 (1991): 4–14.
12. William Stevenson Smith, "Old Kingdom Sculpture," *American Journal of Archaeology* 45 (1941): 525.
13. George Andrew Reisner, *A History of the Giza Necropolis*, vol. 1 (Cambridge, MA: Harvard University Press, 1942), p. 46, fig. 8; Bolshakov, "What Did Ankh-haf Look Like?" p. 9, fig. 6.
14. Foreign archeological expeditions in Egypt operated under a license from the Egyptian Department of Antiquities. The expeditions bore all the costs of excavation and ensured that the objects were safely retrieved and properly documented. In return, they received a share of the finds. From the 1880s to the 1920s the excavators' share was half of the finds. In 1924–25, a new regulation left determination of the excavators' portion entirely to the discretion of the Department of Antiquities. As a rule, objects of unique historical importance or those needed to fill out the collections of the Cairo Museum stayed in Egypt, although exceptions could be made. Reisner, who had excellent relations with the Egyptian officials, was the only one of the foreign excavators who did not protest the new rules. The same year that the Egyptians awarded the bust of Ankhhaf to Boston, they kept the entire contents of the tomb of Queen Hetepheres, mother of Khufu, which Reisner discovered the same year as the bust and had received much more publicity. See Dows Dunham, "The Portrait Bust of Prince Ankhhaf," *Bulletin of the Museum of Fine Arts* 37, no. 221 (June 1939): 42–43.
15. Dows Dunham, statement to Trustees, June 1928, curatorial files, Department of Ancient Egyptian,

Nubian, and Near Eastern Art. For the outer coffin of Djehutynakht (MFA 20.1822–26), see Rita E. Freed et al., *The Secrets of Tomb 10A: Egypt 2000 BC*, exh. cat. (Boston: MFA Publications, 2009), pp. 106–24. The Museum constructed its first ever climate-controlled case for the fragile bust's display. See Gänsicke et al., "The Ancient Egyptian Collection at the Museum of Fine Arts, Boston," pp. 208–9, fig. 17.

16. "Report of the Director," *Sixty-Ninth Annual Report for the Year 1944* (Museum of Fine Arts, Boston, 1945): 16.
17. Dows Dunham, "An Experiment with an Egyptian Portrait," *Bulletin of the Museum of Fine Arts* 41, no. 243 (February 1943): 10.
18. These were the *Seated Scribe* in the Louvre and the so-called *Sheikh el-Beled* in the Egyptian Museum, Cairo. See Lawrence M. Berman, *The Priest, the Prince, and the Pasha: The Life and Afterlife of an Ancient Egyptian Sculpture* (Boston: MFA Publications, 2015), pp. 99–102.
19. The first Greek portraits with individual facial features appear outside of Athens in the sixth century BCE, in Athens not until the late fourth century; Paul Zanker, *Roman Portraits: Sculptures in Stone and Bronze in the Collection of the Metropolitan Museum of Art* (New York: Metropolitan Museum of Art, 2016), pp. 2–5.
20. Dows Dunham, "Portraiture in Egyptian Art," *Bulletin of the Museum of Fine Arts* 41, no. 246 (December 1943): 69.

Individuality

1. From Abydos, Petrie excavations, 1903. Cairo JE 36143; Mohamed Saleh and Hourig Sourouzian, *The Egyptian Museum Cairo: Official Catalogue* (Mainz: Philipp von Zabern, 1987), no. 28.
2. From Giza, Mariette excavations, 1860, Cairo JE 10062; Saleh and Sourouzian, *The Egyptian Museum Cairo*, no. 31.
3. George A. Reisner, *Mycerinus: The Temples of the Third Pyramid at Giza* (Cambridge, MA: Harvard University Press, 1931), p. 108. These numbers do not take into consideration the hundreds of fragments of statues smashed to pieces.
4. For the large fragments, see Reisner, *Mycerinus*, p. 108, no. 1; p. 18; pp. 22–23.
5. G[eorge] A[ndrew] R[eisner], "The Harvard University—Museum of Fine Arts Expedition," *Museum of Fine Arts Bulletin* 9, no. 50 (April 1911): 17.
6. See Dows Dunham, "Successive Installations of a Statue of King Mycerinus," *Bulletin of the Museum of Fine Arts* 33, no. 196 (April 1935): 21–25. The parts restored are: the right shoulder, most of the right arm, the lower parts of the left arm, the lappets of the headdress, the lower torso, both legs from mid-calves down, the feet with the exception of the left toes and a small part of the base, and the major part of the seat and base.
7. *Handbook of the Museum of Fine Arts, Boston* (Boston: Museum of Fine Arts, 1911), p. 16.
8. Henry G. Fischer, "An Elusive Shape within the Fisted Hands of Egyptian Statues," *Metropolitan Museum Journal* 10 (1975): 9–21.
9. See for example Peter Lacovara and C. Nicholas Reeves, "The Colossal Statue of Mycerinus Reconsidered," *Revue d'Egyptologie* 38 (1987): 111–115 and pls. 3–4.
10. For example: "The head seems small in proportion to the large shoulders and the bold musculature of the body, but accentuates the impression of power and majesty which emanate from the ruler." Hourig Sourouzian, "Old Kingdom Sculpture," in Alan B. Lloyd, ed., *A Companion to Ancient Egypt* (Chichester, England: Wiley, 2014), p. 863.
11. W. Stevenson Smith, *The Art and Architecture of Ancient Egypt*, rev. William Kelly Simpson (New Haven: Yale University Press, 1998), pp. 52, 60; Mark Lehner and Zahi Hawass, *Giza and the Pyramids: The Definitive History* (Chicago: University of Chicago Press, 2017), p. 255.
12. Now in the British Museum, EA 6647. See Lehner and Hawass, *Giza and the Pyramids*, p. 251, fig. 11.10.
13. Reisner divided the statuary from Giza into two different schools. The earlier of the two, whom he called Sculptor A, worked in a more severe style. He would have done the pair statue as well as the limestone portrait heads. The other, Sculptor B, created the colossal seated Menkaura, the Boston triad, and perhaps Ankhhaf, all characterized by a greater realism and softness in the modeling. See Reisner, *Mycerinus*, pp. 127–29; Smith, *Egyptian Sculpture and Painting*, pp. 19–20; Smith, *Art and Architecture of Ancient Egypt*, pp. 56–60.
14. She may have been Khamerernebty I, buried in a rock-cut tomb behind Khafra's valley temple, or she may have been Khentkawes, the owner of a large funerary monument adjacent to Menkaura's valley temple; Lehner and Hawass, *Giza and the Pyramids*, p. 282.
15. Khuenra's scribe statue is at the MFA (13.3140); see *MFA Highlights: Arts of Ancient Egypt* (Boston: MFA Publications, 2003), p. 88.
16. See Erik Hornung, Rolf Krauss, and David Warburton, *Ancient Egyptian Chronology* (Leiden: Brill, 2006), p. 485. A fragmentary list of kings preserved on a papyrus from the time of Ramesses II (1279–1213 BCE) gives the length of Menkaura's reign as [1]8 or [2]8 years.

17. Herodotus, *The Histories*, trans. Aubrey de Sélincourt (Harmondsworth, England: Penguin Books, 1954), p. 180.
18. Reisner, in *Giza Necropolis*, p. 27, describes it as a community of living spirits.
19. Twenty-four of the portrait heads come from tombs that date from the earliest construction phases in the western cemetery. See Massimiliano Nuzzolo, "The 'Reserve Heads': Some Remarks on Their Function and Meaning," in Nigel Strudwick and Helen Strudwick, eds., *Old Kingdom, New Perspectives: Egyptian Art and Archaeology 2750–2150 BC* (Oxford: Oxbow Books, 2001), p. 204.
20. These scholars include Ludwig Borchardt and Hermann Junker. In German they are called *Ersatzköpfe* (replacement heads); in French, *têtes de réserve* (reserve heads) or *têtes de remplacement* (replacement heads).
21. See, for example, Salima Ikram and Aidan Dodson, *The Mummy in Ancient Egypt: Equipping the Dead for Eternity* (London: Thames and Hudson, 1998), pp. 109–112.
22. Smith, *Egyptian Sculpture and Painting*, pp. 23–28; Smith, *Art and Architecture of Ancient Egypt*, p. 56. The most complete example of such a body covering is MFA 39.828; see *Egyptian Art in the Age of the Pyramids*, exh. cat. (New York: Metropolitan Museum of Art, 1999), pp. 476–477, no. 197.
23. Oric Bates, "Report on the Department of Ancient Art," *Museum of Fine Arts, Boston: Thirty-first Annual Report for the Year 1906* (Cambridge, MA: University Press, 1907): 75, no. 7. See also O[ric] B[ates], "Sculptures from the Excavations at Gizeh, 1905–1906," *Museum of Fine Arts Bulletin* 5, no. 26 (June 1907): 20.
24. See *Egyptian Art in the Age of the Pyramids*, p. 237n17.
25. The five relief portraits of Nofer are illustrated on one page in Peter Der Manuelian, *Mastabas of Nucleus Cemetery G 2100: Major Mastabas*, Giza Mastabas 8:1 (Boston: Museum of Fine Arts, 2009), p. 201, figs. 6.85–89; compare Reisner, *Giza Necropolis*, pls. 30–33.
26. Smith, *Egyptian Sculpture and Painting*, pp. 22–23.
27. See *Egyptian Art in the Age of the Pyramids*, no. 44, pp. 229–231.
28. Smith, *Art and Architecture of Ancient Egypt*, p. 55, fig. 102.
29. *Egyptian Art in the Age of the Pyramids*, p. 31, fig. 15a-b; p. 231, figs. 9–10.

Renaissances and Revivals

1. See George A. Reisner, "The Tomb of Hepzefa, Nomarch of Siûṭ," *Journal of Egyptian Archaeology* 5 (1918): 79–98.
2. Jochem Kahl, *Ancient Asyut: The First Synthesis after 300 Years of Research* (Wiesbaden: Harrassowitz, 2007), pp. 87–92.
3. See Rita E. Freed, "Art of the Middle Kingdom," in *The Secrets of Tomb 10A: Egypt 2000 BC*, exh. cat. (Boston: MFA Publications, 2009), pp. 75–76; Rita Freed, "Les portraits royaux de Sésostris III," in Palais des Beaux-Arts de Lille, *Sésostris III, pharaon de légende*, exh. cat. (Heule: Éditions Snoeck, 2014), pp. 34–35.
4. See Marianne Eaton-Krauss, *The Representations of Statuary in Private Tombs of the Old Kingdom* (Wiesbaden: Harrassowitz, 1984), pp. 87–89.
5. Entry by staff member Louis Caulton West, Archives, Department of Ancient Egyptian, Nubian, and Near Eastern Art, MFA.
6. MFA 14.724; Reisner, *Excavations at Kerma*, pl. 7.2.
7. See Elizabeth Joanna Minor, "The Use of Egyptian Material Culture in Nubian Burials of the Classic Kerma Period" (Ph.D. diss., UC Berkeley, 2012), pp. 70–74.
8. Minor, "The Use of Egyptian Material Culture in Nubian Burials of the Classic Kerma Period," pp. 55–65.
9. See Prudence O. Harpur, Joan Aruz, and Françoise Talon, eds., *The Royal City of Susa: Ancient Near Eastern Treasures in the Louvre*, exh. cat. (New York: The Metropolitan Museum of Art, 1992), pp. 159–182.
10. See Adela Oppenheim et al., *Ancient Egypt Transformed: The Middle Kingdom*, exh. cat. (New York: Metropolitan Museum of Art, 2015), no. 26, pp. 83–84 (Dahshur), and pp. 318–319 (Abydos).
11. Miriam Lichtheim, *Ancient Egyptian Literature*, vol. 1: *The Old and Middle Kingdoms* (Berkeley and Los Angeles: University of California Press, 1973), pp. 119–120. For the stele, see Oppenheim et al., *Ancient Egypt Transformed*, no. 100, p. 167.
12. Lichtheim, *Ancient Egyptian Literature*, vol. 1, p. 68.
13. Lawrence M. Berman, "Amenhotep III and His Times," in Arielle P. Kozloff and Betsy M. Bryan with Lawrence M. Berman, *Egypt's Dazzling Sun: Amenhotep III and His World*, exh. cat. (Cleveland: Cleveland Museum of Art, 1992), p. 48.
14. See Sylvia Schoske, "Historisches Bewusstsein in der ägyptischer Kunst: Beobachtungen an der Münchner Statue des Bekenchons," *Münchner Jahrbuch der bildenden Kunst* 38 (1987): 22–24; Hourig Sourouzian, "La statue d'Amenhotep fils de Hapou âgé, un chef-d'oeuvre de la XVIIIe dynastie," *Mitteilungen des Deutschen Archäologischen Instituts, Abteilung Kairo* 47 (1991): 341–355.
15. See Dietrich Wildung, *Egyptian Saints: Deification in Pharaonic Egypt* (New York: New York University Press, 1977).

16. See Edna R. Russmann, "Aspects of Egyptian Art: Archaism," in Edna R. Russmann, *Eternal Egypt: Masterworks of Ancient Art from the British Museum*, exh. cat. (Berkeley: University of California Press, 2001), pp. 40–44.
17. See Lehner and Hawass, *Giza and the Pyramids*, pp. 493–525.
18. "Dr. Reisner believes all these statues as belonging to the 4th dynasty. Borchardt, who has only seen photos of them, Firth, who succeeds Reisner in Nubia, Edgar, and Bates, say they belong to the 26th dynasty, when the Temple was repaired"; Oric Bates and Albert Lythgoe, "Egyptian Antiquities Found in 1906–1908," curatorial files, Museum of Fine Arts, Boston.
19. Steven Blake Shubert, "Realistic Currents in Portrait Sculpture of the Saite and Persian Periods in Egypt," *The Journal for the Society for the Study of Egyptian Antiquities* 19 (1989): 35.
20. Bernard V. Bothmer, "The Block Statue of Ankh-Khonsu in Boston and Cairo (Membra Dispersa V), with a Contribution by Herman de Meulenaere," in Madeleine E. Cody, ed., *Egyptian Art: Selected Writings of Bernard V. Bothmer* (Oxford: Oxford University Press, 2004), pp. 337–354; Jack A. Josephson and Mamdouh Mohamed Eldamaty, *Catalogue général of Egyptian Antiquities in the Cairo Museum, nrs. 48601–48649: Statues of the XXVth and XXVIth Dynasties* (Cairo: Supreme Council of Antiquities Press, 1999), no. 48635, pp. 82–87, pl. 35.
21. Bothmer, "Ankh-Khonsu in Boston and Cairo," pp. 344–347; Josephson and Eldamaty, *Statues of the XXVth and XXVIth Dynasties*, no. 48624, pp. 54–58, pl. 24.
22. Edna R. Russmann and David Finn, *Egyptian Sculpture: Cairo and Luxor* (Austin: University of Texas Press, 1989), p. 89. It has not been sufficiently recognized just how much the idealizing style of the Late Period owes to the Eighteenth Dynasty.

Mavericks and Glamour Kings

1. Gay Robins, "The Names of Hatshepsut as King," *Journal of Egyptian Archaeology* 85 (1999): 103–12.
2. Labib Habachi, *The Obelisks of Egypt: Skyscrapers of the Past* (Cairo: The American Research Center in Egypt Press, 1984), p. 60.
3. Miriam Lichtheim, *Ancient Egyptian Literature: A Book of Readings*, vol. 2, *The New Kingdom* (Berkeley: University of California Press, 1976), pp. 25–29.
4. William Stevenson Smith, "Recent Discoveries in the Egyptian Department, II: Two Fragments from Hatshepsut's Southern Obelisk," *Bulletin of the Museum of Fine Arts* 40, no. 239 (June 1942): 45–49; Nancy Thomas, ed., *The American Discovery of Ancient Egypt*, exh. cat. (Los Angeles: Los Angeles County Museum of Art, 1995), p. 175, no. 77 (entry by Joyce Haynes); Catharine H. Roehrig, with Renée Dreyfus and Cathleen A. Keller, eds., *Hatshepsut: From Queen to Pharaoh*, exh. cat. (New York: Metropolitan Museum of Art, 2005), p. 152, no. 78 (entry by Catharine H. Roehrig). Other fragments of this obelisk are in Liverpool and Sydney, Australia; see Habachi, *The Obelisks of Egypt*, p. 60. A small fragment in Glasgow was destroyed during World War II.
5. Lawrence M. Berman, "The Prehistory of the Egyptian Department of the Museum of Fine Arts, Boston," in Mamdouh Eldamaty and May Trad, eds., *Egyptian Museum Collections around the World* (Cairo: Supreme Council of Antiquities, 2002), vol. 1, pp. 122–23; idem, "Egypt Lost and Found in Boston," in Rita E. Freed, Lawrence M. Berman, and Denise M. Doxey, *MFA Highlights: Arts of Ancient Egypt* (Boston: MFA Publications, 2003), pp. 19–21; Andrew Oliver, *American Travelers on the Nile: Early U.S. Visitors to Egypt, 1774–1839* (Cairo: American University in Cairo Press, 2014), pp. 188–92.
6. See Smith, "Recent Discoveries," p. 46; William Stevenson Smith, *Ancient Egypt as Represented in the Museum of Fine Arts, Boston* (Boston: Museum of Fine Arts, 1960), p. 116.
7. The first and third sarcophagi are in Cairo (JE 42032 and 37678). See Peter Der Manuelian and Christian E. Loeben, "New Light on the Recarved Sarcophagus of Hatshepsut and Thutmose I in Boston," *Journal of Egyptian Archaeology* 79 (1993): 121–55; Der Manuelian and Loeben, "From Daughter to Father: The Recarved Egyptian Sarcophagus of Queen Hatshepsut and King Thutmose III," *Journal of the Museum of Fine Arts, Boston* 5 (1993): 24–61.
8. See Catharine H. Roehrig, "The Two Tombs of Hatshepsut," in Roehrig, *Hatshepsut: From Queen to Pharaoh*, pp. 184–87.
9. Theodore M. Davis, *The Tomb of Hâtshopsîtû* (1906; rept. London: Duckworth, 2004), pp. 79–80 and pls. VIII–IX.
10. See Smith, "Recent Discoveries," p. 48; Karol Myśliwiec, *Le portrait royal dans le bas-relief du Nouvel Empire* (Warsaw: Éditions scientifiques de Pologne, 1976), p. 47 and fig. 65; see also Manuelian and Loeben, "The Recarved Sarcophagus of Hatshepsut," pp. 151–52 and pl. XIII, 3; Manuelian and Loeben, "From Daughter to Father," pp. 56–57, fig. 56.
11. See Cathleen A. Keller, "Hatshepsut's Reputation in History," in Roehrig, *Hatshepsut: From Queen to Pharaoh*, pp. 294–97.
12. William A. Moran, *The Amarna Letters* (Baltimore: Johns Hopkins University Press, 1992), pp. 39, 8.

13. Lawrence M. Berman, "Amenhotep III and His Times," in Arielle P. Kozloff and Betsy M. Bryan with Lawrence M. Berman, *Egypt's Dazzling Sun: Amenhotep III and His World*, exh. cat. (Cleveland: Cleveland Museum of Art, 1992), p. 33. The stele from the king's memorial temple is in Cairo, CG 34025.
14. See Betsy M. Bryan, "Designing the Cosmos: Temples and Temple Decoration," in Kozloff and Bryan, *Egypt's Dazzling Sun*, pp. 73–119.
15. Kozloff and Bryan, *Egypt's Dazzling Sun*, p. 97; Betsy M. Bryan, "Antecedents to Amenhotep III," in David O'Connor and Eric H. Cline, eds., *Amenhotep III: Perspectives on His Reign* (Ann Arbor: University of Michigan Press, 1998), p. 32; Betsy M. Bryan, "The Temple of Mut: New Evidence on Hatshepsut's Building Activity," in *Hatshepsut: From Queen to Pharaoh*, pp. 181–83.
16. Kozloff and Bryan, *Egypt's Dazzling Sun*, p. 108, fig. IV.28.
17. An adjoining block is in Copenhagen, Ny Carlsberg Glyptotek ÆIN 1152; see Tine Bagh, *Finds from W. M. F. Petrie's Excavations in Egypt in the Ny Carlsberg Glyptotek* (Copenhagen: Ny Carlsberg Glyptotek, 2011), pp. 47–48, figs. 1.47–49.
18. See Kozloff and Bryan, *Egypt's Dazzling Sun*, pp. 193–211.
19. See W. Raymond Johnson, "The Setting: History, Religion, and Art," in Rita E. Freed, Yvonne J. Markowitz, and Sue H. D'Auria, eds., *Pharaohs of the Sun: Akhenaten, Nefertiti, Tutankhamen*, exh. cat. (Boston: Museum of Fine Arts, 1999), p. 43; Johnson, "Images of Amenhotep III in Thebes: Styles and Intentions," in Lawrence M. Berman, ed., *The Art of Amenhotep III: Art Historical Analysis* (Cleveland: Cleveland Museum of Art, 1990), pp. 36–38.
20. See Berman, in Kozloff and Bryan, *Egypt's Dazzling Sun*, pp. 41–43.
21. See Berman, in Kozloff and Bryan, *Egypt's Dazzling Sun*, pp. 44–56.
22. See further Bryan, in Kozloff and Bryan, *Egypt's Dazzling Sun*, pp. 237–38.
23. Edward A. Tuck to Joseph Randolph Coolidge, Jr., March 29, 1906, curatorial files, Department of Ancient Egyptian, Nubian, and Near Eastern Art, MFA.
24. MFA 29.728, 29.730, 29.731, 29.732, 29.733; Dows Dunham, "Three Inscribed Statues in Boston," *Journal of Egyptian Archaeology* 15 (1929): 164–66; Dunham, *Recollections of an Egyptologist* (Boston: Museum of Fine Arts, 1972), p. 50.
25. Lehner and Hawass, *Giza and the Pyramids*, pp. 222–23.
26. For other examples, see Cyril Aldred, *Akhenaten and Nefertiti*, exh. cat. (Brooklyn: Brooklyn Museum, 1973), p. 99, no. 13.
27. Dorothea Arnold, *The Royal Women of Amarna: Images of Beauty from Ancient Egypt*, exh. cat. (New York: The Metropolitan Museum of Art, 1996), p. 20.
28. Arnold, *Royal Women of Amarna*, p. 55, citing Kurt Gerhardt, "Waren die Köpfchen der Echnaton-Töchter künstlich deformiert?" *Zeitschrift für ägyptische Sprache und Altertumskunde* 94 (1967): 51–56.
29. Rita E. Freed, "Art in the Service of Religion and the State," in Freed, Markowitz, and D'Auria, *Pharaohs of the Sun*, pp. 116, 123. For the inscription, see Labib Habachi, "Varia from the Reign of Akhenaten," *Mitteilungen des Deutschen Archäologischen Instituts Kairo* 20 (1985): 87–88. For the trial piece, see Dows Dunham, "Some New Objects from Tell-el-Amarna," *Bulletin of the Museum of Fine Arts* 35, no. 207 (1937): 12–13.
30. Arnold, *Royal Women of Amarna*, pp. 14–15, 105–106.

Back to the Future

1. These proposed measurements are based on a classic Egyptian grid of 18 squares from the browline to the soles of the feet for a striding statue and 11 squares for a kneeling statue. The head measures about 3 inches from the browline to the junction of the neck and shoulders, equal to 2 squares.
2. C. Ferri Pisani, "Bronzes égyptiens tirés de la collection du Prince Napoléon," *Gazette des beaux-arts* 1 (1859): 281 (as "head of a eunuch").
3. For the full story, see Berman, *The Priest, the Prince, and the Pasha: The Life and Afterlife of an Ancient Egyptian Sculpture* (Boston: MFA Publications, 2015).
4. Bernard V. Bothmer with Herman De Meulenaere and Hans Wolfgang Müller, *Egyptian Sculpture of the Late Period, 700 B.C. to A.D. 100*, exh. cat. (Brooklyn: Brooklyn Museum, 1960), pp. 138–40; restated in Bernard V. Bothmer, "Egyptian Antecedents of Roman Republican Realism," in Madeleine E. Cody, ed., *Egyptian Art: Selected Writings of Bernard V. Bothmer* (Oxford: Oxford University Press, 2004), p. 425.
5. William Stevenson Smith was the first to propose this date; see Smith, *Ancient Egypt as Represented in the Museum of Fine Arts, Boston* (Boston: Museum of Fine Arts, 1942), p. 155. In the sixth edition (1960) the word "probably" in relation to the date has been deleted (p. 176).
6. Emmanuel de Rougé, "Une lettre écrite d'Egypte par M. Mariette," *Comptes-rendus des séances de l'Academie des Inscriptions et Belles-Lettres* 2 (1858): 115–21.
7. See for example Elizabeth Anne Hastings, *The Sculpture from the Sacred Animal Necropolis at North Saqqara 1964–76*, Sixty-first Excavation Memoir

(London: Egypt Exploration Society, 1997), pp. 11–16, nos. 21, 24–25, 27–28, 31, pls. 13, 16–19.

8. See Herodotus 2.37.2–5; Robert B. Strassler, ed., *The Landmark Herodotus: The Histories*, trans. Andrea L. Purvis (New York: Pantheon Books, 2007), pp. 133–34. For more about the priesthood and priestly regulations, see Serge Sauneron, *The Priests of Ancient Egypt*, new ed., trans. David Lorton (Ithaca: Cornell University Press, 2000), esp. pp. 35–42.
9. See Jean-Claude Goyon, "Ptolemaic Egypt: Priests and the Traditional Religion," in *Cleopatra's Egypt: Age of the Ptolemies*, exh. cat. (Brooklyn: Brooklyn Museum, 1988), p. 38, fig. 13; E. Chassinat and Fr. Daumas, *Le temple de Dendara* 8 (Cairo: Institut français d'Archéologie orientale, 1978), pls. 768, 770–72, 793, 796–801.
10. David Klotz, "Replicas of Shu: On the Theological Significance of Naophorous and Theophorous Statues," *Bulletin de l'Institut français d'Archéologie orientale* 114, no. 2 (2014): 322–31.
11. Ibid., p. 330.
12. The statue was purchased in 1965 from Ernst E. Kofler, Lucerne, Switzerland. Its history prior to that is not known.
13. See Jack A. Josephson, "Egyptian Sculpture of the Late Period Revisited," *Journal of the American Research Center in Egypt* 34 (1997): 12–13.
14. Josephson, "Egyptian Sculpture," p. 11n68; Shubert, "Realistic Currents in Portrait Sculpture," p. 40.
15. See David Klotz, "The Peculiar Naophorous Statuette of a Heliopolitan Priest: Hannover, Museum August Kestner 1935.200.510," *Zeitschrift für ägyptische Sprache und Altertumskunde* 139 (2012): 137; Klotz, "Replicas of Shu," pp. 294–96. The progression goes from *naoi* held between the palms of the hand, resting on the ground or on a support, to *naoi* held between the palms of the hands without any support, to *naoi* supported by the tips of the fingers. See Herman De Meulenaere, "Personnages debout tenant un naos dans la statuaire de la Basse Epoque," in Wouter Claes, Herman De Meulenaere, and Stan Hendrickx, eds., *Elkab and Beyond: Studies in Honor of Luc Limme*, Orientalia Lovaniensia Analecta 191 (2009): 223–31.
16. Dieter Arnold, *Temples of the Last Pharaohs* (New York: Oxford University Press, 1999), pp. 131–32, figs. 87–88; and pp. 140–41, figs. 94–95.
17. See Jeffrey Spier, Timothy Potts, and Sara Cole, eds., *Beyond the Nile: Egypt and the Classical World*, exh. cat. (Los Angeles: J. Paul Getty Museum, 2018), pp. 168–69, nos. 100–101.
18. Bothmer et al., *Egyptian Sculpture of the Late Period*, no. 136, pp. 178–79; *Cleopatra's Egypt*, no. 132, pp. 126–27.

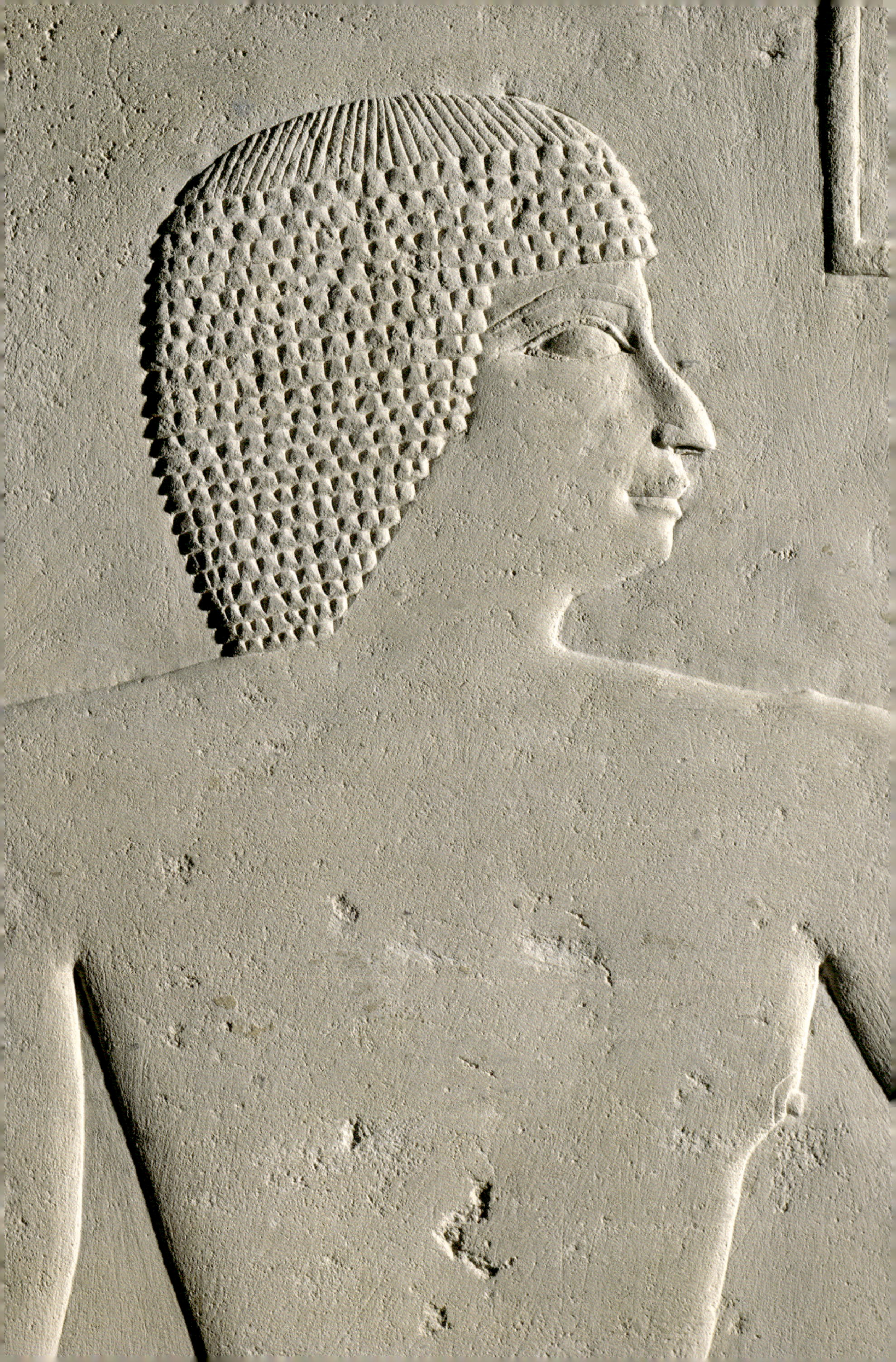

LIST OF ILLUSTRATIONS

Unless indicated otherwise, all objects are in the collections of the Museum of Fine Arts, Boston. Dimensions are given as height × width × depth.

1
Bust of Ankhhaf
Old Kingdom, Dynasty 4, reign of Khafra, 2520–2494 BCE
Painted limestone, h. 50.5 cm (19⅞ in.)
Harvard University–Boston Museum of Fine Arts Expedition, 27.442

2
Joseph Lindon Smith
***Bust of Prince Ankhhaf, Profile View*, 1925**
Oil on canvas, 86 × 54.5 cm (33⅞ × 21½ in.)
Anonymous gift, 27.1468

3
False door of Idu, with engaged bust of Idu in lower section, January 20, 1931
Giza tomb G 7102, reign of Pepy I, 2289–2255 BCE
Photograph by Mohammedani Ibrahim Ibrahim
Harvard University–Boston Museum of Fine Arts Expedition, A6108_NS

4
Fishtail knife inscribed for Khufu
Old Kingdom, Dynasty 4, reign of Khufu, 2551–2528 BCE
Flint, 18.3 × 2.8 cm (7½ × 1⅛ in.)
Harvard University–Boston Museum of Fine Arts Expedition, 11.765

5
Model vessels and offerings found under the bust of Ankhhaf
Old Kingdom, Dynasty 4, reign of Khafra, 2520–2494 BCE
Plaster, largest object h. 4.1 cm (1⅝ in.)
Harvard University–Boston Museum of Fine Arts Expedition

6
Cast of bust of Ankhhaf in modern clothing, about 1943
Museum of Fine Arts, Boston

7
Colossal statue of Menkaura
Old Kingdom, Dynasty 4, reign of Menkaura, 2490–2472 BCE
Travertine (Egyptian alabaster), 243.8 × 115.6 × 83.8 cm (96 × 45½ × 33 in.)
Harvard University–Boston Museum of Fine Arts Expedition, 09.204

8
Head of Menkaura seen through a drain hole, April 14, 1907
Photograph by Said Ahmed Said
Harvard University–Boston Museum of Fine Arts Expedition, B162_NS

19
Seated statue of Hemiunu
Old Kingdom, Dynasty 4, reign of Khufu, 2551–2528 BCE
Limestone, h. 155.5 cm (61¼ in.)
Roemer and Pelizaeus Museum, PM 1962
Photograph © Roemer and Pelizaeus Museum

20
Statue of Lady Sennuwy
Middle Kingdom, Dynasty 12, reign of Senwosret I, 1971–1926 BCE
Granodiorite, overall: 170.2 × 116.2 × 47 cm (67 × 45¾ × 18½ in.)
Harvard University–Boston Museum of Fine Arts Expedition, 14.720

21
Relief of Lady Wadjkaues (detail)
Middle Kingdom, Dynasty 12, reign of Senwosret I, 1971–1926 BCE
Painted limestone, 59 × 37 cm (23¼ × 14⅝ in.)
Seth K. Sweetser Fund, 1972.984

22
Lady Sennuwy as found, December 17, 1913
Photograph by Mohammedani Ibrahim Ibrahim
Harvard University–Boston Museum of Fine Arts Expedition, B2121_NS

23
Head of Senwosret III
Middle Kingdom, Dynasty 12, reign of Senwosret III, 1878–1841 BCE
Yellow quartzite, 45.1 × 34.3 × 43.2 cm (17¾ × 13½ × 17 in.)
The Nelson-Atkins Museum of Art, Kansas City, Missouri, Purchase: William Rockhill Nelson Trust, 62-11
Photograph courtesy The Metropolitan Museum of Art, New York

24
Head of an official (The Josephson Head)
Middle Kingdom, Dynasty 12, reign of Senwosret III, 1878–1841 BCE
Quartzite, 18.5 × 24 × 21 cm (7¼ × 9½ × 8¼ in.)
Partial gift of Magda Saleh and Jack A. Josephson and Museum purchase with funds donated by the Florence E. and Horace L. Mayer Funds, Norma Jean and Stanford Calderwood Discretionary Fund, Norma Jean Calderwood Acquisition Fund, Marilyn M. Simpson Fund, Otis Norcross Fund, Helen and Alice Colburn Fund, William E. Nickerson Fund, Egyptian Curator's Fund, Frederick Brown Fund, Elizabeth Marie Paramino Fund in memory of John F. Paramino, Boston Sculptor, Morris and Louise Rosenthal Fund, Arthur Tracy Cabot Fund, Walter and Celia Gilbert Acquisition Fund, Marshall H. Gould Fund, Arthur Mason Knapp Fund, John Wheelock Elliot and John Morse Elliot Fund, Miguel and Barbara de Bragança Fund, Brian J. Brille Acquisition Fund, Barbara W. and Joanne A. Herman Fund, MFA Senior Associates and MFA Associates Fund for Egyptian Acquisitions, and by exchange from an anonymous gift, 2003.244

25
Statue of Amenhotep son of Hapu as an old man
New Kingdom, Dynasty 18, reign of Amenhotep III, 1390–1352 BCE
Granodiorite, h. 117 cm (46⅛ in.)
Egyptian Museum Cairo, JE 38368 (= CG 42127)
Photograph by Lawrence M. Berman

26
Triad of Menkaura, the goddess Hathor, and the deified Hare nome
Old Kingdom, Dynasty 4, reign of Menkaura, 2490–2472 BCE
Graywacke, 84.5 × 43.5 × 49 cm (33¼ × 17⅛ × 19¼ in.)
Harvard University–Boston Museum of Fine Arts Expedition, 09.200

27
Statue of Khonsuiraa
Late Period, Dynasty 25, 760–660 BCE
Black stone, 43.5 × 12.6 × 13.5 cm (17⅛ × 5 × 5⅜ in.)
Julia Bradford Huntington James Fund and Museum purchase with funds donated by contribution, 07.494

28
Head of a man in a bag wig
Late Period, Dynasty 26, 664–525 BCE
Granodiorite, 22.8 × 18 cm (9 × 7⅛ in.)
Seth K. Sweetser Fund, 37.377

29
Head of Ankhkhonsu
Late Period, Dynasty 26, 664–525 BCE
Graywacke, 19.5 × 18.5 × 15 cm (7⅝ × 7¼ × 5⅞ in.)
Emily Esther Sears Fund, 04.1841

30
Cast of head of Ankhkhonsu joined to body
Body: Egyptian Museum Cairo, JE 37987
Photograph by Bernard Bothmer, courtesy of the Brooklyn Museum

31
Seated statue of Hatshepsut
New Kingdom, Dynasty 18, reign of Hatshepsut, 1473–1458 BCE
Indurated limestone, paint, 213 × 50 × 119 cm (83⅞ × 19⅝ × 46⅞ in.)
Metropolitan Museum of Art, Rogers Fund, 1929, 29.3.2

32
Standing obelisk of Hatshepsut, Karnak, 2005
Photograph by Lawrence M. Berman

33
Fragment from Hatshepsut's fallen obelisk at Karnak (detail)
New Kingdom, Dynasty 18, reign of Hatshepsut, 1473–1458 BCE
Granite, 106 × 45.7 × 22.9 cm (41¾ × 18 × 9 in.)
Gift of heirs of Francis Cabot Lowell, 75.12

34
Sarcophagus of Hatshepsut, recut for her father, Thutmose I
New Kingdom, Dynasty 18, reign of Hatshepsut, 1473–1458 BCE
Painted quartzite, 82 × 225 × 87 cm (32¼ × 88⅝ × 34¼ in.)
Gift of Theodore M. Davis, 04.278.1-2

35
Head of Amenhotep III
New Kingdom, Dynasty 18, reign of Amenhotep III, 1390–1352 BCE
Quartzite, 52.5 × 21.2 × 26.2 cm (20⅝ × 8⅜ × 10⅜ in.)
Museum purchase with funds donated by Miss Anna D. Slocum, 09.288

36
Relief of Amenhotep III and Sekhmet (detail)
New Kingdom, Dynasty 18, reign of Amenhotep III, 1390–1352 BCE
Quartzite, 41 × 65 cm (16⅛ × 25⅝ in.)
Gift of British School of Archaeology in Egypt, 10.650

37
Statuette of Amenhotep III as the god Neferhotep
New Kingdom, Dynasty 18, reign of Amenhotep III, 1390–1352 BCE
Glazed steatite, 13 × 3.8 × 5.3 cm (5⅛ × 1½ × 2⅛ in.)
Gift of Mrs. Horace L. Mayer, 1970.636

38
Statuette of Tiye from a family group
New Kingdom, Dynasty 18, reign of Amenhotep III, 1390–1352 BCE
Glazed steatite, h. 30 cm (11¾ in.)
Musée du Louvre, Paris, E 25493
© Musée du Louvre, Dist. RMN-Grand Palais/Photograph: Christian Decamps/Art Resource, NY

39
Head of Tiye
New Kingdom, Dynasty 18, reign of Amenhotep III, 1390–1352 BCE
Peridotite, 20.3 × 11.5 × 12 cm (8 × 4½ × 4¾ in.)
Gift of Herbert W. Jackson Pasha, 21.2802

40
Head of an official
New Kingdom, Dynasty 18, reign of Amenhotep III, 1390–1352 BCE
Quartzite, h. 20 cm (7⅞ in.)
Marie Antoinette Evans Fund, 29.729

41
Relief of Akhenaten as a sphinx
New Kingdom, Dynasty 18, reign of Akhenaten, 1349–1336 BCE
Limestone, 51 × 105.5 cm (20⅛ × 41½ in.)
Egyptian Curator's Fund, 64.1944

42
Fragment of a column drum featuring the royal family worshipping
New Kingdom, Dynasty 18, reign of Akhenaten, 1349–1336 BCE
Limestone, 22.4 × 52.5 cm (8⅞ × 20⅝ in.)
Mary S. and Edward J. Holmes Fund, 67.637

43
Trial carving of head
New Kingdom, Dynasty 18, reign of Akhenaten, 1349–1336 BCE
Limestone, w. 22 cm (8⅝ in.)
Egypt Exploration Society by subscription, 37.2

44
Relief of princess offering to the Aten
New Kingdom, Dynasty 18, reign of Akhenaten, 1349–1336 BCE
Limestone, 23 × 27 cm (9 × 10⅝ in.)
Charles Amos Cummings Fund, 1971.294

45
Head of Tutankhamen
New Kingdom, Dynasty 18, reign of Tutankhamen, 1336–1327 BCE
Sandstone, 29.6 × 26.5 cm (11⅝ × 10⅜ in.)
Museum purchase with funds donated by Miss Mary S. Ames, 11.1533

55
Statue of Pakhom, governor of Dendara
Greco-Roman Period, Ptolemaic Dynasty, reign of Cleopatra VII, 50–30 BCE
Gray granite, 71.1 × 19.1 × 23.5 cm (28 × 7½ × 9¼ in.)
Detroit Institute of Arts, Founders Society Purchase, William H. Murphy Fund, 51.83

Details and alternate views

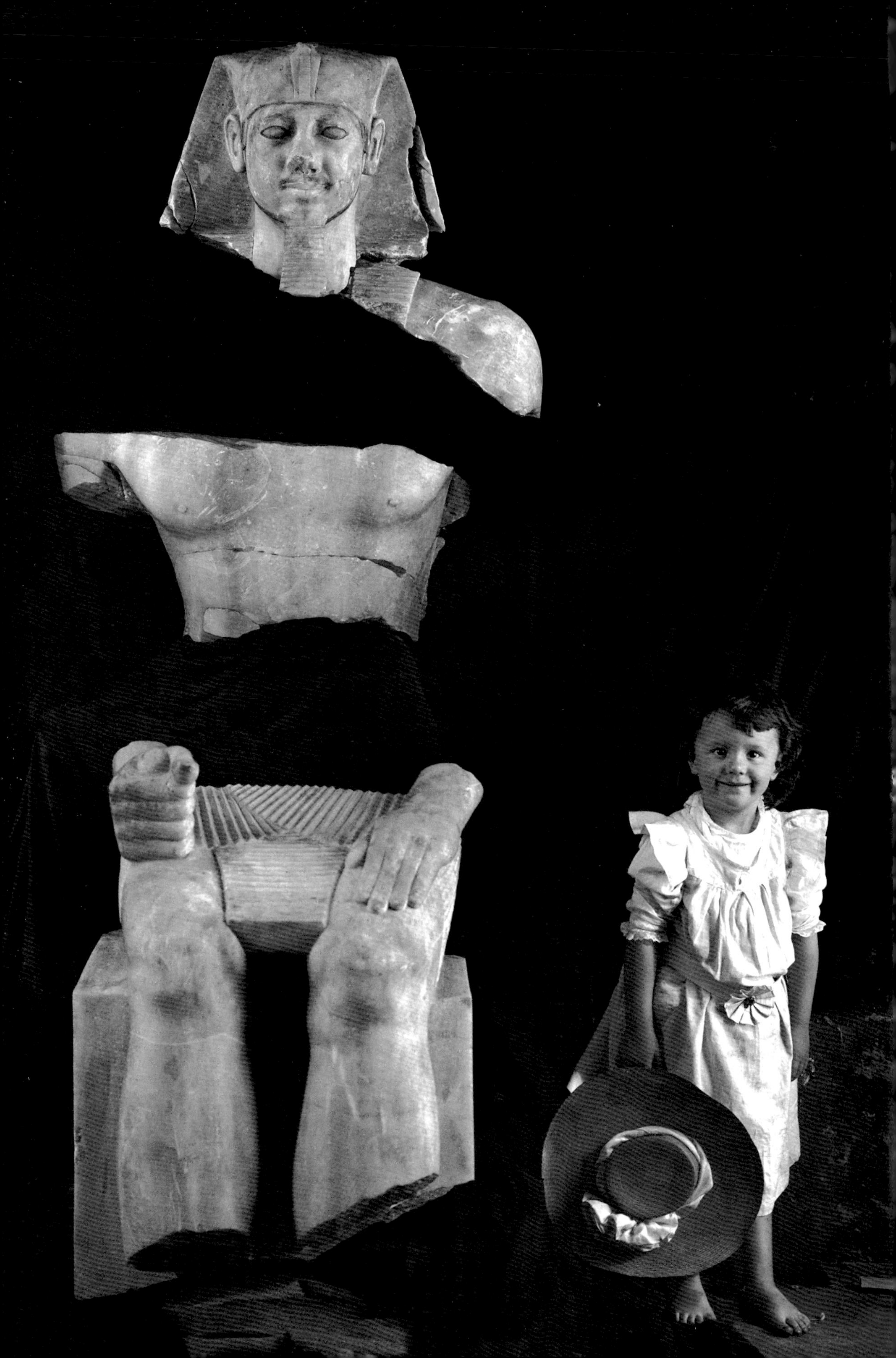

INDEX

References to illustrations are indicated by page numbers in italics.

MFABoston

MFA Publications
Museum of Fine Arts, Boston
465 Huntington Avenue
Boston, Massachusetts 02115
www.mfa.org/publications

Support for this publication provided by the Egyptian Publication Fund at the Museum of Fine Arts, Boston

ISBN 978-0-87846-889-8
Library of Congress Control Number: 2022935921

While the objects in this publication necessarily represent only a small portion of the MFA's holdings, the Museum is proud to be a leader within the American museum community in sharing the objects in its collection via its website. Currently, information about approximately 400,000 objects is available to the public worldwide. To learn more about the MFA's collections, including provenance, publication, and exhibition history, kindly visit www.mfa.org/collections.

For a complete listing of MFA publications, please contact the publisher at the above address, or call 617 369 4233.

Illustrations in this book were photographed by the Imaging Studios, Museum of Fine Arts, Boston, except where otherwise noted.

Cover: Pair statue of Menkaura and queen (alternate view, fig. 12)

Edited by Jennifer Snodgrass
Proofread by Ivy Long
Indexed by Enid Zafran
Designed by Thomas Eykemans, Lucia | Marquand
Production and image research by Diana Sibbald
Typeset in Comma Base by Tina Henderson
Printed on Condat Matt Perigord 150 gsm
Printed and bound at Verona Libri, Verona, Italy

Distributed by
ARTBOOK | D.A.P.
75 Broad Street, Suite 630
New York, New York 10004
www.artbook.com

FIRST EDITION
Printed and bound in Italy
This book was printed on acid-free paper.